Hacker's Playbook: Unraveling the Tactics Behind Cyber Attacks

Table of Content

Chapter 1: The Genesis of Hacking

- Define hacking and its origins in the early days of computing.
- Explore the curiosity-driven motivations of the first hackers.
- Highlight key figures in the history of hacking, such as Kevin Mitnick and Adrian Lamo.
- Discuss their contributions to shaping the hacking culture.
- Trace the evolution of hacking techniques from simple exploits to more sophisticated methods.
- Discuss notable hacking incidents that marked turning points.
- Examine the blurred lines between hacking as a skill and hacking as a criminal act.
- Discuss the emergence of ethical hacking as a response.
- Explore how hacking has influenced the development of cybersecurity measures.
- Discuss the symbiotic relationship between hackers and the security industry.

Chapter 2: The Art of Social Engineering

- Define social engineering and its significance in the realm of cybersecurity.
- Discuss the psychological aspects of manipulation.
- Explore historical examples of social engineering, including espionage and espionage techniques.
- Discuss the transition to digital social engineering.
- Outline various tactics used by social engineers, such as phishing, pretexting, and baiting.
- Provide real-world examples to illustrate each technique.
- Discuss why humans are often the weakest link in cybersecurity.
- Explore the psychology behind successful social engineering attacks.
- Highlight notorious social engineering incidents and their impact.
- Discuss how individuals and organizations fell victim to social engineering.

Chapter 3: Malware Mayhem

- Define malware and its broad categories, including viruses, worms, and trojans.
- Discuss the motives behind creating and distributing malware.
- Explore the timeline of significant malware outbreaks, from early computer viruses to modern-day ransomware.
- Discuss the technological advancements driving malware development.
- Break down the components of malware and how it operates within a system.
- Discuss the techniques malware uses to evade detection.
- Explore the various ways malware spreads, including email attachments, infected websites, and malicious downloads.
- Discuss the role of social engineering in malware distribution.
- Highlight famous malware attacks and their impact on individuals and organizations.
- Discuss the lessons learned from these incidents.

Chapter 4: The Cryptic World of Cryptocurrency

- Define cryptocurrency and its underlying blockchain technology.
- Discuss the decentralization and anonymity aspects of cryptocurrencies.
- Explore how hackers exploit vulnerabilities in cryptocurrency exchanges and wallets.
- Discuss notable cryptocurrency hacking incidents.
- Discuss the connection between ransomware attacks and demands for payment in cryptocurrency.
- Explore the challenges of tracing and recovering cryptocurrency payments.
- Highlight instances of fraudulent initial coin offerings (ICOs) and cryptocurrency scams.
- Discuss the impact on investors and regulatory responses.
- Explore potential vulnerabilities in blockchain technology that hackers may exploit.
- Discuss the ongoing efforts to enhance the security of blockchain networks.

Chapter 5: Advanced Persistent Threats (APTs)

- Define Advanced Persistent Threats and their characteristics.
- Discuss the long-term nature of APT campaigns.
- Explore notable APT campaigns, such as Stuxnet and Operation Aurora.
- Discuss the motivations and targets of these sophisticated attacks.
- Discuss the difficulties in attributing APTs to specific threat actors.
- Explore the role of false flags and misdirection in APT campaigns.
- Break down the stages of an APT attack, including reconnaissance, initial compromise, persistence, and exfiltration.
- Discuss the meticulous planning and execution involved.
- Explore the industries and sectors commonly targeted by APT groups.
- Discuss the geopolitical motivations behind APT campaigns.

Chapter 6: The Underground Economy

- Define the concept of the dark web and the underground economy.
- Discuss the anonymity and encryption methods used in the underground.
- Explore markets where cybercriminals buy and sell stolen data, hacking tools, and other illicit goods.
- Discuss the range of products available on these platforms.
- Discuss the predominant use of cryptocurrency for transactions in the underground economy.
- Explore the challenges of tracking and regulating these transactions.
- Explore services offered in the underground, including hacking-for-hire and DDoS attacks.
- Discuss the motivations of individuals providing such services.
- Trace the evolution of online forums where cybercriminals communicate and collaborate.
- Discuss the role of these forums in knowledge sharing and skill development.

Chapter 7: The Cat-and-Mouse Game of Cybersecurity

- Define the dynamic nature of the cybersecurity landscape.
- Discuss the constant evolution of cyber threats.
- Explore the factors that give hackers an advantage in the ongoing cyber warfare.
- Discuss the rapid adaptation of hacking techniques.
- Highlight advancements in cybersecurity technologies and strategies.
- Discuss the role of artificial intelligence and machine learning in threat detection.
- Discuss the importance of effective incident response plans.
- Explore the concept of cyber hygiene and its role in preventing cyber attacks.
- Discuss the importance of information sharing and collaboration among cybersecurity professionals.
- Explore initiatives that promote global cooperation against cyber threats.

Chapter 8: Ethical Hacking and Cybersecurity Defense

- Define ethical hacking and its role in cybersecurity defense.
- Discuss the ethical hacker's mission to identify and patch vulnerabilities.
- Explore the shift in perception from hacking as a criminal act to ethical hacking as a valuable profession.
- Discuss the ethical considerations of hacking for defensive purposes.
- Explore prominent certifications for ethical hackers, such as Certified Ethical Hacker (CEH) and Offensive Security Certified Professional (OSCP).
- Discuss the importance of ongoing training in the rapidly evolving field.
- Define penetration testing and its role in identifying vulnerabilities.
- Discuss real-world examples of successful penetration tests.
- Explore the concept of bug bounty programs and their role in crowdsourcing cybersecurity testing.
- Discuss the benefits and challenges of bug bounty initiatives.

Introduction

In a contemporary landscape overshadowed by the omnipresence of technology, where our lives are intricately interwoven with the digital realm, there exists an elusive and concealed underbelly—a clandestine world where hackers, like unseen puppeteers, orchestrate a dance of manipulation, infiltration, and disruption. "Hacker's Playbook: Unraveling the Tactics Behind Cyber Attacks" invites readers on a captivating and immersive exploration into this mysterious and often nefarious domain of cyber warfare. The narrative unfolds as a riveting journey, delving deep into the shadows to reveal the complex strategies employed by hackers, offering a rare and enlightening glimpse into the pages of their clandestine playbook.

At the heart of this narrative lies an acknowledgment of the omnipresent threat that looms over our interconnected lives, as individuals and institutions navigate a landscape where the virtual and the tangible seamlessly converge. The term "hacker" ceases to be a mere buzzword and transforms into a protagonist, albeit a shadowy one, with the power to sway the course of our digitally-dependent existence. The exploration begins by dissecting the anatomy of cyber attacks, unraveling the layers of sophistication that characterize these intrusions. It transcends the simplistic portrayal of hackers as mere malevolent actors, instead, painting a nuanced picture of individuals wielding a diverse set of skills in a realm where boundaries are porous and consequences profound.

The narrative intricately weaves through the historical tapestry of cyber warfare, tracing the evolution of hacking from its nascent days to the present era of sophisticated cyber threats. The dichotomy between the pioneers who sought to explore the digital frontier and those who exploit its vulnerabilities for malicious intent becomes a focal point. Drawing parallels between the hackers of yesteryears—often driven by curiosity or a desire for exploration—and their modern counterparts who operate within the shadows of organized cybercrime, the narrative navigates the ethical labyrinth that defines hacking as both an art and a weapon.

As the journey progresses, the playbook of hackers unfolds like a dark and cryptic manuscript, revealing the diverse tactics employed to breach digital fortifications. The narrative unveils the intricacies of social engineering, phishing attacks, and malware deployment, peeling back the layers of obfuscation that shroud these techniques. The reader is immersed in the cat-and-mouse game between security experts and hackers, where each innovation in defense is met with a countermeasure born out of the ingenuity of those who thrive in the shadows.

The global nature of cyber warfare becomes apparent as the narrative expands beyond individual hackers to encompass state-sponsored cyber attacks. The geopolitical dimensions of hacking come to the forefront, with nations engaging in a covert battle for digital supremacy. The narrative elucidates the blurred lines between cyber espionage, cybercrime, and hacktivism, highlighting the interconnectedness of these seemingly disparate realms. The consequences of these geopolitical cyber maneuvers ripple across borders, impacting not only governments and corporations but also the lives of individuals caught in the crossfire.

Amidst the tension and intrigue, the narrative weaves in the ethical considerations that accompany the exploration of hacking's playbook. It prompts reflection on the fine line between the virtuous pursuit of securing digital landscapes and the morally ambiguous realm of hacking for personal gain or malicious intent. The narrative grapples with questions of accountability, responsibility, and the ethical imperative to safeguard the digital commons from those who seek to exploit its vulnerabilities.

In the final chapters of this gripping exploration, the narrative takes a forward-looking stance, contemplating the future of cyber warfare and the evolving dynamics between defenders and adversaries. The increasing integration of artificial intelligence, the advent of quantum computing, and the expanding attack surface of the Internet of Things add layers of complexity to the already intricate dance between hackers and those who strive to protect digital infrastructures.

"Hacker's Playbook: Unraveling the Tactics Behind Cyber Attacks" concludes as more than a narrative; it serves as a call to action. The reader is left with a profound awareness of the stakes involved in the ongoing battle for cyber resilience. It beckons individuals, organizations, and nations to confront the challenges of the digital age head-on, fostering a collective commitment to fortify the vulnerable seams of our interconnected world. The narrative leaves an indelible imprint, urging society to confront the dark underbelly of the digital realm with a sense of vigilance, understanding, and a relentless pursuit of technological evolution that prioritizes security without sacrificing innovation.

Chapter 1: The Genesis of Hacking

Define hacking and its origins in the early days of computing.

Hacking, in the realm of computing, can be broadly defined as the exploration, manipulation, or unauthorized access to computer systems or networks with the intent of gaining information, altering data, or disrupting normal operations. The origins of hacking trace back to the early days of computing, a time when the concept of computer security was still in its infancy. In the 1950s and 1960s, as mainframe computers emerged, a culture of curiosity and experimentation began to flourish among early computer enthusiasts and programmers. These individuals, driven by a passion for understanding the inner workings of these machines, engaged in what could be considered benign hacking - exploring the capabilities and limitations of the newly emerging technology. However, it was during the 1970s that the term "hacker" started to take on a more ambiguous connotation.

The Homebrew Computer Club, founded in 1975 in Silicon Valley, played a pivotal role in shaping the early hacker culture. This club brought together like-minded individuals, including Steve Wozniak and Steve Jobs, who later co-founded Apple Inc. The club members shared a common interest in tinkering with computers and pushing the boundaries of what these machines could achieve. Around the same time, the advent of the ARPANET, the precursor to the modern internet, further fueled the exploration of computer systems. The notion of hacking, at this stage, was not necessarily associated with malicious intent; rather, it embodied the spirit of exploration and a desire to understand the inner workings of complex systems.

As computers became more prevalent in the 1980s, so did the darker side of hacking. With the rise of personal computers and interconnected networks, opportunities for unauthorized access and data manipulation increased. The line between benign exploration and malicious intrusion began to blur. In this era, hackers started to distinguish themselves into various categories based on their motives. "White hat" hackers focused on using their skills to enhance security, identifying vulnerabilities to help organizations strengthen their systems. Conversely, "black hat" hackers engaged in activities with malicious intent, such as unauthorized access, data theft, and system disruptions.

The 1980s also witnessed the emergence of notable hacking incidents, contributing to the evolving public perception of hackers. One of the most infamous cases was the Morris Worm, unleashed in 1988 by Robert Tappan Morris, a graduate student at Cornell University. The worm was intended to measure the size of the internet but ended up causing widespread disruption, infecting thousands of computers and highlighting the potential dangers of malicious hacking. This incident led to the first conviction under the Computer Fraud and Abuse Act (CFAA) in the United States.

As the 1990s unfolded, hacking took on new dimensions with the rise of hacktivism, a form of hacking motivated by political or social causes. Groups like the Chaos Computer Club in Germany and the Cult of the Dead Cow in the United States gained attention for their combination of technical skills and ideological motivations. The internet became a battleground for hacktivists, who used their abilities to promote free speech, challenge censorship, and raise awareness about various social issues.

Simultaneously, the term "cracker" emerged to distinguish those hackers who engaged in malicious activities, such as breaking software protection mechanisms or distributing malware. The evolution of hacking nomenclature reflected the increasing diversity of motives within the hacking community. In the late 1990s and early 2000s, the world witnessed a series of high-profile hacking incidents, including the attacks on prominent websites and the defacement of digital platforms. Notably, the hacking group Lizard Squad gained notoriety for its distributed denial-of-service (DDoS) attacks on gaming networks and other online services.

The 21st century brought about a paradigm shift in the nature of hacking with the emergence of state-sponsored cyber-espionage and cyber warfare. Nation-states began to invest heavily in developing cyber capabilities to conduct intelligence gathering, sabotage, and influence operations in the digital realm. The Stuxnet worm, discovered in 2010 and believed to be a product of joint efforts by the United States and Israel, exemplified the intersection of hacking, espionage, and geopolitical conflict. This sophisticated malware was designed to target Iran's nuclear facilities, marking a new era where the digital realm became a battleground for geopolitical interests.

The rise of hacktivism and state-sponsored hacking also prompted a renewed focus on cybersecurity. Governments and organizations around the world began to invest in cybersecurity measures to protect critical infrastructure, sensitive data, and national security interests. The hacking landscape continued to evolve with the emergence of advanced persistent threats (APTs) - long-term and targeted cyber-espionage campaigns often attributed to nation-states.

The past decade has seen an exponential increase in the frequency and sophistication of cyber attacks. Major incidents, such as the SolarWinds supply chain attack in 2020, underscore the vulnerabilities inherent in interconnected digital systems. As technology continues to advance, so do the capabilities of hackers, making it an ongoing challenge for cybersecurity professionals to stay ahead of emerging threats.

In conclusion, the history of hacking in the early days of computing reflects a complex evolution from a culture of curiosity and exploration to a landscape marked by diverse motives, including malicious intent, hacktivism, and state-sponsored activities. The narrative of hacking has intertwined with the broader story of technological advancement, societal changes, and geopolitical tensions. As we navigate the digital age, the challenges posed by hacking persist, necessitating ongoing efforts to strike a balance between innovation, security, and ethical considerations in the ever-expanding realm of cyberspace.

Explore the curiosity-driven motivations of the first hackers.

The curiosity-driven motivations of the first hackers find their roots in the nascent days of computing, a time when the concept of computer security was in its infancy, and a pioneering spirit of exploration permeated the culture of early computer enthusiasts. In the 1950s and 1960s, as mainframe computers began to emerge, these machines were primarily the domain of researchers, engineers, and scientists. The limited accessibility and exclusive nature of these early computers fostered a close-knit community of individuals who shared a profound fascination with the potential of these new machines.

The first hackers were motivated by an insatiable curiosity to understand the inner workings of the newly developed computing systems. These pioneers saw the computer not merely as a tool but as a complex and intriguing entity that held the promise of unlocking unprecedented possibilities. Their motivations were rooted in a genuine passion for exploration, a desire to push the boundaries of what was known and understood about these technological marvels. The early hackers were driven by a sense of intellectual adventure, an innate need to comprehend the intricacies of the machines that were reshaping the landscape of information processing.

During this period, access to computers was limited, and the resources available were scarce. The curiosity-driven hackers were often individuals who sought creative ways to gain access to computer systems, overcoming barriers imposed by institutions that controlled these machines. Their efforts were not malicious but driven by a genuine thirst for knowledge and a belief that understanding the inner workings of computers could lead to innovations and advancements. The lack of formalized security measures in these early systems meant that individuals could explore and experiment without the fear of legal consequences.

The Homebrew Computer Club, founded in 1975 in Silicon Valley, played a pivotal role in fostering this curiosity-driven hacker culture. The club brought together like-minded individuals who were fascinated by the potential of personal computers. Members, including luminaries like Steve Wozniak and Steve Jobs, shared a common ethos of exploration and collaboration. The Homebrew Computer Club provided a space for these early hackers to showcase their creations, exchange ideas, and inspire each other to delve deeper into the world of computing.

The curiosity that fueled the first hackers was not limited to hardware alone; it extended to the software and the code that governed the behavior of these machines. Programmers and hackers alike were drawn to the challenge of understanding and manipulating code, deciphering the intricacies of programming languages, and exploring the potential for creating new software. This curiosity-driven exploration laid the foundation for the hacker ethos that celebrated the mastery of both hardware and software, a holistic understanding that distinguished hackers from mere users of technology.

In the absence of formal computer science education and established norms, the early hackers were largely self-taught and learned through hands-on experience. This autodidactic approach further fueled their curiosity, as each discovery and breakthrough provided a sense of accomplishment and validation. The early hackers were trailblazers, navigating uncharted territory with an experimental mindset, driven by the belief that their contributions could shape the future of computing.

The advent of the ARPANET, the precursor to the modern internet, in the late 1960s and early 1970s further expanded the canvas for exploration. The interconnected nature of the ARPANET allowed hackers to communicate and collaborate over vast distances, creating a virtual community where ideas could be shared and refined. The curiosity-driven hackers of this era were not confined by geographical limitations; they formed a global network of individuals who were united by their passion for uncovering the mysteries of computing.

While the motivations of the first hackers were primarily rooted in curiosity and exploration, the evolving landscape of computing also introduced ethical considerations. The distinction between benign exploration and potentially harmful activities began to blur as the capabilities of computers expanded, and the potential for unintended consequences became apparent. The Morris Worm incident in 1988, unleashed by a graduate student exploring the size of the internet, exemplified how a curiosity-driven endeavor could inadvertently lead to widespread disruption.

In conclusion, the curiosity-driven motivations of the first hackers were embedded in a unique historical context where computing technology was in its infancy, and a small community of enthusiasts sought to unravel its potential. These early hackers were united by a shared passion for exploration, a genuine curiosity to understand and manipulate the burgeoning world of computers. Their endeavors laid the foundation for a culture that celebrated innovation, creativity, and a hands-on approach to learning. As the digital landscape evolved, so too did the motivations and consequences of hacking, but the curiosity-driven spirit of the first hackers remains an enduring and integral aspect of the ever-evolving world of computing.

Highlight key figures in the history of hacking, such as Kevin Mitnick and Adrian Lamo.

In the annals of hacking history, certain key figures have emerged whose exploits and contributions have left an indelible mark on the evolving landscape of cybersecurity. Among these luminaries is

Kevin Mitnick, a name synonymous with both the notoriety of early hacking and the redemption that can come through rehabilitation. Mitnick gained prominence in the 1980s and 1990s as one of the world's most wanted computer criminals. His exploits involved infiltrating computer systems of major corporations, government agencies, and telecommunication companies. Mitnick's hacking skills were formidable, characterized by social engineering tactics and a deep understanding of computer systems. His elusive nature earned him the moniker of the "Condor," as he evaded law enforcement for years.

Mitnick's hacking journey took a dramatic turn in 1995 when he was apprehended by the FBI, marking the end of his notorious hacking career. The legal battle that ensued culminated in his sentencing to five years in prison, with an additional three years of supervised release. During his time in prison, Mitnick underwent a transformation, not only in terms of his personal outlook but also in his approach to technology. He used his incarceration as an opportunity to gain a formal education in computer networks and security, turning away from malicious hacking and towards ethical cybersecurity practices.

Upon his release in 2000, Kevin Mitnick reinvented himself as a cybersecurity consultant, author, and speaker. His experiences provided valuable insights into the vulnerabilities of computer systems, and he became an advocate for strengthening cybersecurity measures. Mitnick's journey from notorious hacker to respected cybersecurity expert serves as a compelling narrative of redemption and the potential for individuals to channel their skills towards positive ends.

Another key figure in the history of hacking is Adrian Lamo, a figure whose actions were driven by a complex interplay of ethical considerations and the legal consequences of his choices. Lamo gained notoriety in 2003 when he breached the security of major corporations, including Microsoft and Yahoo. However, it was his involvement in a high-profile case in 2010 that brought him into the spotlight. Lamo reported Chelsea Manning, then an intelligence analyst in the U.S. Army, to authorities for leaking classified documents to WikiLeaks.

Lamo's decision to turn in Manning sparked intense debates about ethics within the hacking community. While some viewed him as a whistleblower who prioritized national security, others saw him as a traitor to the hacker ethos of solidarity and resistance against authority. Lamo's complex legacy highlights the ethical dilemmas that can arise within the hacking subculture and underscores the tension between personal values and societal responsibilities.

The hacking landscape has also been shaped by figures like Julian Assange, the founder of WikiLeaks, who played a pivotal role in the publication of classified information provided by whistleblowers. Assange's influence extended beyond hacking into the realm of information dissemination and transparency. WikiLeaks, under Assange's leadership, became a platform for leaking sensitive government documents, sparking controversies and legal battles. Assange's impact on the intersection of hacking, journalism, and activism underscores the evolving nature of information warfare in the digital age.

The emergence of hacktivist groups introduced figures like Jeremy Hammond, a member of the hacktivist collective Anonymous. Hammond gained notoriety for his involvement in high-profile cyber attacks, including the breach of the private intelligence firm Stratfor in 2011. His motivations were rooted in political activism, and he saw hacking as a means to expose corruption and challenge oppressive systems. Hammond's actions, like those of other hacktivists, blurred the lines between traditional hacking, activism, and civil disobedience, illustrating the growing influence of hacktivism as a form of digital protest.

In the realm of state-sponsored hacking, figures like Edward Snowden became central to the global discourse on government surveillance and privacy. Snowden, a former NSA contractor, leaked a trove of classified documents in 2013, revealing extensive surveillance programs conducted by the U.S. government. His actions sparked international debates on the balance between national security and individual privacy, reshaping public perceptions of government surveillance practices. Snowden's revelations had far-reaching consequences, leading to legal reforms, increased awareness of digital privacy issues, and a reevaluation of the role of whistleblowers in a digital age.

The history of hacking also features individuals like Gary McKinnon, a British hacker known for his alleged intrusion into U.S. military and NASA computer systems. McKinnon claimed that he was searching for evidence of UFOs and free energy technology cover-ups. His case garnered attention due to extradition proceedings initiated by the U.S. government, highlighting the challenges and legal complexities surrounding transnational cybercrime.

The list of key figures in hacking history is extensive and diverse, reflecting the multifaceted nature of this subculture. Each individual has contributed to shaping the narrative of hacking, whether through notoriety, activism, or ethical considerations. As the digital landscape continues to evolve, new figures will inevitably emerge, leaving their own imprint on the ever-changing dynamics of hacking and cybersecurity.

Discuss their contributions to shaping the hacking culture.

The contributions of key figures such as Kevin Mitnick, Adrian Lamo, Julian Assange, Jeremy Hammond, Edward Snowden, and Gary McKinnon have played a profound role in shaping the complex and multifaceted culture of hacking. Each individual's actions and motivations have left a lasting impact on the trajectory of hacking, influencing not only the technical aspects of cyber activity but also the ethical, legal, and societal dimensions that define this subculture.

Kevin Mitnick's contributions to the hacking culture are marked by the duality of his narrative – from notorious hacker to ethical cybersecurity consultant. In the early years of his hacking career, Mitnick's exploits exemplified a deep understanding of computer systems and a knack for social engineering. His actions, while illegal, demonstrated the vulnerabilities of early computer networks and underscored the need for improved cybersecurity measures. However, it was Mitnick's post-incarceration transformation that became equally significant. By embracing ethical hacking and sharing his experiences, Mitnick contributed to the evolving narrative that hackers could transition from the shadows to become valuable assets in the fight against cyber threats. His journey became a cautionary tale and an inspiration for those seeking redemption and a legitimate path in the field of cybersecurity.

Adrian Lamo's contributions to hacking culture are marked by a complex interplay of ethical choices and the consequences of those choices. Lamo's infiltration of major corporations showcased the vulnerabilities of digital systems but it was his decision to report Chelsea Manning, a fellow hacker and whistleblower, that ignited debates within the hacking community. Lamo's actions raised ethical questions about loyalty, responsibility, and the blurry line between hacking and whistleblowing. His legacy serves as a reminder of the ethical dilemmas that hackers may face, navigating the fine line between activism, accountability, and the legal consequences of their choices.

Julian Assange, the founder of WikiLeaks, played a pivotal role in shaping the hacking culture by elevating it from the realm of clandestine activities to a form of information warfare and transparency advocacy. Assange's contributions extended beyond traditional hacking, focusing on the publication of classified information provided by whistleblowers. WikiLeaks became a platform for exposing government secrets, challenging oppressive regimes, and advocating for freedom of information. Assange's approach stirred controversy, raising questions about the responsibilities of those who wield the power to disseminate sensitive information. His impact on the intersection of hacking, journalism, and activism underscores the shifting landscape of information dissemination in the digital age.

Jeremy Hammond, as a prominent member of the hacktivist collective Anonymous, contributed to shaping the hacking culture by fusing technical prowess with political activism. Hammond's involvement in high-profile cyber attacks, including the breach of Stratfor, exemplified the emergence of hacktivism as a potent form of digital protest. His actions were driven by a desire to expose corruption and challenge oppressive systems, reflecting a growing trend where hacking became a tool for political dissent. Hammond's contributions highlighted the potential of hacking as a means of civil disobedience, blurring the lines between traditional cyber activities and activism in the digital realm.

Edward Snowden's monumental contributions to the hacking culture revolve around exposing extensive government surveillance programs and sparking a global conversation on digital privacy. Snowden's leak of classified documents in 2013 brought to light the scale of mass surveillance conducted by the U.S. government. His revelations prompted widespread public discourse on the balance between national security and individual privacy, leading to legal reforms and increased awareness of digital rights. Snowden's actions elevated the role of whistleblowers in the digital age, challenging the notion of government secrecy and reshaping the discourse on the ethical responsibilities of those with insider knowledge.

Gary McKinnon's contributions to the hacking culture are notable for their unique context, as he claimed to be driven by a quest for uncovering evidence of UFOs and free energy technology cover-ups. While his actions, including alleged intrusion into U.S. military and NASA systems, were met with legal repercussions, McKinnon's case raised questions about the motivations behind hacking and the complexities of cross-border cybercrime. His contributions underscore the diversity of motives within the hacking community, ranging from political activism to unconventional quests for hidden knowledge.

Collectively, the contributions of these key figures have woven a rich tapestry that defines the hacking culture. They have illuminated the intricate interplay between technical expertise, ethical considerations, and the societal implications of hacking activities. The narratives of Mitnick's redemption, Lamo's ethical dilemma, Assange's information warfare, Hammond's hacktivism, Snowden's digital whistleblowing, and McKinnon's unconventional quest collectively showcase the multifaceted nature of hacking as a subculture that transcends mere technical expertise. As technology continues to advance, the legacies of these figures will undoubtedly influence the evolving dynamics of hacking, cybersecurity, and the ethical considerations surrounding digital activism and information disclosure.

Trace the evolution of hacking techniques from simple exploits to more sophisticated methods.

The evolution of hacking techniques is a captivating journey that mirrors the rapid advancements in computer technology and the perpetual cat-and-mouse game between hackers and cybersecurity professionals. In the early days of computing, hacking techniques were relatively straightforward, driven more by curiosity and a desire for exploration than malicious intent. The 1960s and 1970s witnessed the emergence of what can be considered the pioneering era of hacking, marked by the exploits of individuals like Kevin Mitnick. At this stage, hacking often involved gaining unauthorized access to computer systems using basic techniques such as password guessing, exploiting weak system configurations, or leveraging social engineering tactics. The security measures in place during this era were rudimentary compared to today's standards, making it relatively easier for hackers to navigate through digital systems.

The 1980s ushered in a new phase of hacking characterized by the advent of personal computers and interconnected networks. Hacking techniques evolved in tandem with the expanding digital landscape. The Morris Worm incident in 1988, created by Robert Tappan Morris, showcased a shift from relatively simple exploits to more sophisticated methods. The worm exploited vulnerabilities in Unix systems, spreading rapidly and causing widespread disruption. The incident underscored the potential for malicious code to propagate on a large scale and raised awareness about the importance of securing interconnected computer networks.

As the 1990s unfolded, hacking techniques continued to advance, propelled by the increasing popularity of the internet. The rise of script kiddies, individuals who lacked deep technical knowledge but used readily available hacking tools, marked a notable trend. Automated tools and scripts enabled less skilled individuals to engage in hacking activities, contributing to a broader and more decentralized hacking landscape. Additionally, the era saw the emergence of techniques like packet sniffing, where hackers intercepted and analyzed network traffic to glean sensitive information such as login credentials. The democratization of hacking tools and techniques during this period expanded the pool of potential threat actors.

The late 1990s and early 2000s witnessed a surge in the sophistication of hacking techniques, driven in part by the increasing prevalence of e-commerce and online transactions. Techniques such as SQL injection and cross-site scripting (XSS) became prominent as attackers sought to exploit vulnerabilities in web applications. SQL injection, for instance, involved manipulating a website's database through user input fields, allowing hackers to extract, modify, or delete sensitive information. These techniques represented a shift from traditional system-focused hacking to a more targeted approach aimed at compromising web-based services and applications.

The emergence of distributed denial-of-service (DDoS) attacks in the late 1990s marked another milestone in the evolution of hacking techniques. Attackers leveraged networks of compromised computers, known as botnets, to flood target systems with traffic, rendering them inaccessible. DDoS attacks became a favored tool for hacktivists and cybercriminals seeking to disrupt online services, extort organizations, or advance political agendas. The scale and impact of DDoS attacks demonstrated the potential for cyber threats to transcend individual systems and target the availability of entire online platforms.

The 21st century brought about a paradigm shift with the rise of advanced persistent threats (APTs), a category of hacking techniques characterized by sophisticated, long-term campaigns often attributed to nation-states. APTs involve a combination of advanced technical capabilities, meticulous planning, and a persistent, stealthy approach. Stuxnet, discovered in 2010 and believed to be a product of joint efforts by the United States and Israel, exemplified the convergence of hacking, espionage, and geopolitical conflict. Stuxnet targeted Iran's nuclear facilities, using a combination of zero-day exploits and advanced evasion techniques to compromise air-gapped systems.

The evolution of hacking techniques continued to accelerate with the increasing interconnectedness of digital systems and the proliferation of mobile devices. Exploits targeting vulnerabilities in mobile operating systems, such as iOS and Android, became prevalent. Techniques like jailbreaking and rooting, which aimed to bypass the built-in security measures of mobile devices, gained traction. Mobile malware, designed to compromise smartphones and tablets, emerged as a significant threat vector, reflecting the shift in user behavior towards mobile computing.

In recent years, hacking techniques have evolved in response to the growing complexity of IT environments and the integration of emerging technologies. The widespread adoption of cloud computing introduced new attack vectors, with hackers targeting misconfigurations in cloud infrastructure and exploiting vulnerabilities in cloud-based services. Phishing attacks, where attackers use deceptive emails or messages to trick individuals into revealing sensitive information, evolved to become more sophisticated, incorporating social engineering tactics to increase their effectiveness.

The rise of ransomware represents a particularly impactful evolution in hacking techniques. Ransomware attacks involve encrypting the victim's data and demanding a ransom for its release. The use of advanced encryption algorithms and the anonymization of cryptocurrency payments have made it challenging for victims and law enforcement to trace and apprehend the perpetrators. Notable ransomware incidents, such as the WannaCry attack in 2017, demonstrated the potential for widespread disruption and financial impact.

The advent of artificial intelligence (AI) and machine learning has introduced a new dimension to hacking techniques. Attackers leverage AI to automate tasks such as reconnaissance, vulnerability scanning, and even the generation of sophisticated phishing emails. Conversely, cybersecurity professionals deploy AI to enhance threat detection, analyze patterns, and respond to evolving cyber threats in real-time. This AI-driven arms race has elevated the complexity of cyber operations on both sides of the spectrum.

In conclusion, the evolution of hacking techniques mirrors the relentless pace of technological progress and the dynamic nature of the cybersecurity landscape. From the early days of curiosity-driven exploration to the present era of sophisticated APTs and AI-driven attacks, hackers have continually adapted their methods to exploit emerging vulnerabilities. The evolution is marked by a progression from simple exploits and manual intrusion techniques to automated, stealthy, and highly targeted approaches. As the digital realm continues to evolve, the ongoing challenge for cybersecurity professionals is to anticipate and counteract the next wave of innovative hacking techniques, leveraging technology, collaboration, and proactive defense strategies to stay ahead of the ever-adapting threat landscape.

Discuss notable hacking incidents that marked turning points.

The history of hacking is punctuated by notable incidents that have served as turning points, reshaping the landscape of cybersecurity and influencing the trajectory of digital security practices. One such turning point occurred in 1988 with the emergence of the Morris Worm, a computer worm written by Robert Tappan Morris. Designed to measure the size of the internet, the worm inadvertently caused widespread disruption, infecting thousands of computers and highlighting the potential dangers of unchecked malware. The incident marked a pivotal moment, drawing attention to the vulnerabilities of interconnected computer networks and prompting increased efforts to develop more robust cybersecurity measures.

The early 2000s witnessed the rise of Code Red and Nimda, two significant incidents that underscored the global impact of large-scale cyber attacks. The Code Red worm, discovered in 2001, targeted Microsoft IIS web servers and spread rapidly, defacing websites with the message "HELLO! Welcome to http://www.worm.com! Hacked By Chinese!" Nimda, which emerged in 2001 as well, was a hybrid worm that combined features of viruses, worms, and malicious scripts. Nimda's ability to propagate through multiple vectors, including email attachments and network shares, showcased the increasing sophistication of cyber threats. These incidents prompted a heightened awareness of the need for coordinated international efforts to combat cyber attacks and demonstrated the potential for widespread disruption caused by malicious code.

The Stuxnet worm, discovered in 2010, marked a paradigm shift in hacking incidents, introducing the world to the concept of a state-sponsored cyber-weapon. Believed to be a joint effort by the United States and Israel, Stuxnet was designed to target Iran's nuclear facilities, specifically its uranium enrichment program. The worm demonstrated an unprecedented level of complexity, using multiple zero-day vulnerabilities and sophisticated evasion techniques. Stuxnet not only caused physical damage to Iran's nuclear infrastructure but also ushered in an era where cyber operations became intertwined with geopolitical conflicts. The incident highlighted the strategic use of hacking tools as instruments of national power, blurring the lines between traditional warfare and cyber operations.

The Sony Pictures hack in 2014 marked a turning point in the realm of cyber attacks with its combination of destructive intent and geopolitical implications. Attributed to North Korea, the attack was a response to the planned release of the film "The Interview," which depicted a fictional assassination attempt on North Korean leader Kim Jong-un. The hackers, known as the Guardians of Peace, not only stole and leaked sensitive corporate data but also executed a destructive wiper malware, crippling the organization's computer systems. The incident underscored the potential for cyber attacks to extend beyond data theft and disruption to include geopolitical retaliation and the suppression of free expression.

The WannaCry ransomware attack in 2017 represented a watershed moment in the evolution of cyber threats. Exploiting a vulnerability in Microsoft Windows, WannaCry spread rapidly across the globe, infecting hundreds of thousands of computers in over 150 countries. The attack demonstrated the wide-reaching impact of ransomware, affecting critical infrastructure, healthcare systems, and businesses. The use of sophisticated encryption algorithms and the demand for ransom payments in cryptocurrency highlighted the financial motives driving modern cybercriminals. The incident prompted renewed urgency in addressing software vulnerabilities, improving patch management practices, and developing strategies to mitigate the impact of ransomware attacks.

The SolarWinds supply chain attack, discovered in late 2020, marked a highly sophisticated and far-reaching intrusion with significant implications for cybersecurity. The attack targeted the software supply chain, compromising the SolarWinds Orion platform, which is widely used for network management. The attackers, believed to be a Russian state-sponsored group, inserted a malicious backdoor into software updates, enabling them to infiltrate numerous organizations, including U.S. government agencies and major corporations. The incident exposed the vulnerability of software supply chains and underscored the challenges of defending against advanced persistent threats (APTs) with the capacity for patient and stealthy infiltration.

The Colonial Pipeline ransomware attack in 2021 highlighted the tangible consequences of cyber attacks on critical infrastructure. A ransomware group known as DarkSide targeted the Colonial Pipeline, a major fuel pipeline system in the United States. The attack disrupted fuel supplies along the East Coast, leading to panic buying and fuel shortages. The incident underscored the vulnerability of critical infrastructure to cyber threats and emphasized the need for enhanced cybersecurity measures in sectors that directly impact public safety and national security.

Each of these hacking incidents represents a turning point in the evolution of cybersecurity, influencing the development of defensive strategies, shaping public perceptions of digital threats, and prompting regulatory responses. From the early days of worms and viruses to state-sponsored cyber-espionage and ransomware attacks on critical infrastructure, these incidents have collectively contributed to the ongoing evolution of the cybersecurity landscape. The lessons learned from these turning points continue to inform the efforts of cybersecurity professionals, policymakers, and technology innovators as they work to stay ahead of emerging threats in an increasingly interconnected and digital world.

Examine the blurred lines between hacking as a skill and hacking as a criminal act.

The blurred lines between hacking as a skill and hacking as a criminal act have been a constant and complex theme in the evolution of the digital landscape. At its core, hacking represents a set of technical skills and knowledge that can be applied for various purposes, ranging from ethical and constructive uses to malicious and criminal activities. The term "hacking" itself has undergone a semantic transformation over the years, evolving from its original meaning of playful exploration and experimentation with technology to encompass a broader spectrum of activities, including those with criminal intent.

In the early days of computing, hackers were often individuals driven by a genuine curiosity to understand and explore the intricacies of computer systems. Hacking, in this context, was more about the thrill of discovery and the intellectual challenge of pushing the boundaries of technology. These early hackers were not necessarily motivated by malicious intent but were instead pioneers who contributed to the development of computing and the shaping of cybersecurity practices.

However, as technology advanced and computer systems became more integral to everyday life, the motivations and actions of hackers began to diversify. The advent of the internet provided hackers with unprecedented opportunities to exploit vulnerabilities, and the lines between hacking as a skill and criminal activity started to blur. The transition from benign exploration to malicious intrusion became more pronounced, especially with the increasing interconnectedness of digital systems.

The 1980s witnessed a shift in the perception of hackers as individuals who engaged in unauthorized access to computer systems

for various purposes, including stealing information, spreading malware, or disrupting services. The term "cracker" emerged to distinguish those hackers who engaged in malicious activities, highlighting
the growing recognition of hacking as a potential criminal act. Legal
frameworks, such as the Computer Fraud and Abuse Act (CFAA)
in the United States, were enacted to address unauthorized access to
computer systems and curb criminal hacking activities.

The hacker subculture became more nuanced, with individuals
falling along a spectrum that ranged from "white hat" hackers, who
used their skills for ethical and constructive purposes, to "black hat"
hackers, who engaged in criminal activities. The motivations behind
hacking, whether driven by curiosity, activism, financial gain, or a desire for notoriety, contributed to the complexity of defining hacking
solely as a skill or a criminal act. The subculture also saw the emergence of "grey hat" hackers, who operated in a morally ambiguous
space, sometimes engaging in unauthorized activities with the intent
of exposing vulnerabilities and promoting cybersecurity awareness.

The blurred lines were further accentuated by the rise of hacktivism, a form of hacking motivated by political or social causes.
Hacktivist groups, such as Anonymous, used their hacking skills to
advance ideological agendas, challenge censorship, and expose perceived injustices. While hacktivism often involved unauthorized access and disruptive actions, the motivations behind these activities
were not purely criminal; rather, they were rooted in a form of digital
activism seeking to effect change.

The advent of sophisticated cybercrime enterprises in the late
20th century and early 21st century marked a significant shift in the
landscape of hacking. Criminal organizations began leveraging hacking skills for financial gain, engaging in activities such as data theft,
identity fraud, and the development of sophisticated malware for
profit. The commodification of hacking tools on the dark web further contributed to the perception of hacking as a criminal enter-

prise, with individuals and groups selling their expertise to the highest bidder.

State-sponsored hacking introduced another layer of complexity to the blurred lines between hacking as a skill and a criminal act. Nation-states began investing heavily in developing cyber capabilities for intelligence gathering, economic espionage, and even sabotage. The Stuxnet worm, discovered in 2010 and believed to be a product of joint efforts by the United States and Israel, exemplified the intersection of hacking, geopolitical conflict, and the strategic use of digital weapons. State-sponsored hacking activities, while often aligned with national interests, raised ethical questions about the boundaries of acceptable behavior in cyberspace and the potential for geopolitical tensions to manifest in the digital realm.

The rise of ransomware in recent years has further muddled the distinctions between hacking as a skill and criminal activity. Ransomware attacks involve the use of sophisticated encryption to lock victims out of their own systems, with attackers demanding a ransom for the release of the data. The ransomware ecosystem has become highly organized, with ransomware-as-a-service (RaaS) models allowing even those with limited technical skills to engage in cyber extortion. The financial motivations behind ransomware attacks, coupled with the use of cryptocurrencies for ransom payments, have elevated these activities to a level of criminal sophistication that extends beyond mere technical prowess.

Ethical hacking, or "white hat" hacking, has emerged as a counterforce to criminal hacking activities. Ethical hackers use their skills to identify and address vulnerabilities in computer systems, helping organizations strengthen their cybersecurity defenses. Bug bounty programs, where organizations reward individuals for responsibly disclosing security flaws, provide a legitimate outlet for hackers to apply their skills in a constructive manner. The field of ethical hacking has gained recognition and legitimacy, with certifications such as

Certified Ethical Hacker (CEH) becoming widely recognized in the cybersecurity industry.

The ongoing debate over the ethics of hacking and the role of hacktivism in promoting social and political change further complicates the distinctions between hacking as a skill and a criminal act. Some argue that hacktivism serves as a digital form of civil disobedience, challenging oppressive regimes and corporate entities. Others contend that any unauthorized access or disruption, regardless of the underlying motivations, constitutes a criminal act.

The legal landscape surrounding hacking remains dynamic and varies across jurisdictions. The prosecution of hackers often hinges on the intent behind their actions, with legal frameworks attempting to differentiate between those who seek to exploit vulnerabilities for criminal gain and those who aim to expose weaknesses for the greater good. However, the enforcement of cybercrime laws faces challenges, particularly when hackers operate across international borders or when their activities are seen as politically motivated.

In conclusion, the blurred lines between hacking as a skill and hacking as a criminal act reflect the intricate interplay of technological advancement, societal values, and legal frameworks. The evolution of hacking from a subculture rooted in curiosity to a landscape populated by diverse actors with varied motivations has contributed to the complexity of defining hacking strictly as a skill or a criminal activity. As technology continues to advance, the ethical considerations surrounding hacking will remain a subject of ongoing discourse, demanding a nuanced understanding that acknowledges the multifaceted nature of hacking in the digital age.

Discuss the emergence of ethical hacking as a response.

The emergence of ethical hacking, also known as penetration testing or white hat hacking, represents a proactive and constructive response to the evolving landscape of cybersecurity threats. Ethical hacking is rooted in the recognition that, in order to defend against malicious hackers and cybercriminals, organizations need individuals with similar skills and knowledge to identify and address vulnerabilities before they can be exploited for nefarious purposes. This paradigm shift from viewing all hacking activities as inherently malicious to acknowledging the potential positive contributions of skilled individuals has transformed the perception of hacking within the cybersecurity community.

In the early days of computing, hacking was predominantly associated with curiosity-driven exploration and experimentation. As technology advanced, and the interconnectedness of digital systems increased, the motivations behind hacking diversified, leading to a surge in malicious activities. The 1980s witnessed the emergence of computer security concerns, prompting the need for defensive strategies against unauthorized access, data breaches, and system compromises. Ethical hacking arose as a response to this growing threat landscape, with the fundamental idea that the best defense against hackers is often a skilled and knowledgeable offense.

The first inklings of ethical hacking were evident in the work of early computer security pioneers who sought to understand and address vulnerabilities in computer systems. The Computer Emergency Response Team (CERT), established in 1988, played a crucial role in coordinating responses to computer security incidents and facilitating the exchange of information within the cybersecurity community. While CERT focused on incident response and coordination, its activities laid the groundwork for the collaborative approach that would become central to ethical hacking practices.

The concept of ethical hacking gained further traction in the 1990s as cybersecurity professionals recognized the need for proactive measures to assess and strengthen the security posture of systems. The Certified Ethical Hacker (CEH) certification, introduced by the International Council of E-Commerce Consultants (EC-Council) in 2003, formalized the training and recognition of individuals engaged in ethical hacking. The CEH certification aimed to establish a standard for ethical hacking practices and provide a framework for professionals to acquire the necessary skills and knowledge.

Ethical hacking involves simulating real-world cyber attacks to identify vulnerabilities in systems, networks, and applications. Ethical hackers, often employed by organizations or working as independent consultants, use the same techniques and tools as malicious hackers to uncover weaknesses in security defenses. However, their motivations are aligned with the goal of improving security rather than exploiting vulnerabilities for malicious purposes. By adopting the mindset of a potential adversary, ethical hackers help organizations understand and address their security vulnerabilities before they can be exploited by cybercriminals.

The adoption of ethical hacking practices has become increasingly widespread across industries, driven by the realization that cybersecurity is a continuous and dynamic process. Organizations recognize the need to move beyond reactive security measures and embrace a proactive approach that involves regularly assessing and fortifying their defenses. Ethical hacking provides a controlled environment for organizations to evaluate their security posture, identify weaknesses, and implement effective countermeasures.

One of the key drivers for the growth of ethical hacking is the dynamic and rapidly evolving nature of cyber threats. As cybercriminals continuously develop new techniques and exploit emerging vulnerabilities, ethical hackers serve as a valuable line of defense by staying abreast of the latest trends in hacking and security. The practice of ethical hacking involves conducting regular penetration tests, vulnerability assessments, and security audits to ensure that an organization's defenses remain robust and resilient in the face of evolving threats.

The integration of ethical hacking into organizational cybersecurity strategies is not only a response to the external threat landscape but also a proactive measure to comply with regulatory requirements and industry standards. Many regulatory frameworks, such as the Payment Card Industry Data Security Standard (PCI DSS) and the Health Insurance Portability and Accountability Act (HIPAA), mandate regular security assessments and penetration testing to safeguard sensitive data and ensure the integrity of critical systems. Ethical hacking provides a systematic and methodical approach to meeting these compliance requirements, helping organizations demonstrate due diligence in protecting their digital assets.

The scope of ethical hacking extends beyond traditional network and system assessments to encompass a wide range of technologies and platforms. Mobile devices, web applications, cloud infrastructure, and Internet of Things (IoT) devices are now integral components of organizational IT ecosystems, and ethical hackers adapt their methodologies to evaluate the security of these diverse elements. The versatility of ethical hacking practices allows organizations to comprehensively assess their entire attack surface and identify potential vectors of exploitation.

Ethical hacking is characterized by a strong emphasis on collaboration and knowledge-sharing within the cybersecurity community. Bug bounty programs, which incentivize independent researchers to discover and responsibly disclose vulnerabilities, have become a popular mechanism for organizations to harness the collective intelligence of the global hacking community. Platforms such as HackerOne and Bugcrowd facilitate the coordination of bug bounty programs, enabling ethical hackers to contribute to the security of a wide range of applications and services.

The ethical hacking community has grown exponentially, fostering a culture of continuous learning and skill development. Conferences, such as DEF CON and Black Hat, provide platforms for ethical hackers to exchange ideas, showcase their findings, and engage with cybersecurity professionals, researchers, and enthusiasts. The collaborative nature of these events facilitates the dissemination of knowledge and best practices, contributing to the ongoing refinement and evolution of ethical hacking techniques.

The emergence of automation and artificial intelligence (AI) in cybersecurity has also influenced the practice of ethical hacking. Automated tools assist ethical hackers in performing routine tasks, such as vulnerability scanning and reconnaissance, allowing them to focus on more complex and nuanced aspects of security assessments. However, the human element remains crucial in ethical hacking, as skilled professionals bring contextual understanding, creativity, and intuition to the identification and exploitation of vulnerabilities that automated tools may overlook.

The integration of ethical hacking into the fabric of organizational cybersecurity has evolved from a niche practice to a mainstream necessity. As the frequency and sophistication of cyber attacks continue to escalate, ethical hacking serves as a linchpin in the defense against evolving threats. The collaborative and knowledge-sharing aspects of ethical hacking contribute not only to individual skill development but also to the resilience of the broader cybersecurity ecosystem. Ethical hacking represents a dynamic and adaptive response to the challenges posed by an ever-changing digital landscape, embodying the principle that, in the realm of cybersecurity, the best defense is a well-informed and skilled offense.

Explore how hacking has influenced the development of cybersecurity measures.

The symbiotic relationship between hacking and the development of cybersecurity measures has been a defining characteristic of the digital age. As hackers have continually sought to exploit vulnerabilities and compromise digital systems, the field of cybersecurity has evolved in response, adapting and innovating to mitigate the ever-expanding threat landscape. This intricate dance between attackers and defenders has significantly shaped the strategies, technologies, and methodologies employed in the ongoing battle to secure digital assets and protect sensitive information.

The early days of hacking, characterized by curious exploration and a desire to understand and manipulate computer systems, laid the foundation for cybersecurity considerations. As computing technology advanced, the first instances of unauthorized access and exploitation of vulnerabilities emerged. In response, rudimentary security measures were introduced, focusing on access controls and basic authentication mechanisms. The emergence of viruses and worms in the 1980s prompted the development of antivirus software as a reactive measure to detect and remove malicious code. The cat-and-mouse game between hackers and early cybersecurity efforts highlighted the need for more sophisticated defensive strategies.

The Morris Worm incident in 1988 marked a turning point, showcasing the potential for malicious code to propagate rapidly and disrupt interconnected computer networks. This incident prompted a paradigm shift, leading to increased awareness of the need for proactive cybersecurity measures. The field of intrusion detection and prevention systems began to gain prominence, aiming to identify and block unauthorized access and malicious activities within networks. The Morris Worm incident underscored the importance of not only protecting individual systems but also addressing vulnerabilities that could be exploited on a broader scale.

The 1990s witnessed a proliferation of hacking activities, with individuals and groups exploiting weaknesses in operating systems, applications, and network protocols. In response, the cybersecurity landscape expanded to encompass a broader array of defensive measures. Firewalls emerged as a critical component of network security, acting as barriers to unauthorized access and helping organizations control the flow of traffic. Encryption technologies became more prevalent, providing a means to secure data in transit and protect sensitive information from interception.

The rise of web-based applications and e-commerce in the late 1990s brought about new challenges, as hackers sought to exploit vulnerabilities in web servers and applications. Cross-site scripting (XSS) and SQL injection attacks became prevalent, prompting the development of secure coding practices and application security testing methodologies. The field of web application security evolved to address the unique threats posed by the dynamic nature of online interactions, emphasizing the importance of input validation and secure coding standards.

The early 2000s witnessed a surge in distributed denial-of-service (DDoS) attacks, which aimed to overwhelm and disrupt online services. DDoS mitigation strategies, including the use of specialized hardware and cloud-based services, became essential components of cybersecurity defenses. The recognition that cybersecurity required a holistic approach led to the development of frameworks and best practices, such as the ISO/IEC 27001 standard for information security management systems, providing organizations with guidelines for implementing comprehensive security measures.

The increasing sophistication of cyber threats prompted the development of threat intelligence and analysis capabilities. Cybersecurity professionals began actively monitoring and analyzing the tactics, techniques, and procedures employed by hackers to anticipate and mitigate potential attacks. Information sharing within the cybersecurity community became crucial, leading to the establishment of Information Sharing and Analysis Centers (ISACs) and collaborative platforms where organizations could share threat intelligence and insights.

The mid-2000s saw the proliferation of advanced persistent threats (APTs), sophisticated and targeted cyber attacks often attributed to nation-states. APTs emphasized the need for organizations to adopt a proactive and continuous approach to cybersecurity. Security frameworks, such as the NIST Cybersecurity Framework, emerged to guide organizations in managing cybersecurity risks effectively. These frameworks emphasized the importance of identifying, protecting, detecting, responding to, and recovering from cybersecurity incidents, aligning cybersecurity efforts with broader risk management strategies.

The advent of mobile computing and the widespread use of smartphones introduced new attack vectors, prompting the development of mobile security measures. Mobile device management (MDM) solutions, secure coding practices for mobile applications, and biometric authentication technologies became integral components of mobile cybersecurity. The complexity of the cybersecurity landscape led to the recognition that a one-size-fits-all approach was inadequate, prompting the development of adaptive security measures that could dynamically respond to evolving threats.

The rise of ransomware in the 2010s marked a significant shift in cybercriminal tactics, with attackers encrypting data and demanding ransom payments for its release. The development of effective backup and recovery strategies became crucial for organizations to mitigate the impact of ransomware attacks. Security awareness training for employees gained prominence as a proactive measure to reduce the likelihood of successful phishing attacks, a common vector for delivering ransomware.

The integration of artificial intelligence (AI) and machine learning (ML) into cybersecurity marked a new era in the battle against cyber threats. AI-driven technologies enable organizations to automate threat detection, analyze vast amounts of data for anomalous patterns, and respond to cybersecurity incidents in real-time. The use of behavioral analytics and anomaly detection became essential for identifying malicious activities that traditional signature-based approaches might miss.

The evolution of cloud computing introduced new considerations for cybersecurity, as organizations transitioned from on-premises infrastructure to cloud-based services. Cloud security measures, including identity and access management (IAM), encryption of data at rest and in transit, and security configurations for cloud services, became paramount. The shared responsibility model emphasized the collaborative effort between cloud service providers and customers to secure cloud environments effectively.

The development of a robust cybersecurity workforce became a critical aspect of defending against evolving threats. Recognizing the shortage of skilled cybersecurity professionals, educational programs and certifications, such as Certified Information Systems Security Professional (CISSP) and Certified Ethical Hacker (CEH), gained prominence. Industry collaboration with academic institutions and the establishment of cybersecurity training programs aimed to address the skills gap and cultivate a new generation of cybersecurity experts.

As cyber threats continue to evolve, the integration of automation, orchestration, and response (SOAR) technologies has become essential for streamlining cybersecurity operations. SOAR platforms enable organizations to automate routine tasks, orchestrate complex security workflows, and respond rapidly to cyber incidents. The use of threat hunting techniques, where cybersecurity professionals actively seek out potential threats within their environments, has become a proactive measure to identify and neutralize threats before they cause significant harm.

The regulatory landscape has also played a pivotal role in shaping cybersecurity measures. Data protection regulations, such as the General Data Protection Regulation (GDPR), mandate stringent requirements for the protection of personal data and impose significant penalties for non-compliance. The emphasis on privacy and data protection has led organizations to prioritize cybersecurity measures that safeguard sensitive information and ensure compliance with regulatory frameworks.

In conclusion, the dynamic interplay between hacking and the development of cybersecurity measures has been a driving force in shaping the field of cybersecurity. From the early days of curiosity-driven exploration to the sophisticated and targeted cyber threats of today, cybersecurity has evolved to become a multidimensional discipline that encompasses a wide range of technologies, methodologies, and best practices. The ongoing innovation in cybersecurity is a testament to the resilience and adaptability of defenders in the face of relentless and ever-evolving cyber threats.

Discuss the symbiotic relationship between hackers and the security industry.

The symbiotic relationship between hackers and the security industry represents a dynamic and complex interplay that has significantly shaped the evolution of cybersecurity. At its core, this relationship reflects the constant push and pull between those seeking to exploit vulnerabilities for various motives and the defenders working diligently to safeguard digital systems and information. While hackers and the security industry may seem at odds, their interactions have fostered a continual cycle of innovation, adaptation, and the development of increasingly sophisticated tools and strategies on both sides of the cybersecurity spectrum.

Hackers, often driven by curiosity, the pursuit of knowledge, or various motivations ranging from activism to criminal intent, have historically been the catalysts for change in the security landscape. The early days of hacking, characterized by pioneers exploring the potential of computer systems, laid the groundwork for the development of security measures. As hacking activities evolved to include malicious intent, the security industry responded by devising methods to detect, prevent, and mitigate unauthorized access and exploitation of vulnerabilities.

The symbiotic relationship is evident in the concept of ethical hacking, where individuals with hacking skills apply their expertise to identify and address vulnerabilities in systems, networks, and applications. Ethical hackers, also known as white hat hackers, play a crucial role in helping organizations stay one step ahead of malicious actors. They employ the same techniques and tools as their less ethical counterparts but do so with the intention of improving security rather than compromising it. Ethical hacking programs, often conducted through bug bounty initiatives, engage hackers to discover and responsibly disclose vulnerabilities, turning a potential threat into a collaborative effort to enhance cybersecurity.

The adversarial nature of hacking has fueled the constant evolution of cybersecurity technologies and strategies. As hackers develop new techniques and exploit emerging vulnerabilities, the security industry responds with innovations aimed at detecting, preventing, and mitigating these threats. This reactive and adaptive approach has led to the creation of antivirus software, intrusion detection systems, firewalls, and a myriad of other security solutions. The cyclical nature of this relationship is evident as new security measures prompt hackers to devise creative ways to bypass them, driving the need for continuous improvement and innovation in the security industry.

The emergence of threat intelligence as a discipline reflects the growing sophistication of both hackers and security professionals. Threat intelligence involves the collection, analysis, and dissemination of information about cyber threats, including the tactics, techniques, and procedures employed by hackers. This intelligence is a crucial resource for organizations seeking to anticipate and defend against cyber threats. The collaboration between the security industry and the hacking community in sharing threat intelligence has become essential for staying ahead of evolving attack vectors and tactics.

Bug bounty programs exemplify the cooperative aspect of the relationship between hackers and the security industry. These programs, initiated by organizations to encourage ethical hackers to identify and responsibly disclose vulnerabilities, represent a paradigm shift in viewing hackers as potential allies in the fight against cyber threats. Companies recognize the value of tapping into the diverse skills and perspectives of the global hacking community, turning what might be adversarial relationships into mutually beneficial collaborations. Bug bounty programs not only enhance security but also contribute to building a positive rapport between ethical hackers and organizations.

The development of cybersecurity certifications and training programs reflects the growing demand for skilled professionals in both offensive and defensive roles. Certifications such as Certified Ethical Hacker (CEH) and Offensive Security Certified Professional (OSCP) provide ethical hackers with recognized credentials, validating their skills and expertise. Similarly, defenders in the security industry pursue certifications like Certified Information Systems Security Professional (CISSP) and Certified Information Security Manager (CISM) to demonstrate their proficiency in designing and implementing robust security measures. The existence of these certifications underscores the mutual dependence between hackers and the security industry, with both sides investing in education and skill development.

The rise of nation-state-sponsored hacking has introduced a new dimension to the relationship between hackers and the security industry. State-sponsored actors leverage advanced cyber capabilities for espionage, political influence, and even sabotage. The security industry, in response, must contend with threats that surpass the capabilities of individual hackers or criminal organizations. The evolving tactics of nation-state actors challenge the industry to develop more sophisticated defenses, including advanced threat detection, attribution capabilities, and strategies to protect critical infrastructure from geopolitical cyber threats.

The continuous cycle of hacking and defense has fueled the development of threat hunting as a proactive cybersecurity measure. Threat hunting involves actively searching for signs of malicious activity within an organization's network, rather than waiting for automated systems to detect known threats. This approach recognizes the limitations of purely reactive measures and leverages human expertise to uncover subtle indicators of compromise that may go undetected by automated systems. The collaboration between threat hunters and ethical hackers emphasizes the human element in cybersecurity, acknowledging the importance of intuition and creativity in identifying emerging threats.

The advent of artificial intelligence (AI) and machine learning (ML) has introduced a new era in the relationship between hackers and the security industry. Hackers leverage AI to automate and enhance their attacks, using machine learning algorithms to analyze vast amounts of data and optimize their strategies. In response, the security industry harnesses AI and ML to bolster threat detection, automate routine tasks, and analyze patterns indicative of malicious activity. The race to develop more advanced AI-driven tools represents a contemporary battleground where both hackers and defenders seek to outsmart each other in a rapidly evolving technological landscape.

The increasing interconnectedness of digital systems, coupled with the proliferation of Internet of Things (IoT) devices, has expanded the attack surface, providing hackers with new vectors to exploit. The security industry grapples with the challenge of securing diverse and interconnected ecosystems, incorporating measures to protect not only traditional IT infrastructure but also smart devices, industrial control systems, and critical infrastructure. This evolving landscape highlights the need for a holistic and adaptive approach to cybersecurity that considers the complex interdependencies of modern digital ecosystems.

Legal and regulatory frameworks play a crucial role in shaping the dynamics of the relationship between hackers and the security industry. Legislation such as the Computer Fraud and Abuse Act (CFAA) in the United States criminalizes unauthorized access to computer systems, providing a legal basis for prosecuting malicious hackers. Conversely, the legal landscape recognizes the constructive role of ethical hacking, with protections in place for individuals who engage in responsible disclosure of vulnerabilities. The legal framework seeks to strike a balance between deterring malicious activities and fostering a cooperative environment where ethical hackers contribute to the improvement of cybersecurity.

In conclusion, the symbiotic relationship between hackers and the security industry is a testament to the dynamic nature of cybersecurity. The constant interplay between offensive and defensive strategies, innovation and adaptation, reflects the inherent complexity of securing digital systems in a rapidly evolving technological landscape. While hackers pose challenges and threats, they also serve as catalysts for the development of increasingly sophisticated security measures. This intricate dance between adversaries and defenders underscores the need for collaboration, continuous learning, and a proactive approach to cybersecurity that anticipates and mitigates emerging threats in a cooperative and mutually beneficial manner.

Chapter 2: The Art of Social Engineering

Define social engineering and its significance in the realm of cybersecurity.

Social engineering, in the context of cybersecurity, refers to the manipulation of individuals to deceive them into divulging sensitive information, performing actions, or compromising security measures. Unlike traditional hacking techniques that exploit technical vulnerabilities, social engineering exploits the human element, taking advantage of psychological and behavioral aspects to achieve malicious objectives. It is a tactic that relies on deception, persuasion, and manipulation to trick individuals into divulging confidential information or taking actions that can compromise the security of systems, networks, or personal data.

The significance of social engineering in the realm of cybersecurity cannot be overstated, as it represents a persistent and evolving threat that targets one of the most vulnerable components of any security infrastructure: human beings. No matter how robust technical safeguards may be, human error and susceptibility to manipulation remain inherent challenges in the cybersecurity landscape. Social engineering attacks come in various forms, ranging from phishing emails and pretexting to impersonation and baiting, all designed to exploit human psychology and trust.

Phishing, one of the most prevalent forms of social engineering, involves the use of deceptive emails, messages, or websites to trick individuals into revealing sensitive information such as login credentials or financial details. These phishing attempts often employ tactics like mimicking trusted entities, creating urgency, or exploiting current events to increase the likelihood of success. Spear phishing, a targeted form of phishing, customizes the attack to specific individuals or organizations, making it even more difficult to detect.

Pretexting involves the creation of a fabricated scenario or pretext to deceive individuals into providing information or performing actions they might not otherwise do. This could include impersonating a colleague, authority figure, or service provider to gain trust and manipulate the target into divulging sensitive information. The success of pretexting relies on the ability to create a plausible and convincing story that aligns with the target's expectations and social norms.

Impersonation, another form of social engineering, occurs when an attacker poses as a trusted individual or entity to manipulate the target. This could involve impersonating a colleague, technical support representative, or even a family member to gain access to information or resources. The psychological impact of believing that one is interacting with a trusted entity often lowers the target's guard, making them more susceptible to manipulation.

Baiting leverages the curiosity or desire for gain in individuals, enticing them to take actions that compromise security. This can involve leaving infected USB drives in public places, promising free downloads, or creating fake promotions that require the user to input sensitive information. By exploiting human tendencies, such as curiosity and the desire for something valuable, baiting attacks seek to compromise systems through the actions of unsuspecting individuals.

The significance of social engineering lies in its ability to bypass traditional security measures by targeting the human element, which is often considered the weakest link in the cybersecurity chain. No matter how advanced or sophisticated the technical defenses may be, human psychology remains susceptible to manipulation, making social engineering attacks highly effective. Moreover, social engineering attacks are adaptable and can evolve to exploit current events, trends, or technological developments, making them a dynamic and persistent threat.

Social engineering attacks can have severe consequences, ranging from financial losses and identity theft to unauthorized access to sensitive systems and data breaches. In the corporate environment, social engineering attacks can lead to the compromise of proprietary information, intellectual property theft, or unauthorized access to critical infrastructure. The reputational damage resulting from successful social engineering attacks can be equally detrimental, eroding trust and credibility in both personal and organizational contexts.

The effectiveness of social engineering attacks often stems from the exploitation of cognitive biases and psychological tendencies that are inherent in human behavior. For example, individuals may exhibit a tendency to trust authority figures, follow social norms, or act impulsively in response to urgency. Social engineers leverage these cognitive biases to manipulate individuals into divulging information or performing actions that compromise security. Understanding the psychology behind social engineering is crucial for developing effective countermeasures and awareness programs.

The significance of social engineering is further magnified in the age of information and interconnectedness. The vast amount of personal information available online provides social engineers with ample material to craft convincing and targeted attacks. Social media platforms, in particular, become valuable sources for gathering information about individuals, their relationships, interests, and activities, enabling attackers to tailor their approaches for maximum effectiveness. The personalization of social engineering attacks makes them more difficult to detect and resist.

Mitigating the risks associated with social engineering requires a multifaceted approach that combines technological defenses, user education, and organizational policies. Technological solutions such as email filtering, spam detection, and advanced threat protection can help identify and block phishing attempts. Multi-factor authentication adds an extra layer of security, making it more challenging for attackers even if credentials are compromised. Regular security awareness training for users, emphasizing the recognition of social engineering tactics and the importance of verifying requests for sensitive information, is essential in building a resilient human firewall.

Organizations must also establish and enforce robust security policies that address social engineering risks. This includes clear protocols for handling sensitive information, reporting suspicious activities, and verifying the identity of individuals making requests for information or access. Regular testing and simulations of social engineering attacks can help organizations evaluate the effectiveness of their security awareness programs and identify areas for improvement.

In conclusion, the significance of social engineering in the realm of cybersecurity lies in its ability to exploit the human element, making it a persistent and evolving threat. The dynamic and adaptable nature of social engineering attacks requires a comprehensive approach that includes technological defenses, user education, and organizational policies. As long as human vulnerabilities persist, social engineering will remain a potent tool in the hands of attackers, emphasizing the ongoing need for vigilance, awareness, and proactive defenses in the ever-changing landscape of cybersecurity.

Discuss the psychological aspects of manipulation.

The psychological aspects of manipulation delve into the intricate mechanisms by which individuals influence, control, or deceive others to achieve specific goals. At the core of manipulation lies a nuanced understanding of human behavior, emotions, and cognitive processes. This psychological interplay involves various factors, including perception, persuasion, social dynamics, and emotional responses, each contributing to the effectiveness of manipulative tactics. Whether in interpersonal relationships, social interactions, or broader societal contexts, the study of manipulation unveils the complex ways in which individuals navigate and exploit the vulnerabilities of the human psyche.

Perception plays a pivotal role in the psychology of manipulation, influencing how individuals interpret and make sense of the world around them. Manipulators often leverage cognitive biases, which are systematic patterns of deviation from norm or rationality in judgment, to shape perceptions in their favor. Confirmation bias, for example, leads individuals to interpret information in a way that confirms their preexisting beliefs. Manipulators exploit this tendency by selectively presenting information that aligns with their objectives, reinforcing the target's existing beliefs and making them more susceptible to manipulation.

Persuasion, a central element of manipulation, involves the art of influencing someone's beliefs, attitudes, or behaviors. The study of persuasion draws from psychological principles such as the elaboration likelihood model, which explains the varying routes individuals take to process persuasive messages. Manipulators adeptly tailor their communication strategies based on the target's receptiveness, motivation, and cognitive processing style. Emotional appeals, social validation, and the use of authority figures are common tools in the manipulator's arsenal, as they seek to exert influence by shaping the target's perceptions and decision-making processes.

The social dynamics of manipulation explore the ways in which individuals navigate relationships and power structures to achieve their objectives. Social influence theories, such as social identity theory and conformity, provide insights into how individuals align their beliefs and behaviors with those of a social group. Manipulators exploit these dynamics by creating or manipulating social norms, fostering a sense of belonging or exclusion, and leveraging the desire for social approval. By tapping into the social fabric of human interactions, manipulators can induce conformity and mold the behaviors of others to suit their aims.

Emotional manipulation delves into the realm of exploiting emotions to control or influence individuals. Emotional intelligence, the ability to recognize, understand, and manage one's own emotions and those of others, plays a crucial role in both perpetrating and resisting emotional manipulation. Manipulators may use tactics such as gaslighting, guilt-tripping, or playing on insecurities to evoke specific emotional responses in their targets. Understanding the emotional landscape allows manipulators to create situations that foster dependency, erode self-esteem, or induce fear, thereby gaining control over their targets.

The psychology of manipulation is intricately linked to the concept of power and control. Social power theories, including French and Raven's taxonomy of power bases, identify sources of power such as legitimate authority, reward, coercive force, expertise, and referent power. Manipulators strategically wield these power bases to assert control over others. For instance, an authority figure may exploit their legitimate power, while a charismatic individual may rely on referent power to sway opinions and garner support. The dynamics of power and control are pervasive in manipulative relationships, whether in personal, professional, or societal contexts.

Cognitive dissonance, a psychological theory developed by Leon Festinger, elucidates the discomfort individuals feel when holding conflicting beliefs or attitudes. Manipulators leverage cognitive dissonance by creating situations where the target's actions or beliefs are inconsistent with their self-image or values. This discomfort motivates individuals to reconcile the inconsistency, often by adjusting their beliefs or behaviors to align with the manipulator's agenda. The manipulation process exploits the innate human drive to maintain cognitive consistency and reduce psychological discomfort.

The concept of reciprocity, rooted in social psychology, illuminates the psychological principle that individuals feel compelled to return favors or acts of kindness. Manipulators capitalize on this inclination by employing tactics such as the "door-in-the-face" technique, where an initial exaggerated request is followed by a more reasonable one. The target, feeling a sense of indebtedness, is more likely to comply with the second, seemingly more reasonable request. Reciprocity creates a psychological obligation, and manipulators deftly use it to elicit compliance and control.

An understanding of the psychology of authority sheds light on how individuals respond to figures of power and influence. Stanley Milgram's famous obedience experiments demonstrated the extent to which individuals would comply with authority figures, even to the point of causing harm to others. Manipulators exploit this tendency by assuming or feigning authority, using titles, uniforms, or symbols of power to coerce compliance. The psychology of authority underscores the malleability of human behavior in the face of perceived authority figures.

The role of trust in manipulation is a nuanced aspect of human psychology. Trust is a fundamental component of social interactions, underpinning relationships and collaborations. Manipulators often build trust with their targets, creating a veneer of authenticity and reliability. Once trust is established, manipulators can then exploit it to deceive, coerce, or influence the target. Trust becomes a tool in the manipulator's repertoire, allowing them to navigate social dynamics with a degree of control over the perceptions and actions of others.

Cultural and societal influences shape the landscape of manipulation, introducing additional layers of complexity. Cultural norms, values, and expectations influence the strategies and tactics employed by manipulators. Additionally, societal structures and power dynamics can create environments that either facilitate or inhibit manipulation. Social norms and expectations become tools in the manipulator's arsenal, as they leverage cultural and societal contexts to achieve their objectives.

The ethical dimensions of manipulation underscore the importance of considering the consequences and implications of manipulative tactics. While manipulation is often associated with negative connotations, not all instances of influence or persuasion are inherently unethical. Ethical considerations involve questions of intent, transparency, and the impact on the well-being of individuals. Manipulative tactics that exploit vulnerabilities, coerce individuals into actions against their will, or cause harm are generally considered unethical. Ethical decision-making in the realm of manipulation requires a nuanced understanding of the balance between influence and coercion, transparency and deception.

In conclusion, the psychological aspects of manipulation delve into the intricate ways in which individuals influence, control, or deceive others to achieve specific goals. Understanding the dynamics of perception, persuasion, social influence, emotions, power, and trust provides insights into the mechanisms by which manipulation operates. Whether in interpersonal relationships, social interactions, or broader societal contexts, the study of manipulation unveils the complex ways in which individuals navigate and exploit the vulnerabilities of the human psyche. Recognizing these psychological dynamics is essential for individuals to guard against manipulation and for society to develop ethical frameworks that mitigate the risks associated with manipulative tactics.

Explore historical examples of social engineering, including espionage and espionage techniques.

Throughout history, social engineering has played a pivotal role in espionage, with various examples showcasing the effectiveness of manipulating individuals and exploiting their trust to gain access to sensitive information. One notable historical example dates back to World War II, where British intelligence employed social engineering techniques to deceive the Germans during the Allied invasion of Normandy in 1944. As part of Operation Bodyguard, a comprehensive deception plan, British agents engaged in disinformation campaigns, created fictitious military units, and manipulated German perception through double agents. The goal was to mislead the Germans about the location and timing of the D-Day landings, ultimately contributing to the success of the Allied invasion.

The Cold War era witnessed an escalation of social engineering techniques in the realm of espionage, with both the United States and the Soviet Union employing elaborate schemes to manipulate individuals for intelligence gains. A notable example is the case of the Cambridge Spy Ring, a group of British agents recruited by the Soviet Union during the 1930s and 1940s. This clandestine group, including individuals such as Kim Philby and Guy Burgess, successfully infiltrated British intelligence agencies. Through social engineering, these agents exploited personal relationships, loyalty, and ideological convictions to access classified information, providing the Soviets with valuable intelligence for years.

The Stasi, East Germany's Ministry for State Security, represents another historical example of social engineering employed for espionage purposes. During the Cold War, the Stasi developed extensive networks of informants within East Germany, relying on the pervasive use of social engineering tactics to recruit and control individuals. The Stasi's success in infiltrating various aspects of society, including workplaces, universities, and even families, exemplifies the effectiveness of manipulating interpersonal relationships and exploiting trust to gather intelligence.

In the realm of cyber espionage, the case of Kevin Mitnick, a notorious hacker in the late 20th century, provides insight into the use of social engineering to breach digital security. Mitnick, once one of the FBI's most-wanted cybercriminals, relied on his social engineering skills to manipulate individuals within organizations and gain unauthorized access to computer systems. His tactics included pretexting, posing as trusted figures, and exploiting human factors to extract sensitive information. Mitnick's exploits underscore the vulnerability of human psychology in the face of well-crafted social engineering attacks.

In the context of modern espionage, the case of Anna Chapman, a Russian spy arrested in the United States in 2010, illustrates the continued relevance of social engineering in intelligence operations. Chapman and her fellow spies infiltrated American society, using social engineering to establish relationships with influential individuals. Employing tactics reminiscent of traditional espionage, such as covert communications and coded messages, the group leveraged social engineering to navigate the intricacies of human relationships and gather intelligence.

China's cyber espionage campaigns provide contemporary examples of the fusion of traditional espionage techniques with sophisticated social engineering in the digital age. APT (Advanced Persistent Threat) groups associated with the Chinese government, such as APT 10 and APT 41, have been implicated in extensive cyber espionage operations. These groups employ social engineering tactics, including spear-phishing emails and targeted attacks, to compromise individuals within targeted organizations. By exploiting trust relationships and manipulating human behavior, these actors gain unauthorized access to sensitive information and intellectual property.

The Edward Snowden affair in 2013 revealed a different facet of social engineering in the context of intelligence operations. Snowden, a contractor for the National Security Agency (NSA), exploited his insider status and social engineering skills to access and leak classified information regarding mass surveillance programs. Snowden's actions underscore the vulnerability of organizations to insider threats facilitated by social engineering, highlighting the need for robust security measures to mitigate such risks.

The use of social engineering techniques by intelligence agencies extends beyond individual spies to broader disinformation campaigns aimed at manipulating public opinion. The Russian interference in the 2016 United States presidential election serves as a prominent example. Russian operatives, through entities like the Internet Research Agency, engaged in extensive social engineering efforts on social media platforms to sow discord, spread disinformation, and influence public sentiment. By leveraging psychological tactics and exploiting existing societal divisions, these campaigns showcased the power of social engineering in shaping perceptions on a mass scale.

In recent years, the emergence of deepfake technology has added a new dimension to social engineering in espionage. Deepfakes involve the use of artificial intelligence to create realistic but fabricated audio and video content. This technology can be exploited by intelligence actors to manipulate public figures' statements or create deceptive content for disinformation campaigns. The potential impact on public trust and the manipulation of narratives through deepfakes underscore the evolving landscape of social engineering in the digital age.

The historical examples of social engineering in espionage demonstrate the enduring effectiveness of manipulating individuals and exploiting human psychology for intelligence gains. Whether through traditional espionage tactics, cyber operations, or disinformation campaigns, the art of social engineering continues to be a formidable tool in the arsenal of intelligence agencies. As technology advances and new forms of manipulation emerge, the importance of understanding and mitigating the psychological aspects of social engineering remains a critical aspect of modern counterintelligence efforts.

Discuss the transition to digital social engineering.

The transition to digital social engineering represents a paradigm shift in the methods employed by malicious actors to manipulate individuals and exploit human psychology for various nefarious purposes. As society undergoes an unprecedented digital transformation, so too have the techniques of social engineering evolved to leverage the interconnected nature of the online world. This transition is marked by a convergence of traditional manipulation tactics with the technological capabilities of the digital age, resulting in a potent and widespread threat landscape that extends from individual phishing attempts to sophisticated state-sponsored cyber operations.

The advent of digital social engineering has been propelled by the increasing reliance on digital technologies in all aspects of life. With the proliferation of the internet, social media platforms, and digital communication channels, individuals find themselves more interconnected than ever before. This connectivity presents both opportunities and challenges, as it becomes the foundation upon which digital social engineering tactics are built. The transition to the digital realm has expanded the attack surface, providing malicious actors with a vast landscape to exploit and a multitude of vectors to employ in their social engineering campaigns.

Phishing, a classic form of social engineering, has seamlessly adapted to the digital landscape, becoming one of the most prevalent and effective techniques employed by cybercriminals. Digital phishing attacks involve the use of deceptive emails, messages, or websites to trick individuals into divulging sensitive information such as login credentials or financial details. Malicious actors craft sophisticated phishing emails that mimic trusted entities, leveraging psychological tactics to create a sense of urgency or fear that prompts the recipient to act impulsively. The ubiquity of email communication and the interconnected nature of online identities make phishing a versatile and widely used digital social engineering tool.

Spear phishing, a targeted and personalized form of phishing, exemplifies the precision achievable in the digital realm. Malicious actors, often armed with information gathered from social media and other online sources, tailor their phishing attempts to specific individuals or organizations. By referencing personal details, relationships, or recent activities, spear phishing emails create a false sense of familiarity and legitimacy, increasing the likelihood of success. This level of personalization was not easily achievable in traditional forms of social engineering and highlights the evolution of these techniques in the digital age.

The rise of social media platforms has provided fertile ground for digital social engineering to thrive. Malicious actors exploit the wealth of personal information voluntarily shared by individuals on these platforms to craft targeted attacks. Impersonation, a classic social engineering tactic, takes on new dimensions as cybercriminals create fake profiles, mimicking friends, colleagues, or trusted entities to establish connections with potential targets. The digital environment amplifies the impact of impersonation, as the ease of creating and disseminating false information allows for rapid and widespread manipulation.

Digital social engineering extends beyond individual attacks to encompass more sophisticated and large-scale operations, often associated with state-sponsored or politically motivated actors. Influence campaigns leverage social engineering tactics to manipulate public opinion, spread disinformation, and sow discord in digital spaces. The use of fake accounts, automated bots, and orchestrated narratives exploits the interconnected nature of online communities, amplifying the impact of these campaigns. The transition to digital platforms has allowed for the weaponization of information at an unprecedented scale, posing significant challenges to the integrity of online discourse and democratic processes.

The realm of digital social engineering is not limited to deception for financial gain or political influence; it also encompasses the manipulation of individuals within organizations. Business email compromise (BEC) attacks exemplify the convergence of traditional social engineering with digital techniques. In a BEC attack, cybercriminals compromise email accounts or impersonate high-ranking executives to deceive employees into transferring funds or disclosing sensitive information. The use of social engineering tactics, coupled with the intimate knowledge of organizational dynamics gleaned from digital reconnaissance, makes BEC attacks a potent threat to businesses across industries.

As digital communication becomes more prevalent, the art of pretexting has evolved to exploit new avenues for manipulation. Pretexting involves the creation of a fabricated scenario or pretext to deceive individuals into providing information or performing actions they might not otherwise do. In the digital realm, cybercriminals may employ sophisticated social engineering schemes, such as posing as IT support to gain remote access or masquerading as a trusted service provider to trick individuals into revealing sensitive information. The seamless integration of pretexting into digital communication channels underscores the adaptability of social engineering techniques in the face of technological advancements.

The psychology of social engineering remains a critical aspect of its digital manifestation. Malicious actors leverage cognitive biases, emotional triggers, and social dynamics to manipulate individuals online. The ease of information dissemination in the digital age facilitates the creation of convincing narratives that exploit cognitive biases such as confirmation bias, where individuals tend to interpret information in a way that confirms their preexisting beliefs. Emotional manipulation thrives in the digital realm, as cybercriminals use sensationalism, fear, or empathy to elicit specific responses from targets, prompting them to click on malicious links, disclose information, or take other actions.

The digital transition of social engineering is also marked by the emergence of novel threats, such as deepfakes. Deepfake technology leverages artificial intelligence to create realistic but fabricated audio and video content, often featuring manipulated appearances or voices of individuals. While initially associated with entertainment, deepfakes present a new frontier for digital social engineering, allowing malicious actors to convincingly impersonate public figures or manipulate content to deceive and manipulate audiences. The potential impact on trust, authenticity, and the veracity of digital information raises profound challenges for individuals and organizations alike.

Digital social engineering techniques have also found their way into the realm of cyberespionage. State-sponsored actors deploy sophisticated social engineering tactics to infiltrate organizations, government agencies, or critical infrastructure. APT (Advanced Persistent Threat) groups associated with nation-states engage in long-term, targeted campaigns that often involve digital social engineering to compromise high-value targets. These campaigns may include tactics such as establishing fake personas, exploiting relationships, and using psychological manipulation to coerce individuals into divulging sensitive information.

The integration of artificial intelligence (AI) into digital social engineering marks another significant development. AI-driven tools enable cybercriminals to automate and enhance their attacks, using machine learning algorithms to analyze vast amounts of data for personalized and convincing manipulations. Natural language processing allows for more realistic and contextually relevant phishing messages, while AI-driven chatbots simulate human interactions in real-time, amplifying the potential for digital social engineering attacks to scale and adapt dynamically.

The transition to digital social engineering demands a holistic approach to cybersecurity that encompasses technological defenses, user education, and organizational policies. Technological solutions, including advanced email filtering, endpoint protection, and threat intelligence, are crucial for detecting and mitigating digital social engineering attacks. However, the human factor remains a linchpin in the defense against such tactics. User education programs that raise awareness about common social engineering tactics, promote critical thinking, and emphasize the importance of verifying requests for sensitive information are integral to building a resilient human firewall in the digital age.

Organizations must also establish and enforce robust security policies that address digital social engineering risks. This includes implementing multi-factor authentication, restricting access to sensitive information, and conducting regular security awareness training. Additionally, incident response plans should be developed to enable organizations to quickly detect, contain, and remediate the impact of successful digital social engineering attacks. Collaboration between industry stakeholders, government agencies, and cybersecurity professionals is essential to staying ahead of evolving threats in the dynamic landscape of digital social engineering.

In conclusion, the transition to digital social engineering represents a dynamic evolution of traditional manipulation tactics in the face of technological advancements. From phishing and impersonation to influence campaigns and deepfakes, the digital age has provided malicious actors with a vast array of tools to exploit human psychology for various purposes. The interconnected nature of the online world amplifies the impact of social engineering, necessitating a comprehensive and adaptive approach to cybersecurity. As technology continues to advance, understanding the nuances of digital social engineering and implementing proactive defenses remain critical to mitigating the risks posed by this ever-evolving threat landscape.

Outline various tactics used by social engineers, such as phishing, pretexting, and baiting.

Social engineers employ a diverse range of tactics, exploiting human psychology and trust to achieve their objectives. Phishing, a pervasive and effective method, involves the use of deceptive emails, messages, or websites to trick individuals into divulging sensitive information such as passwords or financial details. These messages often mimic trusted entities, creating a false sense of urgency or fear to prompt recipients to act impulsively. Phishing attacks have evolved in sophistication, employing convincing replicas of legitimate websites and leveraging psychological triggers to manipulate individuals in both personal and professional settings.

Pretexting is another social engineering tactic that involves the creation of a fabricated scenario or pretext to deceive individuals into providing information or performing actions they might not otherwise do. This method often entails the impersonation of a trusted figure, such as a colleague, authority figure, or service provider. By crafting a plausible narrative and exploiting human tendencies to trust and assist others, pretexting allows social engineers to manipulate individuals into revealing sensitive information or granting unauthorized access.

Baiting, as a social engineering tactic, leverages curiosity or the desire for gain to entice individuals into taking actions that compromise security. This may involve leaving infected USB drives in public places, creating fake promotions that require the user to input sensitive information, or promising free downloads that deliver malicious payloads. Baiting exploits human vulnerabilities, capitalizing on the natural inclination to seek rewards or explore enticing opportunities. The tactic highlights the interplay between psychological triggers and the lure of potential benefits in the context of social engineering.

Impersonation is a classic social engineering technique wherein attackers pose as trusted individuals or entities to manipulate targets. This can occur through various channels, including in-person interactions, phone calls, or digital communication. Social engineers may impersonate colleagues, technical support representatives, or even family members to gain trust and manipulate targets into revealing information or performing actions against their best interests. Impersonation relies on the psychology of trust and authority, exploiting the natural inclination to comply with requests from perceived trustworthy sources.

Quid pro quo is a social engineering tactic that involves the exchange of something valuable for information or access. In this scenario, social engineers offer a perceived benefit, such as a service or assistance, in exchange for specific information or actions from the target. This tactic exploits the psychological principle of reciprocity, where individuals feel compelled to return favors or acts of kindness. By presenting themselves as helpful, social engineers manipulate targets into providing information or access that they would not otherwise disclose.

Tailgating, also known as piggybacking, is a physical social engineering tactic that involves an unauthorized person following an authorized individual into a secure location. By exploiting the natural tendency to hold doors open for others or the reluctance to confront someone who appears to belong, social engineers gain physical access to restricted areas. Tailgating underscores the importance of human interactions and social norms in physical security, highlighting how individuals may inadvertently facilitate security breaches through courtesy or social pressure.

Quizzes and surveys represent social engineering tactics that exploit individuals' willingness to share personal information willingly. Social engineers may design quizzes or surveys that appear innocuous or entertaining, enticing individuals to provide information about themselves. This seemingly harmless engagement can result in the collection of valuable data, such as birthdates, preferences, or security-related information, which can be exploited for malicious purposes. The tactic capitalizes on individuals' trust and the desire for engagement in online activities.

Pharming is a more technically sophisticated form of social engineering that involves the redirection of website traffic to fraudulent sites without the users' knowledge. Attackers manipulate the Domain Name System (DNS) or compromise routers to reroute users to malicious websites designed to collect sensitive information. Pharming exploits individuals' trust in the legitimacy of websites and the assumption that they have arrived at the intended destination. The tactic highlights the intersection of technical manipulation and human trust in the context of online interactions.

Online dating scams represent a social engineering tactic that exploits individuals' emotions and desire for connection. In these scams, attackers create fake online personas, establish romantic relationships with targets, and eventually request money or sensitive information under various pretenses. The emotional investment in the relationship and the trust established over time make individuals more susceptible to manipulation. Online dating scams highlight the exploitation of emotional vulnerabilities as a potent social engineering tactic.

Influence campaigns are social engineering tactics that operate on a larger scale, often driven by political or ideological motives. These campaigns leverage various methods, including disinformation, manipulation of online discourse, and the creation of fake personas to influence public opinion. By exploiting cognitive biases, amplifying existing divisions, and shaping narratives, influence campaigns seek to sway public sentiment, undermine trust in institutions, and achieve broader societal impacts. These tactics demonstrate the intersection of social engineering with broader socio-political dynamics in the digital age.

The use of deepfake technology represents an emerging social engineering tactic that involves the creation of realistic but fabricated audio and video content. Deepfakes use artificial intelligence to manipulate the appearance or voice of individuals, making it difficult to discern between genuine and manipulated content. This tactic raises concerns about the potential for malicious actors to impersonate public figures, manipulate media narratives, or deceive individuals on a large scale. Deepfakes underscore the evolving nature of social engineering in the context of advancing technologies.

In conclusion, social engineers employ a wide array of tactics that exploit human psychology, trust, and vulnerabilities to achieve their objectives. From traditional methods such as phishing and impersonation to more sophisticated techniques like deepfakes and influence campaigns, social engineering tactics continue to evolve in response to technological advancements and societal dynamics. Understanding these tactics is crucial for individuals and organizations to enhance their awareness, resilience, and defenses against the multifaceted challenges posed by social engineering in the digital age.

Provide real-world examples to illustrate each technique.

Phishing, a pervasive social engineering tactic, has been employed in numerous real-world examples to compromise sensitive information. In 2016, the campaign targeting the Gmail accounts of political figures and journalists demonstrated the potency of phishing. Attackers sent seemingly innocuous emails containing a fake Google security alert, prompting victims to enter their login credentials on a deceptive website. The attackers successfully gained access to personal emails and sensitive information, highlighting the effectiveness of phishing in exploiting human trust and urgency.

Pretexting has been notably employed in corporate settings to manipulate individuals and extract sensitive information. The 2014

Sony Pictures hack is a prime example, where attackers used pretexting to gather intelligence before launching a destructive cyberattack. Posing as Sony executives, the attackers engaged in convincing email exchanges with employees, gradually extracting valuable information about the company's operations, personnel, and systems. This elaborate pretexting scheme laid the groundwork for the subsequent cyberattack, showcasing the strategic use of deception in the digital realm.

Baiting tactics often exploit the curiosity or desire for gain in individuals. In 2017, the WannaCry ransomware attack leveraged baiting by enticing users to click on seemingly harmless email attachments or links. The attackers capitalized on users' curiosity or interest in the content, embedding malicious software that spread rapidly across networks. The bait, in this case, was the promise of information or content that, once clicked, led to devastating consequences, encrypting files and demanding ransom payments.

Impersonation, a classic social engineering tactic, has been used in various real-world scenarios. In 2019, the "CEO fraud" case involving Nikkei Inc., a Japanese media company, demonstrated the effectiveness of impersonation. Cybercriminals impersonated a company executive in email communication, instructing an employee to transfer funds to a fraudulent account. The employee, believing the request was legitimate due to the impersonation, transferred a substantial amount of money. This real-world example highlights how impersonation exploits authority and trust within organizational structures.

Quid pro quo attacks, exchanging something valuable for information, have been witnessed in the realm of cybersecurity. In 2011, the RSA SecurID breach was initiated through a quid pro quo tactic. Attackers posed as trusted vendors, offering a presentation on a relevant topic to RSA employees. In exchange for the presentation, the attackers requested and received a file containing malware. This file ultimately led to the compromise of RSA's SecurID tokens, affecting the security of numerous organizations. The quid pro quo approach demonstrated the exploitation of trust in vendor relationships for malicious purposes.

Tailgating, a physical social engineering tactic, was exemplified in the case of the famous art heist at the Isabella Stewart Gardner Museum in 1990. Two individuals dressed as police officers approached the museum's entrance, claiming to be responding to a disturbance. By exploiting the staff's natural inclination to assist law enforcement, the impostors gained entry and executed a heist, stealing thirteen pieces of artwork. The tailgating tactic showcased how social engineering extends beyond digital realms to exploit human interactions in physical security contexts.

Quizzes and surveys are often used to exploit individuals' willingness to share personal information. In 2018, the "This Is Your Digital Life" app on Facebook gained notoriety for harvesting user data through a personality quiz. While the app purported to be a harmless quiz, it collected not only the data of those who participated but also the data of their Facebook friends. This large-scale data harvesting operation, conducted under the guise of a quiz, illustrated the potential consequences of individuals willingly sharing personal information online.

Online dating scams, leveraging emotional manipulation, have affected individuals seeking companionship. The "Catfish" phenomenon gained attention through the MTV documentary series, highlighting cases where individuals engaged in online relationships with fabricated personas. These scammers exploited emotional vulnerabilities, creating fake identities to forge connections with unsuspecting individuals. The emotional investment in these relationships often led to financial exploitation, demonstrating how online dating scams prey on the desire for emotional connection.

Influence campaigns, as seen in the Russian interference in the 2016 U.S. presidential election, involve the strategic use of disinformation to sway public opinion. Russian operatives created fake personas on social media platforms, disseminating divisive content and amplifying existing societal tensions. By manipulating narratives and exploiting cognitive biases, the influence campaign aimed to sow discord and undermine trust in democratic institutions. This real-world example showcased the impact of influence campaigns on a large scale, demonstrating the potential for social engineering to shape public sentiment.

Deepfakes, an emerging social engineering tactic, pose a significant threat to authenticity and trust in digital content. In 2019, a deepfake video featuring Facebook CEO Mark Zuckerberg circulated online, showcasing the technology's ability to convincingly manipulate audio-visual content. While this particular instance was created for satirical purposes, it underscored the potential for malicious actors to use deepfakes for deception, manipulation, or spreading false information. The episode highlighted the evolving landscape of social engineering in the era of advanced technologies.

These real-world examples illustrate the diverse tactics employed by social engineers, ranging from classic methods like phishing and impersonation to emerging threats like deepfakes and influence campaigns. Understanding these tactics is essential for individuals, organizations, and societies to develop effective countermeasures, enhance awareness, and fortify defenses against the multifaceted challenges posed by social engineering in various contexts.

Discuss why humans are often the weakest link in cybersecurity.

Humans are often considered the weakest link in cybersecurity due to a combination of psychological, social, and technological factors that make individuals susceptible to various cyber threats. One fundamental aspect contributing to this vulnerability is the inherent complexity of human behavior and cognition. While technology can be designed with stringent security measures, human decision-making introduces a level of unpredictability and variability that creates challenges for maintaining a secure cyber environment. Cognitive biases, such as overconfidence, confirmation bias, and the illusion of invulnerability, play a significant role in shaping individuals' perceptions of risk and their ability to recognize and respond to potential cyber threats.

Social engineering exploits the intricacies of human psychology, making individuals susceptible to manipulation and deception. Attackers leverage the innate human tendency to trust, creating scenarios or personas that appear trustworthy. Whether through phishing emails, impersonation, or pretexting, social engineering tactics rely on human emotions, trust, and the desire to help others. The persuasive nature of social engineering preys on fundamental aspects of human interaction, exploiting the social fabric that binds individuals together.

The rapid evolution of technology has outpaced the development of cybersecurity awareness and education among the general population. Many individuals lack the necessary knowledge to discern between legitimate and malicious online activities. This knowledge gap is further exacerbated by the fast-paced nature of technological advancements, making it challenging for individuals to keep up with the latest cybersecurity threats and best practices. As a result, individuals may inadvertently engage in risky online behaviors, such as clicking on malicious links or downloading malware, due to a lack of awareness and understanding.

Moreover, the ubiquity of digital devices in everyday life contributes to the human factor in cybersecurity vulnerabilities. The increasing dependence on smartphones, laptops, and other connected devices creates a larger attack surface for cybercriminals. Individuals often prioritize convenience over security, leading to lax practices such as using weak passwords, neglecting software updates, or accessing sensitive information over unsecured networks. The integration of technology into every facet of daily life means that lapses in cybersecurity hygiene can have far-reaching consequences.

Another key aspect of human vulnerability in cybersecurity is the challenge of maintaining a balance between security and user experience. Stringent security measures can be perceived as inconvenient or burdensome by users, leading to the circumvention of security protocols or the use of weak passwords. The tension between security and user convenience is a delicate balance that organizations must navigate to ensure that security measures do not impede productivity and user satisfaction. Finding this balance requires a user-centric approach that considers human factors in the design of cybersecurity solutions.

Additionally, the emotional aspect of cybersecurity plays a crucial role in individuals' responses to threats. Fear, uncertainty, and a lack of familiarity with cybersecurity concepts can evoke emotional responses that hinder rational decision-making. Cybersecurity incidents often induce panic or anxiety, leading individuals to act impulsively or irrationally. The emotional dimension of cybersecurity underscores the need for effective communication and education to empower individuals to make informed decisions and respond calmly in the face of cyber threats.

The human factor in cybersecurity is further complicated by the dynamic and interconnected nature of modern society. Interpersonal relationships, organizational structures, and societal norms all contribute to the complexity of human interactions in cyberspace. The interconnectedness of individuals within social networks creates pathways for the rapid spread of cyber threats, such as malware or phishing attacks, within communities. Trust within these networks, while essential for collaboration and communication, also becomes an avenue for exploitation by malicious actors engaging in social engineering tactics.

Moreover, the prevalence of insider threats highlights the role of human actors within organizations as potential vulnerabilities. Insider threats can manifest as intentional malicious actions or unintentional mistakes made by employees. Whether through negligence, lack of awareness, or disgruntlement, individuals with access to organizational systems and data can pose significant risks. Balancing the need for trust and collaboration with the necessity of monitoring and mitigating insider threats is a complex challenge for organizations.

The inherent variability in human behavior and the diverse ways individuals interact with technology make it challenging to implement one-size-fits-all cybersecurity solutions. Tailoring cybersecurity measures to account for individual differences, preferences, and behaviors is a nuanced task that requires a deep understanding of human psychology. It also involves addressing the broader socio-technical context in which individuals operate, recognizing that cybersecurity is not solely a technical issue but a multidimensional challenge that encompasses human, organizational, and societal dimensions.

Addressing the human factor in cybersecurity requires a holistic and multifaceted approach. Education and awareness programs play a crucial role in empowering individuals with the knowledge and skills needed to recognize and respond to cyber threats. Cybersecurity training should focus not only on technical aspects but also on behavioral aspects, fostering a culture of security awareness within organizations and society at large. Additionally, organizations must invest in user-friendly security solutions that prioritize both effectiveness and user experience, minimizing the friction between security measures and productivity.

Furthermore, the importance of cultivating a cybersecurity culture within organizations cannot be overstated. Establishing a culture of security involves fostering a sense of collective responsibility, where every individual understands their role in maintaining a secure environment. This includes promoting open communication about cybersecurity issues, encouraging reporting of suspicious activities, and creating an environment where individuals feel supported rather than blamed for security incidents. A positive cybersecurity culture enhances resilience by leveraging the collective vigilance of all individuals within an organization.

As technology continues to advance and cyber threats evolve, the human factor in cybersecurity will remain a critical aspect of defense strategies. Recognizing and addressing the vulnerabilities associated with human behavior, cognition, and interaction with technology is essential for building robust and resilient cybersecurity ecosystems. By embracing a holistic understanding of the human factor, organizations and society can forge a path towards a more secure and cyber-aware future.

Explore the psychology behind successful social engineering attacks.

The psychology behind successful social engineering attacks is deeply rooted in an intricate understanding of human behavior, cognitive biases, and the dynamics of trust and manipulation. At its core, social engineering exploits the vulnerabilities inherent in the human psyche, leveraging psychological principles to deceive individuals and elicit specific responses. One key aspect is the principle of trust, a fundamental component of human relationships. Successful social engineers adeptly manipulate this trust, often posing as trustworthy entities or individuals to lower their targets' guard. This manipulation is often achieved through careful observation of social norms, linguistic patterns, and contextual cues, allowing the attacker to craft a convincing façade that aligns with the expectations of the targeted individual.

Cognitive biases play a pivotal role in successful social engineering attacks, as attackers exploit these systematic patterns of deviation from norm or rationality in judgment. One prominent bias is the confirmation bias, where individuals tend to interpret information in a way that confirms their preexisting beliefs. Social engineers capitalize on this bias by tailoring their messages to align with the target's existing beliefs or expectations, making the deceptive content more convincing and less likely to be scrutinized. Another cognitive bias, the authority bias, involves individuals' inclination to obey or follow the guidance of perceived authorities. Social engineers often impersonate figures of authority, such as IT personnel, executives, or trusted service providers, to manipulate targets into complying with requests or divulging sensitive information.

The psychology of urgency and scarcity also plays a significant role in successful social engineering attacks. By creating a sense of urgency or presenting an opportunity that appears scarce, attackers exploit individuals' instinctive reactions to act quickly and seize valuable resources. This tactic triggers emotional responses that bypass rational decision-making processes, leading individuals to overlook potential red flags and prioritize immediate action. Phishing emails often leverage these psychological triggers, using urgency to prompt individuals to click on malicious links, download attachments, or disclose sensitive information before careful scrutiny.

Social engineers are adept at exploiting the innate human desire for social connection and cooperation. This is evident in tactics such as pretexting, where attackers create fabricated scenarios that appeal to individuals' willingness to help or cooperate. By presenting a plausible pretext, often involving a personal or professional need, social engineers manipulate targets into providing information or performing actions that they would not typically consider. This taps into the social instinct of reciprocity, where individuals feel compelled to reciprocate when someone has done something for them.

The emotional dimension of successful social engineering attacks is particularly powerful. Social engineers leverage emotions such as fear, curiosity, greed, or empathy to influence their targets' behavior. Fear-based tactics, such as threats of legal action or impending security breaches, trigger emotional responses that override rational thought, compelling individuals to take immediate actions to alleviate the perceived threat. Curiosity is exploited through enticing messages or links that prompt individuals to click without fully assessing the potential risks. Similarly, greed or the promise of financial gain can lead individuals to divulge sensitive information or engage in risky behaviors. By understanding and manipulating these emotional triggers, social engineers effectively control their targets' reactions.

The reciprocity principle, a social norm ingrained in human interactions, is a key psychological lever in social engineering attacks. Individuals naturally feel obligated to reciprocate when they receive a favor or gift, and social engineers exploit this tendency to create a sense of indebtedness. By offering something of perceived value, whether in the form of apparent assistance, free downloads, or exclusive access, attackers stimulate a psychological obligation that encourages targets to provide information or perform actions in return. This reciprocity-driven dynamic builds trust and cooperation, creating an opening for social engineers to achieve their objectives.

Understanding the psychology of authority figures is essential for successful social engineering attacks. The Milgram experiment, conducted in the early 1960s, demonstrated individuals' tendency to obey authority figures even when asked to perform actions contrary to their moral beliefs. Social engineers capitalize on this obedience to authority, often posing as figures with perceived power or expertise. Whether claiming to be IT support, law enforcement, or executives, attackers exploit the automatic deference individuals often afford to authority figures, making them more susceptible to manipulation and compliance with seemingly legitimate requests.

The principle of social proof, derived from the concept that individuals look to others for guidance in uncertain situations, is a psychological trigger that social engineers skillfully exploit. By creating an illusion of consensus or presenting fabricated evidence of others' actions, attackers induce individuals to follow suit. This herd mentality is evident in tactics like phishing emails claiming to be from colleagues or friends who have already taken certain actions, fostering a false sense of security and encouraging the target to replicate the perceived behavior.

Recency bias, a cognitive bias where individuals give more weight to recent events in their decision-making, is another psychological element leveraged in successful social engineering attacks. Attackers may exploit recent news, events, or trends to craft convincing narratives that align with individuals' current concerns or interests. By incorporating these elements into their tactics, social engineers increase the likelihood that targets will be emotionally engaged and less likely to question the authenticity of the presented information.

The psychology behind successful social engineering attacks also involves exploiting the tendency of individuals to rely on heuristics or mental shortcuts in decision-making. These cognitive shortcuts, while efficient in everyday decision-making, can be manipulated to deceive individuals. Social engineers create scenarios that trigger automatic responses based on ingrained mental patterns, leading individuals to make decisions without engaging in critical thinking. This is particularly evident in phishing attacks that imitate familiar communication patterns or use familiar logos, triggering heuristics that contribute to the success of the deception.

In conclusion, the psychology behind successful social engineering attacks is a sophisticated interplay of trust, cognitive biases, emotional triggers, and social dynamics. Social engineers leverage their understanding of human behavior to exploit weaknesses in decision-making processes, effectively manipulating individuals into divulging information or performing actions against their best interests. As technology continues to advance, the psychological dimensions of social engineering remain a critical focus for cybersecurity efforts, emphasizing the need for robust awareness programs, user education, and proactive defenses that account for the intricacies of human psychology in the digital age.

Highlight notorious social engineering incidents and their impact.

One of the most notorious social engineering incidents in recent history was the "Spear Phishing" attack on the Democratic National Committee (DNC) in 2016. Widely believed to be orchestrated by Russian hackers, this sophisticated social engineering campaign involved the use of targeted phishing emails to compromise the email accounts of key DNC members. By carefully crafting emails that appeared legitimate and exploiting human curiosity and trust, the attackers successfully tricked individuals into clicking on malicious links or providing their login credentials. The impact was profound, as sensitive emails were exposed, leading to political turmoil, public outrage, and a pervasive sense of mistrust in the democratic process. The incident underscored the potential of social engineering to influence political landscapes on a global scale.

In 2013, the "Target Data Breach" marked a significant social engineering attack that targeted a major retail corporation. Cyber-criminals gained access to Target's network through a third-party HVAC vendor, illustrating how attackers exploit trusted relationships in supply chains. The attackers deployed a sophisticated phishing campaign that tricked employees of the HVAC vendor into providing their credentials. Subsequently, the attackers navigated through Target's systems, eventually compromising credit card information and personal data of millions of customers. The aftermath included financial losses, damage to Target's reputation, and increased awareness of the potential vulnerabilities within interconnected business ecosystems.

The "CEO Fraud" incident involving the Austrian aerospace manufacturer FACC in 2016 exemplifies the effectiveness of social engineering in exploiting authority and trust. In this case, cyber-criminals impersonated the CEO through email communication, instructing employees to transfer approximately €50 million to fraud-ulent accounts. The attackers leveraged social engineering tactics to create a sense of urgency and authority, bypassing normal verification processes. The financial impact was substantial, showcasing how a well-executed social engineering attack could override traditional se-curity measures and result in significant financial losses for organiza-tions.

The "WannaCry" ransomware attack in 2017 is another notable incident with social engineering at its core. The ransomware exploit-ed a vulnerability in Microsoft Windows systems, spreading rapidly across networks. The initial infection vector, however, was a phishing email that tricked individuals into clicking on a malicious link. The attackers preyed on the urgency and fear associated with ran-somware, encrypting files on infected computers and demanding payment in cryptocurrency for their release. The widespread impact affected organizations globally, including healthcare institutions, highlighting the cascading consequences of a social engineering at-tack on critical infrastructure and public services.

In 2014, the "Sony Pictures Hack" demonstrated the effective-ness of social engineering through a combination of spear phishing and psychological manipulation. The attackers, believed to be as-sociated with North Korea, conducted an extensive campaign that involved sending phishing emails to Sony employees. These emails, carefully crafted to appear legitimate, exploited employees' curiosity and trust. The attackers then escalated their tactics by engaging in psychological warfare, threatening to release sensitive data and embarrassing emails if certain demands were not met. The incident resulted in significant damage to Sony's reputation, financial losses, and raised questions about the intersection of cyber threats and geopolitical tensions.

The "CryptoLocker" ransomware attack in 2013 showcased the adaptability of social engineering in the context of financial extortion. The ransomware was typically distributed through phishing emails containing malicious attachments or links. Once activated, CryptoLocker encrypted files on the victim's computer and demanded payment in Bitcoin for the decryption key. The attackers played on the fear of losing valuable personal or business data, compelling individuals to pay the ransom. This incident highlighted the psychological impact of social engineering, as victims faced the emotional dilemma of either losing critical data or succumbing to the extortion demands.

In the realm of social media, the "Twitter Bitcoin Scam" of 2020 demonstrated the exploitation of trust and authority on a platform used by millions. High-profile Twitter accounts, including those of prominent individuals like Elon Musk, Barack Obama, and Bill Gates, were compromised in a coordinated social engineering attack. The attackers posted tweets promoting a Bitcoin scam, urging followers to send cryptocurrency to a specified address with the false promise of doubling their investment. The incident not only highlighted the vulnerability of even the most influential social media accounts but also showcased the real-time and widespread impact of social engineering on public perception and financial transactions.

The "Bangladesh Bank Heist" of 2016 is a notable example of social engineering targeting the financial sector. Cybercriminals used a combination of malware and social engineering to compromise the security of Bangladesh Bank's systems. The attackers, posing as bank officials, sent multiple fraudulent transfer requests to the Federal Reserve Bank of New York, requesting the transfer of nearly $1 billion. While the majority of the requests were blocked, the attackers still managed to divert $81 million to accounts in the Philippines. The incident highlighted the intersection of technical vulnerabilities and social engineering tactics in orchestrating a large-scale financial heist.

The "Emotet" malware campaign, active since 2014, showcases the evolution and persistence of social engineering tactics. Emotet initially functioned as a banking trojan but later transformed into a multifaceted threat that spread through malicious email attachments. The social engineering aspect involved deceptive emails that appeared to be legitimate documents, such as invoices or shipping information. Once opened, these attachments would deploy Emotet, enabling further cybercriminal activities, including data theft and the distribution of other malware. The campaign illustrated the ongoing effectiveness of social engineering in delivering malware and compromising systems.

The "LinkedIn Phishing Campaign" of 2020 targeted professionals using the popular networking platform. Attackers created fake LinkedIn profiles and sent connection requests to individuals, appearing as legitimate business associates. Subsequently, they engaged in conversation, sharing malicious links disguised as job offers or business opportunities. The campaign demonstrated how social engineers leverage the trust associated with professional networking platforms to deliver phishing attacks tailored to specific individuals. The impact extended beyond individual victims, as compromised accounts could be used for further social engineering or targeted attacks within professional networks.

These notorious social engineering incidents underscore the diverse tactics employed by attackers to exploit human psychology, trust, and vulnerabilities. From politically motivated attacks like the DNC spear phishing to financially driven exploits such as the Bangladesh Bank heist, social engineering remains a potent and adaptable tool in the hands of cybercriminals. These incidents also emphasize the need for continuous cybersecurity awareness, education, and proactive defenses that address the multifaceted challenges posed by social engineering in various contexts.

Discuss how individuals and organizations fell victim to social engineering.

Individuals and organizations have fallen victim to social engineering attacks due to a myriad of factors, ranging from psychological vulnerabilities to the increasing sophistication of attackers. One common avenue through which individuals are targeted is phishing, where attackers employ deceptive emails, messages, or websites to trick individuals into divulging sensitive information. Phishing attacks often play on the emotions of recipients, inducing fear or urgency to prompt impulsive actions. For instance, a seemingly urgent email claiming to be from a bank may convince an individual to click on a malicious link and input their login credentials, unknowingly providing access to their financial accounts.

In the corporate landscape, employees have often fallen prey to social engineering tactics through techniques like pretexting. In a pretexting scenario, attackers create a fabricated story or pretext to manipulate individuals into disclosing information. For example, an attacker might pose as a fellow employee or a vendor, claiming an urgent need for specific details. The desire to be helpful or the fear of consequences for refusing such requests can lead employees to inadvertently provide sensitive information, facilitating unauthorized access or data breaches.

Impersonation is another prevalent social engineering technique that exploits the human tendency to trust authoritative figures. Attackers often impersonate executives, IT personnel, or even law enforcement to manipulate targets. In organizations, employees might receive a call from someone claiming to be from the IT department, urgently requesting login credentials for system maintenance. The perceived authority of the caller can override skepticism, leading individuals to comply with requests that compromise organizational security.

The realm of online scams, including romance scams, illustrates how attackers exploit individuals' emotional vulnerabilities. In these scams, perpetrators create fake personas on dating websites or social media platforms to establish romantic relationships with unsuspecting individuals. Over time, a sense of trust and emotional connection is cultivated, and the scammer then fabricates a crisis or financial need, prompting the victim to send money. The emotional investment in the relationship often blinds individuals to the red flags of a scam, showcasing how social engineering preys on human emotions.

Organizations, irrespective of their size or industry, have faced significant threats from social engineering attacks. The "Business Email Compromise" (BEC) attacks, for instance, target organizations by compromising email accounts. Attackers might gain access to an executive's email and use it to send fraudulent requests for financial transactions or sensitive information. The apparent legitimacy of these requests, combined with the pressure to comply with executive directives, can lead employees to unknowingly facilitate financial fraud or data breaches.

The "Vendor Email Compromise" is another variant where attackers compromise a vendor's email account to manipulate ongoing transactions. By intercepting legitimate invoices and subtly altering payment details, attackers trick organizations into transferring funds to fraudulent accounts. The trust established in vendor relationships becomes a vulnerability, allowing attackers to exploit the flow of financial transactions.

Social engineering techniques also extend to exploiting the human tendency to seek rewards or respond to enticing opportunities. Baiting attacks, for instance, involve enticing individuals with promises of free downloads, special offers, or other appealing content. Attackers might leave infected USB drives in public spaces, relying on individuals' curiosity to plug the devices into their computers. Once connected, the malware on the USB drives can compromise systems, illustrating how the lure of potential rewards can lead individuals to compromise their own cybersecurity.

The "Tech Support Scam" is another example where individuals are manipulated into believing that their computers are infected with malware. Attackers often employ pop-up messages or cold calls, claiming to be from reputable tech support services. The fear of computer viruses or compromised security prompts individuals to follow the scammers' instructions, providing remote access to their computers or paying for unnecessary services. In these instances, attackers exploit individuals' lack of technical expertise and the desire to ensure the security of their devices.

The interconnected nature of social relationships within organizations can also be leveraged in attacks such as the "CEO Fraud." In these incidents, attackers impersonate high-ranking executives and send emails to employees in finance or HR departments, instructing them to initiate fraudulent transactions or provide sensitive information. The psychological pressure to comply with seemingly urgent directives from top management can lead employees to bypass normal verification processes, highlighting how the hierarchical structure of organizations can be manipulated in social engineering attacks.

The "Watering Hole" attack is a tactic where attackers compromise websites frequented by their target audience. By infecting these legitimate websites with malware, attackers exploit the trust users place in familiar online spaces. Individuals visiting these compromised sites unknowingly download malware onto their devices, enabling attackers to gain access to sensitive information. This method exemplifies how attackers capitalize on individuals' routine online behaviors and the trust associated with well-known websites.

Social media platforms, integral to modern communication, have become a breeding ground for social engineering attacks. The "Friendship Request Scam" involves attackers creating fake profiles and sending friendship requests to individuals. Once accepted, the attackers may attempt to gather personal information or deploy further attacks. The desire for social connection and the assumption of familiarity with online connections can lead individuals to overlook potential risks, illustrating how social engineering exploits the trust individuals place in their online networks.

In the context of organizational espionage, social engineering plays a crucial role in intelligence gathering. Attackers might pose as journalists, consultants, or industry professionals to gain access to sensitive information. By exploiting individuals' willingness to share information with seemingly trustworthy external parties, attackers can gather strategic intelligence, compromising the organization's competitive position or proprietary knowledge.

Moreover, the blurred lines between personal and professional online activities contribute to the success of social engineering attacks. The "LinkedIn Spear Phishing" incident in 2020 targeted professionals by sending phishing emails disguised as job offers or business opportunities. Leveraging the trust associated with professional networking, attackers tricked individuals into clicking on malicious links or providing login credentials, showcasing how personal and professional realms intertwine, creating opportunities for social engineering attacks to traverse boundaries.

The prevalence of remote work has also introduced new avenues for social engineering attacks. With employees accessing organizational systems from diverse locations, attackers exploit the potential weaknesses in home network security. The "Remote Access Scam" involves attackers posing as IT support personnel, claiming to troubleshoot technical issues for remote employees. By gaining remote access to individuals' computers, attackers can compromise sensitive data or install malware. The trust individuals place in IT support, especially when faced with technical challenges, becomes a vulnerability in this scenario.

The adoption of new technologies has given rise to novel social engineering tactics, such as voice phishing or "vishing." In vishing attacks, attackers use voice communication, often over the phone, to impersonate trusted entities like banks or government agencies. By employing social engineering techniques, such as creating a sense of urgency or fear, attackers manipulate individuals into providing personal information or transferring funds. The auditory nature of vishing leverages the human inclination to trust information conveyed through spoken communication, making it a potent avenue for social engineering attacks.

In conclusion, individuals and organizations fall victim to social engineering attacks due to the intricate interplay of psychological vulnerabilities, trust dynamics, and evolving tactics employed by attackers. From phishing campaigns exploiting human emotions to pretexting schemes leveraging organizational hierarchies, social engineering exploits the human element in cybersecurity. The increasing complexity of these attacks, coupled with the interconnected nature of modern life, underscores the need for robust cybersecurity awareness, continuous education, and proactive defenses that address the multifaceted challenges posed by social engineering in both personal and professional realms.

Chapter 3: Malware Mayhem

Define malware and its broad categories, including viruses, worms, and trojans.

Malware, short for malicious software, refers to any software specifically designed to harm, exploit, or infiltrate computer systems, networks, or devices. Malware encompasses a wide range of malicious programs, each with distinct characteristics and functionalities. Understanding the various categories of malware is crucial for developing effective cybersecurity measures to detect, prevent, and mitigate these threats.

Viruses are a prominent category of malware that attaches itself to legitimate programs or files, spreading when those files are executed. Much like biological viruses, computer viruses replicate and spread, often with the goal of infecting as many files and systems as possible. They can be transmitted through infected email attachments, compromised software downloads, or infected external storage devices. Viruses may have various payloads, including damaging files, stealing information, or providing unauthorized access to the infected system.

Worms are another category of malware that, unlike viruses, can independently spread across networks and systems without requiring a host program. Worms exploit vulnerabilities in network protocols or operating systems to replicate and transmit themselves to other computers. They often have a self-propagating nature, enabling them to quickly spread and infect large numbers of devices. Worms can consume network bandwidth, degrade system performance, and carry payloads that execute malicious actions, such as data theft or system exploitation.

Trojans, named after the ancient Greek story of the wooden horse used to infiltrate Troy, are deceptive programs that disguise themselves as legitimate software to trick users into installing them.

Trojans do not replicate like viruses or worms but focus on delivering malicious payloads once installed on a system. These payloads can include backdoors for unauthorized access, spyware for monitoring activities, or ransomware for encrypting files and demanding payment. Trojans often rely on social engineering techniques to persuade users to execute or install them, making them particularly insidious.

Ransomware is a type of malware that encrypts files on a victim's system, rendering them inaccessible until a ransom is paid to the attacker. Ransomware can spread through various means, including malicious email attachments, compromised websites, or exploit kits. Once activated, it encrypts files using strong encryption algorithms, and the victim is typically presented with a ransom demand accompanied by instructions on how to make the payment, often in cryptocurrency. Paying the ransom does not guarantee the recovery of files, and ethical concerns surround this practice.

Spyware is designed to covertly observe and collect information from a user's device without their knowledge or consent. This information can include keystrokes, login credentials, browsing habits, and sensitive personal or financial data. Spyware often operates stealthily in the background, and users may remain unaware of its presence. It is commonly delivered through Trojans or phishing attacks. The collected data is then transmitted to the attacker, who can use it for various malicious purposes, including identity theft, financial fraud, or corporate espionage.

Adware, short for advertising-supported software, is a type of malware that delivers unwanted advertisements to users. While adware may not be as malicious as other types of malware, it can be intrusive and negatively impact user experience. Adware often accompanies free software downloads, and users may unknowingly install it along with the desired program. Once installed, adware displays pop-up ads, banners, or redirects users to advertising websites.

In some cases, adware may collect user information for targeted advertising, raising privacy concerns.

Rootkits are a particularly stealthy type of malware designed to conceal the presence of other malicious programs or unauthorized activities on a system. Rootkits gain elevated privileges, often exploiting vulnerabilities, to manipulate the operating system's core functions. They can hide files, processes, network connections, or registry entries from traditional security measures, making them difficult to detect. Rootkits may be used as part of a broader attack strategy, allowing attackers to maintain persistent access and control over compromised systems.

Botnets, short for robot networks, are networks of compromised computers, known as bots or zombies, controlled by a single entity, the botmaster. Infected devices in a botnet can be coordinated to perform malicious activities, such as launching distributed denial-of-service (DDoS) attacks, sending spam emails, or conducting large-scale cyber attacks. Botnets are often created by infecting a large number of computers with malware, turning them into unwitting participants in coordinated, malicious campaigns. The scale and distributed nature of botnets make them formidable threats to online security.

Keyloggers, or keystroke loggers, are a type of spyware designed to record and monitor the keystrokes of users, capturing sensitive information such as usernames, passwords, and credit card details. Keyloggers can operate at various levels of a system, from hardware-based solutions to software that runs in the background. They are often deployed stealthily, and users may remain unaware that their keystrokes are being monitored. Keyloggers can be employed for identity theft, unauthorized access, or extracting confidential information.

Fileless malware represents a class of malware that operates without leaving traditional traces on a system's hard drive. Instead of relying on files or executables, fileless malware resides in the system's memory or leverages existing system tools and processes to execute malicious activities. This characteristic makes fileless malware challenging to detect using traditional antivirus solutions that rely on file-based signatures. Fileless malware often exploits vulnerabilities in software or relies on social engineering to trick users into running malicious scripts or commands.

Polymorphic malware is designed to change its code or appearance each time it infects a new system, making it difficult for traditional antivirus programs to detect and prevent. By altering its code, polymorphic malware can evade signature-based detection methods that rely on recognizing known patterns. This adaptive nature allows polymorphic malware to persistently pose a threat and remain undetected by security measures that rely on static indicators. Polymorphic malware may include various malicious functionalities, such as data theft, system exploitation, or serving as a payload delivery mechanism.

Overall, the diverse categories of malware highlight the evolving nature of cyber threats and the need for dynamic and sophisticated cybersecurity measures to counteract these malicious programs. As technology continues to advance, malware developers adapt their strategies, necessitating continuous efforts to enhance detection, prevention, and response mechanisms to safeguard digital ecosystems.

Discuss the motives behind creating and distributing malware.

The motives behind creating and distributing malware are multifaceted, driven by a combination of financial gain, ideological reasons, geopolitical objectives, and a desire for power or notoriety. One prominent motive is the pursuit of financial gains through cybercrime. Malicious actors, often organized crime groups or individual hackers, create and distribute malware with the primary goal of generating profits. This can manifest through various means, including stealing sensitive financial information such as credit card details, login credentials, or engaging in ransomware attacks that demand payment in exchange for restoring access to encrypted files. The lucrative nature of cybercrime has attracted a diverse range of actors, from skilled individuals seeking financial opportunities to sophisticated criminal organizations operating on a global scale.

Another prevalent motive is the pursuit of ideological or political objectives. Hacktivism, a blend of hacking and activism, involves individuals or groups creating and deploying malware to advance social or political causes. Hacktivists may target organizations or government entities perceived as adversaries, aiming to disrupt their operations, expose sensitive information, or promote their own ideological agenda. The motives behind hacktivism can range from advocating for freedom of information to expressing dissent against perceived injustices, making it a form of cyber protest that leverages malware as a tool for activism.

State-sponsored cyberattacks represent a distinct category of malware deployment motivated by geopolitical considerations. Nation-states may develop and distribute malware to achieve strategic objectives, including espionage, sabotage, or exerting influence over other nations. State-sponsored actors often engage in advanced persistent threats (APTs), deploying sophisticated malware to maintain long-term access to targeted systems, gather intelligence, or disrupt the operations of adversaries. The motives behind state-sponsored malware campaigns are rooted in geopolitical rivalries, intelligence gathering, and the pursuit of national interests in the cyber domain.

The motive of gaining power and control is inherent in the creation and distribution of certain types of malware. Botnets, networks of compromised computers controlled by a single entity, provide a means for malicious actors to exert control over a large number of devices. Botnet operators can leverage their control to launch coordinated attacks, such as distributed denial-of-service (DDoS) attacks, steal sensitive information, or use the compromised devices to mine cryptocurrency. The motive for power and control extends beyond immediate financial gains, encompassing the manipulation of digital resources and the potential to influence online activities on a large scale.

Some individuals create and distribute malware driven by a desire for notoriety or a sense of accomplishment. These individuals, often referred to as script kiddies or amateur hackers, may lack sophisticated technical skills but use readily available malware tools or exploit kits to compromise systems. Their motives are rooted in a desire to gain recognition within hacker communities, demonstrate technical prowess, or simply cause chaos and disruption for personal satisfaction. The notoriety gained from successful malware attacks, even on a smaller scale, can contribute to the hacker's reputation within online subcultures.

Espionage and information warfare represent motives behind the creation and distribution of malware with the aim of gathering intelligence or influencing strategic outcomes. Cyberespionage involves the use of malware to infiltrate systems and networks to steal sensitive information, intellectual property, or gain insights into the activities of targeted entities. Nation-states, corporate rivals, or criminal organizations may employ malware for espionage purposes, exploiting vulnerabilities in software or networks to access confidential data. Information warfare extends this concept to the deliberate manipulation of information to achieve strategic goals, utilizing malware as a means of shaping narratives, spreading disinformation, or disrupting communication channels.

The motives behind creating and distributing malware are also influenced by the evolving landscape of cybersecurity and the emergence of new technologies. As digital currencies like Bitcoin gained popularity, cryptocurrency mining malware became a prevalent threat. Malicious actors leverage the processing power of compromised devices to mine cryptocurrencies without the users' knowledge, generating profits through the computational resources of a large botnet. The motive in this context is financial, as attackers seek to exploit the decentralized and pseudonymous nature of cryptocurrencies for monetary gain.

The underground economy of cybercrime has further fueled the motives behind malware creation and distribution. The Dark Web provides a marketplace where malware developers can sell their creations, and aspiring attackers can purchase sophisticated tools and services. Malware-as-a-Service (MaaS) platforms have emerged, allowing individuals with limited technical skills to deploy malware easily. The motives here are intertwined with profit, as developers receive payment for their malware, and buyers seek to exploit these tools for various malicious purposes, including stealing sensitive information or conducting cyberattacks.

The rapid evolution of technology and the increasing connectivity of devices in the Internet of Things (IoT) era have introduced new motives for malware creation. Malicious actors may exploit vulnerabilities in IoT devices to compromise networks, launch attacks, or conduct surveillance. The motives can range from orchestrating large-scale DDoS attacks using compromised IoT devices to conducting industrial espionage by infiltrating interconnected systems. As society becomes more reliant on interconnected technologies, the motives behind malware creation adapt to exploit the expanding attack surface presented by IoT ecosystems.

The motives behind creating and distributing malware are not mutually exclusive, and often, a single malware campaign may encompass multiple motivations. The interconnected nature of the cyber landscape, coupled with the diverse motivations of malicious actors, underscores the complexity of addressing and mitigating the threats posed by malware. As cybersecurity measures evolve, it becomes imperative to understand the underlying motives driving the creation and distribution of malware to develop comprehensive strategies that can effectively counteract these multifaceted threats.

Explore the timeline of significant malware outbreaks, from early computer viruses to modern-day ransomware.

The timeline of significant malware outbreaks spans several decades, reflecting the evolution of cyber threats from early computer viruses to the sophisticated ransomware attacks prevalent in the modern digital landscape. In the early 1970s, the Creeper virus emerged as one of the first instances of self-replicating malware. Operating on the DEC PDP-10 mainframe, Creeper would display the message "I'm the creeper, catch me if you can!" as it moved between machines. Although more of an experiment than a malicious act, Creeper set the stage for the development of computer viruses.

In the 1980s, the concept of computer viruses gained prominence with the emergence of notable malware like the Elk Cloner, targeting Apple II systems. Elk Cloner infected the boot sector of floppy disks, spreading as users exchanged infected disks. This period also witnessed the appearance of the infamous Brain virus, which targeted MS-DOS systems. Brain marked the first IBM PC-compatible virus and included a copyright notice, revealing a shift towards malicious intent.

The 1990s saw a proliferation of viruses and the rise of worms. The Morris Worm, created by Robert Tappan Morris in 1988, infected Unix systems, exploiting vulnerabilities and highlighting the potential for widespread damage. In 1991, the Michelangelo virus gained attention for triggering on March 6, the birthday of the renowned artist. While the actual impact was limited, it heightened public awareness of the potential dangers posed by malware.

The "ILOVEYOU" worm of 2000 marked a significant shift in the scale and impact of malware. Disguised as a love letter, the worm spread through email attachments and infected millions of computers worldwide, causing widespread damage by overwriting files and spreading itself to email contacts. The financial impact was substantial, and ILOVEYOU highlighted the effectiveness of social engineering in tricking users into activating malicious code.

The early 2000s witnessed the emergence of blended threats, combining elements of viruses, worms, and other types of malware. Nimda, appearing in 2001, exemplified this trend by exploiting multiple vulnerabilities, spreading through email and network shares, and infecting web servers. Nimda's rapid propagation showcased the growing sophistication of malware in compromising diverse systems.

In 2003, the Slammer (SQL Slammer) worm targeted Microsoft SQL Server systems, causing widespread internet disruptions. Slammer leveraged a flaw in Microsoft's software, highlighting the critical importance of promptly applying security patches. The following year brought the Sasser worm, exploiting a Windows vulnerability to spread rapidly and disrupt systems. Sasser demonstrated the potential for malware to exploit vulnerabilities for mass propagation.

Around the same period, spyware gained prominence as a distinct category of malware. Claria, formerly known as Gator, exemplified spyware's invasive nature by tracking users' online activities for targeted advertising. While not directly causing system damage, spyware raised privacy concerns and highlighted the need for tools to combat unwanted surveillance.

The mid-2000s witnessed the advent of ransomware, a malicious software variant designed to encrypt files and demand payment for their release. Gpcode, appearing in 2004, was an early example of ransomware that used strong encryption, making file recovery challenging. However, Gpcode's encryption methods were eventually deciphered, marking an early victory for the cybersecurity community.

In 2008, the Conficker worm gained notoriety for its sophisticated propagation methods and ability to evade detection. Exploiting vulnerabilities in Windows systems, Conficker spread rapidly through networks and USB drives, emphasizing the importance of timely software updates and comprehensive security measures.

The Stuxnet worm, discovered in 2010, represented a groundbreaking shift in malware sophistication. Stuxnet specifically targeted supervisory control and data acquisition (SCADA) systems, notably those used in Iran's nuclear program. Its ability to manipulate physical processes marked a departure from traditional cyber threats, showcasing the potential for malware to impact critical infrastructure.

2013 witnessed the emergence of CryptoLocker, a game-changing ransomware variant that utilized robust encryption. CryptoLocker encrypted users' files and demanded payment in Bitcoin for the decryption key. This marked the beginning of a surge in ransomware attacks targeting individuals and organizations alike. The success of CryptoLocker inspired the development of numerous ransomware strains, creating a lucrative underground economy.

The WannaCry ransomware attack of 2017 represented a watershed moment in the evolution of ransomware. Exploiting a Windows vulnerability known as EternalBlue, initially discovered by the NSA and later leaked, WannaCry spread rapidly across networks, impacting organizations globally, including healthcare institutions. The attack underscored the urgency of patching vulnerabilities and raised awareness about the interconnected nature of cyber threats.

2017 also saw the emergence of NotPetya, a destructive ransomware worm with the ability to spread across networks rapidly. While posing as ransomware, NotPetya's primary objective appeared to be data destruction, particularly targeting organizations in Ukraine. The incident highlighted the potential for malware to be used as a tool for geopolitical objectives.

In recent years, ransomware attacks have continued to escalate in scale and impact. The Ryuk ransomware, first identified in 2018, demonstrated a shift towards more targeted attacks on high-profile organizations. Ryuk is often deployed after initial compromise by other malware, highlighting the trend of attackers using multiple tools in sophisticated campaigns.

The SolarWinds supply chain attack, discovered in late 2020, exemplified a new breed of cyber threats. While not traditional malware, this incident involved the compromise of a trusted software vendor to distribute malicious updates to thousands of organizations. The attack demonstrated the potential for compromising the software supply chain to infiltrate high-profile targets.

The evolution of malware outbreaks underscores the dynamic nature of cybersecurity challenges. From the early days of simple viruses to the complex and multifaceted threats of modern ransomware and supply chain attacks, the timeline reflects an ongoing cat-and-mouse game between cyber attackers and defenders. As technology advances, the motives behind malware evolve, and the cybersecurity community must continuously adapt to address emerging threats and safeguard digital ecosystems.

Discuss the technological advancements driving malware development.

Technological advancements have played a pivotal role in driving the development of malware, enabling malicious actors to create more sophisticated and evasive threats. One key factor contributing to the evolution of malware is the increasing complexity of software and hardware architectures. As computing systems have become more intricate, with a myriad of interconnected components, attackers have found new avenues to exploit vulnerabilities. The sheer complexity of modern software applications and operating systems provides ample opportunities for malware developers to discover and capitalize on weaknesses, allowing them to create more potent and elusive forms of malicious software.

The advent of the Internet and the interconnected nature of digital systems have significantly expanded the attack surface for malware. With the proliferation of online services, cloud computing, and the Internet of Things (IoT), attackers have gained access to a vast array of potential targets. Malware can now exploit vulnerabilities not only in traditional computers but also in a diverse range of IoT devices, smart appliances, and other connected systems. This increased attack surface provides fertile ground for the development of malware that can propagate across different types of devices and networks, posing a more extensive and versatile threat.

The rise of sophisticated exploitation techniques has been a driving force behind the evolution of malware. Attackers leverage advanced methods such as zero-day exploits, which target vulnerabilities unknown to software vendors, giving them the advantage of initiating attacks before security patches are developed and deployed. Additionally, attackers employ polymorphic and metamorphic techniques to create malware that can change its code or appearance dynamically, making it challenging for traditional signature-based detection methods to keep pace. These advancements in exploitation techniques empower malware to evade detection and maintain persistence on compromised systems.

The growth of artificial intelligence (AI) and machine learning (ML) has both benefited cybersecurity and introduced new challenges in the realm of malware development. While AI and ML technologies enhance the capabilities of antivirus and intrusion detection systems, enabling them to detect patterns and anomalies, they are also leveraged by malware developers to create more adaptive and evasive threats. Malware can now incorporate AI-driven evasion techniques, learning and adapting to the defensive measures employed by cybersecurity solutions. This cat-and-mouse game between AI-driven defenses and AI-enhanced malware represents a new frontier in the technological arms race within the cybersecurity landscape.

The commodification of cybercrime tools and services on the dark web has lowered the barrier for entry into the world of malware development. Malicious actors can now purchase or rent sophisticated malware, exploit kits, and other tools, even if they lack deep technical expertise. This underground marketplace enables less skilled individuals, commonly referred to as script kiddies, to engage in cybercriminal activities, contributing to the proliferation of malware. The availability of these off-the-shelf malicious tools facilitates the rapid development and deployment of new malware variants by a broader range of actors.

Another technological trend influencing malware development is the increased use of encryption by legitimate applications and communication channels. While encryption enhances privacy and security, it also provides a convenient cover for malware to conceal its communications and activities. Malware developers incorporate encryption and other obfuscation techniques to make their malicious code more challenging to analyze and detect. This encryption-centric approach poses a significant challenge for cybersecurity professionals, as it requires them to develop more sophisticated methods for inspecting encrypted traffic without compromising user privacy.

The growth of cryptocurrencies, such as Bitcoin, has introduced new economic incentives for malware development. Ransomware, in particular, has flourished due to the anonymous and decentralized nature of cryptocurrency transactions. Attackers can demand ransom payments in cryptocurrency, making it more difficult for law enforcement to trace and apprehend them. The financial motivation provided by cryptocurrency-based extortion has led to the refinement and specialization of ransomware strains, with attackers targeting high-value entities, including corporations and critical infrastructure.

Mobile devices have become integral to modern life, and as a result, they have become lucrative targets for malware developers. The widespread use of smartphones and tablets, coupled with the increasing complexity of mobile operating systems, has created new opportunities for malware to thrive. Malicious actors exploit vulnerabilities in mobile apps, app marketplaces, and even device firmware to compromise mobile devices. The proliferation of mobile malware encompasses a variety of threats, including banking trojans, spyware, and mobile ransomware, reflecting the adaptability of malware to different technological environments.

The interconnectedness of critical infrastructure, including energy grids, transportation systems, and healthcare networks, has introduced new possibilities for malware to cause significant real-world impact. Nation-states and advanced persistent threat (APT) groups leverage malware as a tool for cyber-espionage and sabotage, aiming to disrupt the operations of rival nations or gain strategic advantages. The technological sophistication of these attacks often involves the use of malware tailored to specific targets, incorporating advanced evasion techniques and persistence mechanisms.

The evolution of malware has been driven, in part, by the dynamic nature of software development and deployment practices. The prevalence of DevOps and continuous integration/continuous deployment (CI/CD) pipelines has accelerated the release of software updates and patches. Malware developers exploit this rapid pace of development by actively seeking and exploiting vulnerabilities in newly released software versions before organizations can apply security patches. This strategy allows malware to capitalize on the window of vulnerability that exists between the discovery of a software flaw and the deployment of a patch

The development and deployment of malware have also been influenced by the growing adoption of remote work and cloud computing. The decentralization of corporate networks and the reliance on cloud-based services create new opportunities for attackers to exploit weak points in security. Malware developers adapt their tactics to target remote workers, exploiting vulnerabilities in virtual private networks (VPNs) and collaboration tools. Additionally, cloud-based infrastructure provides attackers with a scalable platform for hosting and distributing malware, enabling them to evade traditional network-based defenses.

In conclusion, technological advancements continue to shape the landscape of malware development, fostering the creation of more sophisticated, adaptive, and evasive threats. The interconnectedness of digital systems, the rise of artificial intelligence, the commodification of cybercrime tools, the prevalence of encryption, and the proliferation of mobile and cloud technologies all contribute to the dynamic evolution of malware. As cybersecurity professionals strive to defend against these evolving threats, they must leverage cutting-edge technologies and strategies to stay ahead in the ongoing battle against malicious actors.

Break down the components of malware and how it operates within a system.

Malware, short for malicious software, is a broad category encompassing various types of harmful software designed to compromise the security and functionality of computer systems. The components of malware can be dissected into several key elements, each playing a distinct role in its operation within a system. The first component is the delivery mechanism, the means by which malware infiltrates a system. This can occur through infected email attachments, malicious websites, or compromised software downloads. Once the malware gains entry, the second component, the infection vector, comes into play. This is the method the malware uses to spread and propagate within the system or to other connected systems. Common infection vectors include exploiting vulnerabilities in operating systems or applications, using removable media, or leveraging network connections.

The third component involves the execution phase, where the malware begins its malicious activities. This phase often includes processes like code injection, where the malware inserts its code into legitimate processes to conceal its presence and evade detection. Polymorphic capabilities, a fourth component, enable malware to constantly change its code's appearance, making it challenging for antivirus programs to recognize and eliminate. The fifth component involves establishing persistence, ensuring the malware remains active on the system even after a reboot. This may involve modifying registry entries, creating hidden files, or manipulating startup processes to guarantee continuous operation.

The sixth component revolves around communication, as malware often establishes connections with command and control (C2) servers. This allows attackers to remotely control the infected system, exfiltrate data, or deliver additional payloads. Encryption is frequently employed to obfuscate communication, making it difficult for security measures to detect malicious traffic. The seventh component concerns the payload, the actual malicious actions the malware performs. This can range from data theft and exfiltration to destructive activities like file deletion or system corruption.

The eighth component is evasion tactics, wherein malware employs techniques to avoid detection by security solutions. This may involve detecting virtual environments or sandboxing and altering its behavior accordingly. Rootkit capabilities, the ninth component, allow malware to embed itself deeply within the system, often at the kernel level, making it challenging to detect and remove. The tenth component involves the exploitation of zero-day vulnerabilities, leveraging previously unknown flaws in software or hardware to gain unauthorized access or control.

The eleventh component pertains to the ability of some malware to self-propagate, creating copies of itself to spread to other systems. Worms, for example, use this mechanism to rapidly infect a large number of devices across networks. The twelfth component is the obfuscation of indicators of compromise (IoCs), where malware conceals traces of its presence, such as file names, registry entries, or network activity patterns, to hinder forensic analysis. Finally, the thirteenth component relates to the dynamic nature of malware, with many strains constantly evolving to adapt to changing security measures and exploit emerging vulnerabilities.

In summary, the anatomy of malware comprises various interconnected components, each serving a specific purpose in the malicious lifecycle. From delivery mechanisms to evasion tactics and self-propagation, these elements collectively contribute to the effectiveness and persistence of malware within a targeted system. Understanding these components is crucial for developing effective cybersecurity strategies and implementing robust defense mechanisms to mitigate the ever-growing threat of malicious software.

Discuss the techniques malware uses to evade detection.

Malware developers employ a myriad of sophisticated techniques to evade detection by security solutions, creating a constant challenge for cybersecurity professionals. One common evasion tactic involves the use of polymorphic and metamorphic code. Polymorphic malware dynamically changes its code's appearance while maintaining its core functionality, making it difficult for signature-based antivirus programs to identify patterns and signatures. Metamorphic malware goes a step further, rewriting its entire code structure, presenting an entirely new binary with each iteration, thus thwarting static analysis.

Another evasion technique involves the use of packers and crypters, which compress and encrypt the malware's code to obfuscate its true intent. Packers compress the executable file, making it harder for static analysis tools to inspect the code directly. Crypters, on the other hand, encrypt the malware's code, requiring a decryption routine at runtime, which can be altered with each iteration, making it challenging for signature-based detection methods to identify the malicious payload.

Rootkit capabilities represent a more insidious evasion strategy, as rootkits embed themselves deep within the operating system, often at the kernel level. By manipulating system calls and API functions, rootkits can conceal the presence of malware, making it virtually invisible to traditional antivirus solutions. Additionally, some advanced rootkits use virtualization techniques to run the entire operating system within a virtual environment, further complicating detection efforts.

In the realm of network communication, malware frequently utilizes encryption and tunneling to hide malicious traffic. Secure Sockets Layer (SSL) or Transport Layer Security (TLS) encryption is commonly employed, making it challenging for network-based intrusion detection systems to inspect the contents of the communication. Malware may also use covert channels and steganography to embed malicious data within seemingly innocuous communication, evading signature-based detection mechanisms.

To counteract sandboxing and virtualization-based detection techniques, some malware incorporates sandbox evasion tactics. This includes detecting the presence of virtual environments and altering its behavior accordingly, such as delaying malicious activities or remaining dormant to avoid triggering analysis systems. Sandboxes are often used by security researchers to analyze the behavior of unknown files in a controlled environment, making sandbox evasion a crucial element in the malware's strategy to escape scrutiny.

Furthermore, fileless malware represents a category of threats that operate without leaving a traditional footprint on the file system. Instead of relying on executable files, fileless malware resides in system memory, registry entries, or other system components, making it challenging for signature-based antivirus solutions to detect and mitigate. This technique leverages legitimate system processes and tools, such as PowerShell or WMI, to carry out malicious activities, blending in with normal system behavior.

Malware also exploits zero-day vulnerabilities to evade detection. These vulnerabilities are previously unknown and unpatched software flaws, giving malware an opportunity to infiltrate systems before security updates are available. By taking advantage of these vulnerabilities, malware can avoid known signature-based detection mechanisms, making it critical for organizations to maintain up-to-date software and security patches.

Additionally, some malware leverages anti-emulation techniques, aiming to deceive emulators and analysis tools used by security researchers. By mimicking user interaction, generating fake system calls, or detecting virtualized environments, malware can alter its behavior to appear benign during analysis, only revealing its true nature when executed in a real, unprotected environment.

In conclusion, the techniques employed by malware to evade detection are diverse and continually evolving. From code obfuscation and encryption to rootkit capabilities and zero-day exploits, malware developers employ a sophisticated arsenal of tactics to outsmart traditional security measures. As the threat landscape evolves, cybersecurity professionals must adapt and employ a combination of proactive strategies, including behavior-based analysis, threat intelligence, and continuous monitoring, to effectively detect and mitigate these elusive and dynamic threats.

Explore the various ways malware spreads, including email attachments, infected websites, and malicious downloads.

Malware employs a multitude of cunning methods to propagate and infiltrate computer systems, exploiting vulnerabilities in various online and offline environments. One prevalent avenue for malware dissemination is through email attachments, a method that capitalizes on users' trust in electronic communication. Malicious actors craft emails with seemingly innocuous content, often posing as legitimate entities or presenting urgent messages, enticing recipients to open attached files. These attachments may harbor executable malware, document macros, or scripts that, when activated, initiate the infection process. The success of this method often hinges on social engineering, tricking users into unwittingly executing the malware by exploiting their curiosity, fear, or trust in seemingly familiar senders.

Infected websites represent another prominent vector for malware distribution. Cybercriminals compromise legitimate websites by injecting malicious code or exploiting vulnerabilities in web servers, content management systems, or third-party plugins. Users visiting these compromised sites may unknowingly download malware onto their systems through drive-by downloads or malicious redirects. Malvertising, a technique involving the injection of malicious ads into legitimate online advertising networks, further amplifies the risk, as users can inadvertently download malware simply by interacting with these compromised ads. This method capitalizes on the widespread use of online platforms and the trust users place in familiar websites, turning routine web browsing into a potential source of infection.

Malicious downloads, often facilitated through peer-to-peer (P2P) file-sharing networks, also play a pivotal role in malware dissemination. Malware creators upload infected files to these networks, masquerading as popular or sought-after content, such as software cracks, movies, or music. Unsuspecting users eager to acquire these files may inadvertently download and execute malware, leading to widespread infections. Torrent sites, in particular, are notorious for hosting infected files, as the decentralized nature of P2P networks makes it challenging to regulate and monitor the content shared. This method preys on users' desire for free and easily accessible content, turning their quest for entertainment or software into a potential security risk.

Social engineering tactics extend beyond email attachments, manifesting in other forms to exploit human behavior. Malware developers leverage fake notifications, deceptive pop-ups, or enticing links on social media platforms, convincing users to click on seemingly harmless content. Once clicked, these links may lead to the download and execution of malware, exploiting the users' trust in their social networks and the content shared within them. The virality of social media further amplifies the impact of this method, as one compromised account can potentially disseminate malware to a vast number of interconnected users.

USB drives and other removable media serve as another avenue for malware to spread, often through a technique known as "auto-run" or "auto-play" infection. When users insert an infected USB drive into their system, the malware exploits the auto-run feature to execute itself automatically. This method relies on the ubiquity of removable media in everyday computing environments, as users commonly share files between devices using USB drives, external hard drives, or SD cards. The convenience of these devices becomes a double-edged sword, providing an efficient means of data transfer but also serving as a potential carrier for malware.

Exploitation of software vulnerabilities represents a technical approach to malware propagation, with attackers targeting flaws in operating systems, applications, or plugins. Malware creators develop exploits or take advantage of existing ones to compromise systems without user interaction. Drive-by downloads, often initiated through exploit kits hosted on malicious websites, leverage these vulnerabilities to silently install malware on users' systems when they visit compromised web pages. The success of this method relies on the delayed or absent patching of known vulnerabilities, underscoring the importance of timely software updates and security patches.

Email phishing campaigns, beyond delivering malware through attachments, also utilize deceptive links to redirect users to malicious websites. These phishing sites may mimic legitimate login pages for popular services, tricking users into entering their credentials. Simultaneously, the site may deliver malware through drive-by downloads or other techniques. By combining social engineering with the exploitation of user trust in familiar login interfaces, phishing attacks seamlessly integrate into users' daily online activities, increasing the likelihood of successful malware infections.

In conclusion, the methods through which malware spreads are diverse and ever-evolving, reflecting the adaptability and creativity of malicious actors. From exploiting human psychology through email attachments, infected websites, and social engineering to technical approaches such as malicious downloads, software vulnerabilities, and phishing campaigns, malware leverages a spectrum of vectors to infiltrate systems. As technology advances and users continue to engage with digital environments, understanding these propagation methods becomes crucial for developing robust cybersecurity strategies that safeguard against the multifaceted threat landscape posed by malware.

Discuss the role of social engineering in malware distribution.

Social engineering plays a pivotal and multifaceted role in the distribution of malware, leveraging psychological manipulation to exploit human trust, curiosity, and fear. At its core, social engineering involves manipulating individuals into divulging confidential information, clicking on malicious links, or executing actions that compromise the security of computer systems. One prevalent avenue where social engineering intersects with malware distribution is through phishing attacks, where cybercriminals craft deceptive emails, messages, or communications to trick users into taking unintended actions. These communications often impersonate trusted entities, such as banks, government agencies, or well-known organizations, creating a façade that lures recipients into clicking on malicious links or opening infected attachments. Once engaged, users may unwittingly download and execute malware, as the cybercriminals exploit the inherent trust users place in familiar and seemingly legitimate sources.

Moreover, social engineering extends its influence beyond email-based phishing, infiltrating other communication channels, including social media platforms. Malicious actors create fake profiles or compromise legitimate accounts to disseminate deceptive content, such as links to infected websites or convincing messages that prompt users to install seemingly harmless software. The interconnected nature of social media networks amplifies the reach of these campaigns, enabling malware to spread rapidly through shares, likes, and interactions. By manipulating the social fabric of online communities, cybercriminals exploit users' trust in their connections, turning the very platforms designed for communication and networking into vectors for malware distribution.

Social engineering also capitalizes on human curiosity and the desire for information, often manifesting in the form of enticing content or clickbait. Cybercriminals leverage sensational or intriguing headlines, images, or offers to lure users into clicking on links that lead to malicious websites or initiate downloads. This technique is prevalent on social media, where users are more likely to engage with content that piques their curiosity. The balance between trust and curiosity becomes a delicate dance, with social engineering techniques exploiting these fundamental aspects of human behavior to facilitate the spread of malware.

In addition to exploiting trust and curiosity, social engineering tactics often prey on fear and urgency. Cybercriminals craft messages that convey a sense of urgency, such as security alerts, legal threats, or imminent account closures, compelling users to take immediate action. This urgency overrides rational judgment, leading individuals to hastily click on links or download attachments without scrutinizing the legitimacy of the communication. By manipulating emotions and triggering a sense of panic or fear, social engineering amplifies the effectiveness of malware distribution campaigns.

Social engineering in malware distribution is not limited to online interactions; it extends to the physical realm as well. Techniques like pretexting involve creating fabricated scenarios or personas to manipulate individuals into divulging sensitive information. In the context of malware, pretexting may involve impersonating IT personnel, service providers, or coworkers to gain physical access to a system or to convince users to execute actions that facilitate malware installation. This blend of psychological manipulation with real-world interactions underscores the versatility of social engineering tactics in orchestrating sophisticated attacks.

Another avenue where social engineering intertwines with malware distribution is through the manipulation of software updates and patches. Cybercriminals exploit the trust users place in legitimate software providers by creating fake update notifications or messages that mimic the appearance of authentic prompts. Users, conditioned to prioritize security through regular updates, may unknowingly download and install malware disguised as a critical update. This method leverages the habit of users to promptly address software vulnerabilities, turning a security-conscious behavior into a vulnerability that can be exploited through deceptive social engineering tactics.

Furthermore, social engineering techniques frequently target employees within organizations, with spear-phishing campaigns tailored to exploit specific individuals or departments. By researching targets and crafting personalized messages, cybercriminals increase the likelihood of success in tricking employees into revealing sensitive information, clicking on malicious links, or inadvertently downloading malware. This targeted approach, known as spear-phishing, often precedes more advanced attacks, such as business email compromise or the infiltration of corporate networks.

The role of social engineering in malware distribution extends to the manipulation of software trust relationships. Malicious actors may compromise legitimate software distribution channels or inject malware into seemingly trustworthy applications. Users, conditioned to trust official app stores or software vendors, may unwittingly download and install malware, believing it to be a legitimate and secure application. This tactic exploits the ingrained trust users place in established software sources, emphasizing the nuanced ways in which social engineering can be wielded to infiltrate systems.

In conclusion, social engineering serves as a linchpin in the distribution of malware, employing psychological manipulation to exploit human vulnerabilities. From phishing attacks that leverage trust and curiosity to the manipulation of fear and urgency, social engineering tactics intricately weave into various channels, including email, social media, physical interactions, and software updates. As cybercriminals continually refine and adapt their strategies, understanding the multifaceted role of social engineering is imperative for individuals and organizations alike. Developing robust cybersecurity awareness, implementing effective training programs, and employing technological defenses are essential components of mitigating the impact of social engineering in the ever-evolving landscape of malware distribution.

Highlight famous malware attacks and their impact on individuals and organizations.

The landscape of cybersecurity is punctuated by infamous malware attacks that have left indelible marks on individuals, organizations, and the digital realm as a whole. One such watershed moment occurred with the advent of the "ILOVEYOU" worm in May 2000. Originating in the Philippines, this worm spread rapidly via email, tempting users with an attachment supposedly containing a love letter. Unwitting recipients who opened the attachment found their systems compromised, as the worm proliferated by overwriting files, stealing passwords, and propagating itself to email contacts. The widespread impact of "ILOVEYOU" was unprecedented, infecting millions of systems globally, disrupting email services, and causing an estimated $5.5–$8.7 billion in damages. This incident underscored the vulnerability of early internet users to social engineering tactics and marked a turning point in the urgency for robust cybersecurity measures.

Fast-forward to 2007, the Conficker worm emerged as a formidable threat, exploiting vulnerabilities in Microsoft Windows operating systems. Capable of spreading through network shares and removable media, Conficker evaded traditional security measures by frequently updating itself and employing advanced evasion tactics. It infected millions of computers globally, creating a massive botnet that could be remotely controlled by its operators. The impact of Conficker extended beyond individual users, affecting hospitals, government agencies, and businesses. The worm's ability to disable security services and update mechanisms emphasized the importance of timely patching and the need for collaborative efforts in combating large-scale malware threats.

The Stuxnet worm, discovered in 2010, represented a paradigm shift in malware sophistication and intent. Believed to be a state-sponsored cyberweapon, Stuxnet targeted supervisory control and data acquisition (SCADA) systems used in industrial settings, with a particular focus on Iran's nuclear program. Stuxnet demonstrated a level of complexity rarely seen before, employing multiple zero-day vulnerabilities and advanced techniques to propagate and manipulate programmable logic controllers (PLCs). Its impact went beyond the digital realm, physically damaging Iran's nuclear infrastructure and setting a precedent for cyber-physical attacks. Stuxnet highlighted the evolving landscape of cyber threats, showcasing the potential for malware to bridge the gap between virtual and physical realms with severe real-world consequences.

In 2013, the world witnessed the emergence of the CryptoLocker ransomware, marking a significant shift in malware tactics. CryptoLocker utilized strong encryption to encrypt files on infected systems, demanding a ransom payment in exchange for the decryption key. This marked the rise of ransomware as a lucrative criminal enterprise, targeting individuals and organizations alike. The success of CryptoLocker spawned a wave of copycat attacks, collectively referred to as the "ransomware epidemic." Organizations, healthcare providers, and individuals fell victim to these attacks, facing the dilemma of either paying the ransom or losing access to critical data. The widespread impact of CryptoLocker underscored the need for robust backup strategies, user education, and proactive cybersecurity measures to counter the growing threat of ransomware.

The WannaCry ransomware attack in 2017 became a global cybersecurity crisis, affecting organizations across various sectors, including healthcare, finance, and government. Exploiting a vulnerability in Microsoft Windows that had been patched months earlier, WannaCry spread rapidly, encrypting files and demanding ransom payments in Bitcoin. The worm-like propagation of WannaCry highlighted the interconnected nature of modern networks, as it quickly traversed the globe, infecting over 200,000 systems in more than 150 countries. The attack's impact was particularly severe on healthcare institutions, with disruptions to critical services and patient care. WannaCry served as a wake-up call, emphasizing the importance of timely patching, cybersecurity hygiene, and collaborative efforts to mitigate the global impact of large-scale malware attacks.

The NotPetya ransomware attack in 2017 further escalated the sophistication and destructiveness of malware. Initially disguised as a ransomware attack, NotPetya's true intent was to cause widespread disruption and destruction. Targeting Ukraine, the malware spread globally, affecting multinational companies, critical infrastructure, and government systems. NotPetya utilized a combination of advanced techniques, including exploiting software supply chains and leveraging legitimate administrative tools, to maximize its impact. The attack's collateral damage was extensive, causing billions of dollars in losses, disrupting global shipping, and illustrating the potential for malware to be used as a tool of statecraft. NotPetya challenged traditional notions of ransomware attacks, revealing a new breed of destructive malware with far-reaching consequences.

In 2018, the Triton (or Trisis) malware attack targeted industrial control systems (ICS), specifically safety instrumented systems (SIS), with the potential to cause catastrophic physical harm. This attack marked a significant escalation in the threat landscape, as Triton sought to manipulate the safety mechanisms of a petrochemical plant. The malware was designed to disable or manipulate the SIS, posing a severe risk to the safety and integrity of the industrial processes. While the attack was ultimately detected and thwarted before causing physical harm, Triton highlighted the potential for malware to pose direct threats to human life and critical infrastructure, emphasizing the need for enhanced cybersecurity measures in industrial settings.

The SolarWinds supply chain attack, discovered in late 2020, exemplified the strategic and stealthy nature of modern cyber espionage. A highly sophisticated operation attributed to a state-sponsored actor, the attack involved compromising the software supply chain of SolarWinds, a prominent IT management company. Malicious code was injected into software updates, allowing threat actors to infiltrate thousands of organizations, including government agencies and major corporations. The impact of the SolarWinds attack extended far beyond traditional malware infections, as it underscored the vulnerability of widely used software supply chains and the potential for covert, long-term espionage campaigns.

The Colonial Pipeline ransomware attack in 2021 highlighted the critical role of critical infrastructure in the crosshairs of cyber threats. DarkSide, a ransomware-as-a-service group, targeted the Colonial Pipeline, a major fuel pipeline in the United States. The attack led to the shutdown of the pipeline, causing fuel shortages, panic buying, and disruptions to the fuel supply chain. The incident underscored the vulnerability of critical infrastructure to cyber threats and the potential for real-world consequences, prompting increased attention to cybersecurity resilience in essential services.

Each of these infamous malware attacks has left an enduring impact on the cybersecurity landscape, reshaping perspectives on threat vectors, the potential for cyber-physical harm, and the imperative for robust defense measures. From the early days of worms exploiting human emotions to the modern era of state-sponsored cyber-espionage and ransomware-as-a-service, these incidents have collectively shaped the trajectory of cybersecurity, emphasizing the need for continuous innovation, collaboration, and resilience in the face of evolving and multifaceted cyber threats.

Discuss the lessons learned from these incidents.

The series of infamous malware incidents over the years has provided invaluable lessons that have shaped the field of cybersecurity, prompting individuals, organizations, and governments to adapt their approaches and defenses. The "ILOVEYOU" worm in 2000 highlighted the vulnerability of early internet users to social engineering. The lesson learned from this incident was the importance of cybersecurity awareness and education. Users needed to be vigilant against deceptive emails and attachments, and organizations needed to implement robust email filtering and security measures to detect and prevent such threats. Additionally, the "ILOVEYOU" worm emphasized the need for timely software updates and patch management to address vulnerabilities exploited by malware.

The emergence of the Conficker worm in 2007 underscored the significance of collaboration in combating large-scale malware threats. Conficker's ability to propagate across networks and evade traditional security measures demonstrated the need for a collective response. The lessons learned included the importance of sharing threat intelligence, coordinating efforts across industries, and establishing best practices for network security. The Conficker incident catalyzed the formation of alliances and partnerships within the cybersecurity community, fostering a more collaborative and proactive approach to addressing emerging threats.

Stuxnet, discovered in 2010, showcased the potential for cyber threats to bridge the gap between virtual and physical realms. The lessons learned from Stuxnet included the recognition that cyber-physical attacks could have severe real-world consequences. This realization prompted critical infrastructure sectors to reassess their cybersecurity posture, acknowledging the need for specialized defenses to protect against threats that could impact physical systems. The incident also emphasized the importance of securing supply chains, as Stuxnet exploited vulnerabilities in widely used industrial control systems.

The CryptoLocker ransomware in 2013 marked the rise of ransomware as a lucrative criminal enterprise. The key lesson from CryptoLocker was the critical importance of data backups and recovery strategies. Organizations learned the necessity of regularly backing up critical data and storing backups in isolated environments to prevent them from being compromised by ransomware. The incident also highlighted the need for user education to recognize phishing attempts and the importance of having robust endpoint security solutions to detect and prevent ransomware infections.

The global impact of the WannaCry ransomware attack in 2017 underscored the urgency of timely patching and the consequences of neglecting security updates. The lesson learned was the critical importance of maintaining up-to-date software and promptly applying security patches. The incident prompted organizations to rethink their patch management processes, implement automated patching solutions, and establish a culture of cybersecurity hygiene. It also emphasized the need for organizations to prioritize and allocate resources for cybersecurity, treating it as a fundamental aspect of risk management.

NotPetya, also in 2017, challenged traditional notions of ransomware attacks, revealing a new breed of destructive malware with far-reaching consequences. The key lesson from NotPetya was the potential for malware to be used as a tool of statecraft and the collateral damage it could cause. Organizations learned the importance of having incident response plans that go beyond data recovery to address the broader impact of a cyberattack. The incident also highlighted the need for international norms and agreements in cyberspace to deter and mitigate state-sponsored cyber threats.

The Triton (Trisis) malware attack in 2018 emphasized the critical nature of industrial control systems (ICS) security. The lesson learned from Triton was the necessity of implementing specialized cybersecurity measures for ICS environments. Organizations with critical infrastructure assets realized the importance of conducting thorough risk assessments, implementing network segmentation, and deploying intrusion detection systems tailored to the unique characteristics of industrial networks. Triton prompted increased attention to securing industrial systems against cyber threats that could have severe consequences on safety and operations.

The SolarWinds supply chain attack in 2020 revealed the strategic and stealthy nature of modern cyber espionage. The lesson learned from SolarWinds was the need for enhanced supply chain security and scrutiny. Organizations recognized the importance of vetting and monitoring third-party software providers, conducting thorough security assessments, and implementing measures to detect and respond to supply chain compromises. The incident also underscored the importance of zero-trust architectures and continuous monitoring to identify anomalous behavior within networks.

The Colonial Pipeline ransomware attack in 2021 highlighted the critical role of essential services in the crosshairs of cyber threats. The key lesson from Colonial Pipeline was the need for resilience and continuity planning in critical infrastructure sectors. Organizations realized the importance of regularly testing and updating incident response plans, collaborating with law enforcement, and implementing measures to minimize the impact of disruptions on essential services. The incident also prompted increased attention to cybersecurity regulations and standards for critical infrastructure operators.

Collectively, these incidents have instilled several overarching lessons in the field of cybersecurity. Firstly, the importance of a proactive and collaborative approach is paramount. Cyber threats are dynamic and multifaceted, requiring collective efforts across industries, governments, and the cybersecurity community. Collaboration facilitates the sharing of threat intelligence, best practices, and resources necessary to stay ahead of evolving threats.

Secondly, the lessons underscore the need for a comprehensive and layered defense strategy. Organizations should not solely rely on traditional security measures but should embrace a holistic approach that includes user education, timely patching, robust endpoint security, secure supply chains, and specialized defenses for critical infrastructure.

Thirdly, incident response and resilience planning are critical components of cybersecurity preparedness. Organizations must be equipped to detect, respond to, and recover from cyber incidents swiftly. This involves regular testing of incident response plans, collaboration with law enforcement, and minimizing the potential impact of disruptions on essential services.

Fourthly, the evolving threat landscape demands continuous innovation and adaptation. Cybersecurity is an ongoing process that requires organizations to stay abreast of emerging threats, technologies, and best practices. This adaptability ensures that defenses remain effective against the latest tactics and techniques employed by malicious actors.

Lastly, the lessons highlight the importance of international cooperation and norms in cyberspace. As cyber threats transcend national borders, a collective and coordinated response is essential. Establishing norms, agreements, and frameworks for responsible state behavior in cyberspace can contribute to deterring malicious activities and fostering a more secure digital environment.

In conclusion, the lessons learned from infamous malware incidents provide a roadmap for strengthening cybersecurity practices globally. They emphasize the importance of collaboration, comprehensive defense strategies, incident response preparedness, adaptability, and international cooperation. As the cyber threat landscape continues to evolve, these lessons serve as guideposts for individuals, organizations, and policymakers navigating the complex terrain of cybersecurity.

Chapter 4: The Cryptic World of Cryptocurrency

Define cryptocurrency and its underlying blockchain technology.

Cryptocurrency is a revolutionary form of digital or virtual currency that employs cryptographic techniques to secure financial transactions, regulate the creation of additional units, and verify the transfer of assets. The most prominent example of a cryptocurrency is Bitcoin, introduced in 2009 by an anonymous entity known as Satoshi Nakamoto. Unlike traditional currencies issued by governments, cryptocurrencies operate on decentralized networks based on blockchain technology, which serves as the backbone of their existence.

Blockchain, the underlying technology of cryptocurrencies, is a distributed ledger that records and verifies transactions across a network of computers. It operates on a peer-to-peer network, eliminating the need for central authorities such as banks or governments. The blockchain consists of a chain of blocks, each containing a list of transactions, a timestamp, and a reference to the previous block. This chain is maintained through a consensus mechanism, where nodes on the network must agree on the validity of transactions before they are added to the ledger.

One of the key features of blockchain is its immutability, meaning once a block is added to the chain, it is nearly impossible to alter or tamper with previous transactions. This immutability is achieved through cryptographic hash functions, which generate unique identifiers for each block based on its content. Any attempt to alter the information within a block would require the consensus of the majority of nodes in the network, making it highly secure against fraud or manipulation.

Decentralization is another fundamental characteristic of blockchain technology. Traditional financial systems often rely on a central authority to validate and regulate transactions, but blockchain operates on a peer-to-peer network where every participant has an equal role in the validation process. This decentralization reduces the risk of a single point of failure, enhances security, and fosters transparency.

Smart contracts, self-executing contracts with the terms directly written into code, are another innovative aspect of blockchain technology. These contracts automatically execute and enforce agreed-upon rules when predefined conditions are met, eliminating the need for intermediaries and reducing transaction costs. Ethereum, the second-largest cryptocurrency by market capitalization, is a prominent platform for developing and deploying smart contracts.

The consensus mechanisms employed in blockchain networks ensure that all participants agree on the state of the ledger. Proof of Work (PoW) and Proof of Stake (PoS) are two common consensus mechanisms. PoW, used by Bitcoin, requires participants, known as miners, to solve complex mathematical problems to validate transactions and create new blocks. PoS, on the other hand, relies on participants, known as validators, to stake a certain amount of cryptocurrency as collateral, and the chance of validating a block is determined by the amount staked.

Blockchain technology has transcended its original use case of supporting cryptocurrencies and has found applications in various industries. The concept of a transparent and tamper-resistant ledger has been embraced in sectors such as supply chain management, healthcare, and finance. By providing a verifiable and immutable record of transactions, blockchain enhances accountability, reduces fraud, and streamlines processes.

Despite its numerous advantages, blockchain technology faces challenges and criticisms. Scalability, the ability to handle a large number of transactions simultaneously, remains a concern. The energy consumption associated with PoW consensus mechanisms, particularly in the case of Bitcoin, has raised environmental concerns. Additionally, regulatory uncertainty and the potential for illicit activities in the cryptocurrency space have led to debates about the need for government oversight.

In conclusion, cryptocurrency and blockchain technology represent a transformative force in the realm of finance and beyond. The decentralized, secure, and transparent nature of blockchain has the potential to revolutionize how transactions are conducted and recorded. As the technology continues to evolve and find applications in diverse industries, the future holds both challenges and opportunities for the widespread adoption of this groundbreaking innovation.

Discuss the decentralization and anonymity aspects of cryptocurrencies.

Decentralization and anonymity are two core principles that distinguish cryptocurrencies from traditional financial systems, contributing to their unique characteristics and capabilities. Decentralization, a fundamental concept underlying cryptocurrencies, refers to the distribution of control and validation processes across a network of participants, eliminating the need for a central authority. In traditional financial systems, centralized entities such as banks or governments typically regulate and oversee transactions. Cryptocurrencies, however, operate on decentralized networks, often based on blockchain technology, where each participant, or node, plays a role in the validation and verification of transactions. This decentralized structure not only enhances security by reducing the risk of a single point of failure but also promotes inclusivity, allowing anyone with an internet connection to participate in the network.

Anonymity, on the other hand, addresses the privacy of users involved in cryptocurrency transactions. While it's a common misconception that all cryptocurrencies provide complete anonymity, they often offer a degree of pseudonymity. In the context of cryptocurrencies like Bitcoin, transactions are recorded on the public blockchain, and addresses are pseudonymous strings of characters. Participants in the network are identified by these addresses rather than personal information. However, the level of anonymity varies across different cryptocurrencies, with some employing additional privacy-focused features. For instance, privacy coins like Monero and Zcash utilize advanced cryptographic techniques, such as ring signatures and zk-SNARKs, to enhance the privacy and fungibility of transactions, making it more challenging to trace the origin, destination, and amount involved.

Decentralization and anonymity in cryptocurrencies work in tandem to create a trustless and borderless financial environment. The absence of a central authority means that users can transact directly with one another without intermediaries, fostering financial inclusion, especially in regions with limited access to traditional banking services. Moreover, decentralization aligns with the ethos of financial sovereignty, as users have control over their private keys and, by extension, their funds. This stands in contrast to traditional banking systems, where individuals must trust centralized institutions to safeguard their assets.

The concept of decentralization not only applies to the structure of cryptocurrency networks but also to the issuance of new units of currency. In many cryptocurrencies, the process of creating new units, often referred to as mining, is decentralized and open to participants in the network. Bitcoin, for example, uses a Proof of Work (PoW) consensus mechanism, where miners compete to solve complex mathematical puzzles to validate transactions and add new blocks to the blockchain. This decentralized mining process ensures that no single entity has control over the creation of new units, mitigating the risk of inflation through unchecked currency issuance.

However, decentralization comes with its set of challenges. Scalability, or the ability of a network to handle a growing number of transactions, has been a persistent issue. As more participants join the network, the scalability of certain blockchain networks can be strained, leading to slower transaction speeds and increased fees. Various scaling solutions, such as layer-two protocols and consensus algorithm upgrades, are actively being explored and implemented to address these challenges without compromising the decentralized nature of the networks.

Anonymity in cryptocurrencies, while providing a degree of privacy, has also raised concerns related to illicit activities, such as money laundering and terrorism financing. The pseudonymous nature of transactions on public blockchains can make it challenging for authorities to trace and identify individuals involved in criminal activities. This has led to debates about striking a balance between privacy and regulatory compliance, with some jurisdictions implementing Know Your Customer (KYC) and Anti-Money Laundering (AML) regulations on cryptocurrency exchanges to ensure transparency and accountability.

In the realm of decentralization and anonymity, it is essential to recognize that these principles exist on a spectrum. While cryptocurrencies offer a level of decentralization and pseudonymity, the extent to which they achieve these goals varies. Some projects prioritize decentralization at the expense of transaction speed, while others aim to balance both. Similarly, the pursuit of anonymity involves trade-offs, with privacy-focused cryptocurrencies providing enhanced confidentiality but often facing increased scrutiny from regulators.

The interplay between decentralization and anonymity in cryptocurrencies reflects the ongoing evolution of the technology and its adaptation to societal and regulatory considerations. As the cryptocurrency ecosystem continues to mature, finding the right equilibrium between decentralization, anonymity, and regulatory compliance will be crucial for its acceptance and integration into mainstream financial systems. Striking this balance holds the key to unlocking the full potential of cryptocurrencies as a transformative force in the global financial landscape.

Explore how hackers exploit vulnerabilities in cryptocurrency exchanges and wallets.

Hackers employ various sophisticated techniques to exploit vulnerabilities in cryptocurrency exchanges and wallets, aiming to compromise the security of these platforms and gain unauthorized access to digital assets. One common avenue for exploitation is through weaknesses in the exchange infrastructure. Cryptocurrency exchanges, being online platforms that facilitate the trading of digital assets, are attractive targets for hackers due to the potential for substantial financial gain. Vulnerabilities in the exchange's code, servers, or web applications can be exploited to execute attacks such as SQL injection, cross-site scripting (XSS), and Distributed Denial of Service (DDoS) attacks. SQL injection involves manipulating a database query to gain access to sensitive information, while XSS targets vulnerabilities in web applications, allowing attackers to inject malicious scripts into websites viewed by other users. DDoS attacks, on the other hand, overwhelm the exchange's servers with a flood of traffic, causing disruptions and creating opportunities for other forms of exploitation.

In addition to attacking the infrastructure, hackers often exploit weaknesses in the human element, taking advantage of social engineering and phishing techniques. Social engineering involves manipulating individuals, often employees of exchanges, into divulging sensitive information or performing actions that compromise security. Phishing involves creating deceptive websites or emails that mimic legitimate platforms, tricking users into providing login credentials or private keys. These tactics prey on human error and trust, making them effective strategies for hackers seeking unauthorized access to cryptocurrency exchanges.

Furthermore, vulnerabilities in the code of the cryptocurrency wallets used by individuals to store their digital assets are another target for exploitation. Wallets, whether hardware, software, or online, are essential tools for managing and securing cryptocurrencies. Malicious actors often exploit vulnerabilities in wallet software to compromise the integrity of private keys, the cryptographic keys that grant access to users' funds. In some cases, poorly designed or inadequately tested wallet software may contain bugs or security flaws that hackers can exploit to gain unauthorized access. Additionally, attackers may use malware to target the devices of wallet users, seeking to steal private keys or manipulate transactions.

One prominent method of exploiting vulnerabilities in cryptocurrency wallets is the use of keyloggers and screen recording malware. Keyloggers record the keystrokes of users, capturing sensitive information such as passwords and private keys. Screen recording malware captures the entire screen activity, providing hackers with a visual record of a user's interactions with their wallet. These tools can be surreptitiously installed on a user's device through phishing emails, malicious downloads, or compromised websites, allowing attackers to gain access to private keys and compromise the security of cryptocurrency holdings.

Another technique employed by hackers is the manipulation of software updates for wallets. By compromising the update process, attackers can introduce malicious code into the wallet software, enabling them to steal private keys or manipulate transactions. This method preys on users' trust in official updates, as they may unwittingly download and install compromised versions of wallet software, believing them to be legitimate. Ensuring the authenticity and integrity of software updates is crucial for users to mitigate this type of vulnerability.

Hardware wallets, designed to provide an additional layer of security by keeping private keys offline, are not immune to exploitation. In some cases, attackers have tampered with the hardware itself or exploited vulnerabilities in the firmware. This can involve manipulating the device during the manufacturing process to insert malicious components or compromising the firmware through vulnerabilities in the code. While hardware wallets are generally considered more secure than software wallets, these targeted attacks highlight the importance of thorough security measures at every stage of the hardware wallet's lifecycle.

Moreover, the use of man-in-the-middle (MitM) attacks is another avenue for exploiting vulnerabilities in cryptocurrency wallets. In a MitM attack, an attacker intercepts communication between the user and the wallet, allowing them to eavesdrop on sensitive information or manipulate transactions. This can be achieved through various means, such as compromising public Wi-Fi networks, DNS spoofing, or injecting malicious code into legitimate websites. Users who access their wallets through unsecured networks or fail to verify the authenticity of websites may unknowingly expose themselves to such attacks.

The interconnected nature of the cryptocurrency ecosystem also introduces risks associated with third-party services, such as exchanges and wallet providers. Users often entrust these services with their private keys or rely on them for various cryptocurrency-related functions. However, if these third-party services have vulnerabilities or lack robust security measures, they become attractive targets for hackers aiming to compromise a large number of users simultaneously. The compromise of a single service can have cascading effects, potentially leading to widespread financial losses for users.

In conclusion, the exploitation of vulnerabilities in cryptocurrency exchanges and wallets is a multifaceted challenge that requires a comprehensive approach to security. From infrastructure weaknesses and social engineering tactics to vulnerabilities in wallet software and hardware, hackers continuously evolve their methods to compromise the integrity of the cryptocurrency ecosystem. Addressing these challenges necessitates a combination of robust cybersecurity measures, user education, and ongoing efforts to identify and patch vulnerabilities in both exchange platforms and wallet solutions. As the cryptocurrency space continues to grow, the proactive mitigation of these risks will be essential to ensuring the security and trustworthiness of digital asset management and transactions.

Discuss notable cryptocurrency hacking incidents.

Over the years, the cryptocurrency space has been marred by several notable hacking incidents, each leaving a significant impact on the industry and its participants. One of the earliest and most infamous instances occurred in 2014 with the collapse of Mt. Gox, once the world's largest Bitcoin exchange. Mt. Gox, based in Japan, filed for bankruptcy after revealing that it had lost approximately 850,000 Bitcoins, worth hundreds of millions of dollars at the time, due to a series of security breaches. The incident shed light on the vulnerabilities of centralized exchanges, highlighting the risks associated with entrusting large amounts of cryptocurrency to a single platform. The aftermath of the Mt. Gox debacle prompted increased scrutiny and regulatory efforts within the cryptocurrency ecosystem.

In 2016, a notable hacking incident targeted The DAO (Decentralized Autonomous Organization), a crowdfunding project built on the Ethereum blockchain. The DAO aimed to create a decentralized venture capital fund but suffered a severe security flaw in its smart contract code. Exploiting this vulnerability, an attacker managed to drain one-third of The DAO's funds, amounting to approximately $50 million worth of Ether. The incident led to a contentious hard fork in the Ethereum blockchain, resulting in the creation of Ethereum (ETH) and Ethereum Classic (ETC) as the community debated whether to reverse the exploited transactions. This event underscored the challenges of managing smart contract security and the complexities surrounding community responses to security breaches.

In 2017, the cryptocurrency exchange Bithumb, based in South Korea, experienced a major security breach, with hackers stealing personal information, including email addresses and mobile phone numbers, of over 30,000 users. While the stolen information itself did not directly compromise cryptocurrency holdings, it raised concerns about the security practices of exchanges and the potential for targeted phishing attacks. This incident highlighted the importance of robust cybersecurity measures not only for protecting digital assets but also for safeguarding user data and privacy.

Later in 2017, another significant hacking incident targeted NiceHash, a platform that facilitated the buying and selling of hash power for cryptocurrency mining. Hackers infiltrated the platform, making off with approximately 4,700 Bitcoins, worth tens of millions of dollars. The breach not only resulted in financial losses for NiceHash users but also underscored the vulnerability of mining-related services in the cryptocurrency ecosystem. This incident prompted increased awareness regarding the security of mining platforms and the need for enhanced measures to protect both user funds and the infrastructure supporting cryptocurrency mining.

One of the most prominent and damaging cryptocurrency hacking incidents occurred in January 2018 when Coincheck, a major Japanese cryptocurrency exchange, suffered a security breach. Hackers exploited vulnerabilities in the exchange's security systems, making off with a staggering 523 million NEM tokens, valued at over $500 million at the time. The incident raised concerns about the security practices of exchanges and prompted regulatory authorities in Japan to intensify their oversight of the cryptocurrency industry. It also fueled discussions on the importance of implementing robust security measures, including cold storage for large amounts of digital assets held by exchanges.

Later in 2018, the Italian cryptocurrency exchange BitGrail reported a significant security breach, with hackers making off with 17 million Nano tokens, valued at approximately $170 million. The incident led to a contentious legal battle between BitGrail and the Nano development team, with accusations and counteraccusations regarding the responsibility for the breach. The fallout from the Bit-Grail incident underscored the legal and regulatory challenges surrounding cryptocurrency exchanges and their responsibilities in securing user funds.

In 2019, Cryptopia, a New Zealand-based cryptocurrency exchange, suffered a security breach that resulted in substantial financial losses. Hackers targeted the exchange, stealing a variety of digital assets. The incident prompted Cryptopia to halt its services and eventually file for bankruptcy, leaving users uncertain about the recovery of their funds. This case highlighted the persistent challenges faced by exchanges in maintaining robust security measures and the significant impact of such breaches on both the affected platforms and their users.

In 2020, the decentralized finance (DeFi) space experienced a high-profile hacking incident when the lending platform bZx fell victim to multiple exploits. The attacks exploited vulnerabilities in the smart contract code, resulting in the loss of millions of dollars in various cryptocurrencies. The incidents raised questions about the security and auditing processes within the rapidly evolving DeFi sector, prompting calls for more rigorous testing and evaluation of smart contracts before they are deployed on the blockchain.

The SolarWinds cyberattack, discovered in late 2020, also had implications for the cryptocurrency industry. While not a direct attack on a cryptocurrency platform, the SolarWinds incident highlighted the broader cybersecurity challenges faced by institutions, including those in the financial sector. As various industries grappled with the fallout from the SolarWinds attack, concerns about the potential vulnerabilities of cryptocurrency infrastructure and the need for heightened cybersecurity measures gained prominence.

More recently, in 2021, the decentralized finance platform Poly Network experienced a high-profile exploit, resulting in the theft of over $600 million in various cryptocurrencies. The attacker exploited a vulnerability in the platform's code, allowing them to manipulate the blockchain and transfer substantial amounts of digital assets. However, what set this incident apart was the unexpected turn of events when the hacker, identifying as a white-hat or ethical hacker, returned the stolen funds and engaged in a dialogue with the Poly Network team. This incident highlighted the complex dynamics of security vulnerabilities in the cryptocurrency space and the potential for collaboration between security researchers and platform operators to address such issues

In conclusion, cryptocurrency hacking incidents have been pervasive throughout the industry's development, affecting exchanges, projects, and users alike. These events underscore the ongoing need for rigorous security measures, robust regulatory frameworks, and continuous efforts to educate users about best practices for securing their digital assets. As the cryptocurrency ecosystem continues to evolve, addressing and mitigating the risks associated with hacking incidents remain critical for fostering trust and stability in the broader adoption of digital currencies and blockchain technology.

Discuss the connection between ransomware attacks and demands for payment in cryptocurrency.

The nefarious nexus between ransomware attacks and demands for payment in cryptocurrency has become a prominent and concerning trend in the realm of cybersecurity. Ransomware, a type of malicious software designed to block access to a computer system or files until a sum of money is paid, has evolved into a lucrative criminal enterprise, often facilitated by the anonymity and pseudonymity offered by cryptocurrencies. This symbiotic relationship between ransomware attacks and cryptocurrency payments poses significant challenges for individuals, organizations, and law enforcement agencies alike.

Cryptocurrencies, particularly Bitcoin, have emerged as the preferred method of payment for ransomware operators due to their characteristics of decentralization, pseudo-anonymity, and borderless nature. Bitcoin, being the first and most widely adopted cryptocurrency, has become the default medium of exchange in many ransomware incidents. The decentralized nature of cryptocurrencies allows malicious actors to receive payments without relying on traditional banking systems, making it more challenging for authorities to trace and freeze funds. Pseudo-anonymity, inherent in many cryptocurrency transactions, enables ransomware operators to conceal their identities behind cryptographic addresses, making it difficult for law enforcement to attribute payments to specific individuals.

The modus operandi of a typical ransomware attack involves infiltrating a victim's computer system, encrypting critical files or locking access to the entire system, and subsequently demanding payment in cryptocurrency, usually Bitcoin. This payment is often referred to as a ransom, and the sum can vary widely, ranging from a few hundred dollars to millions, depending on the perceived value of the data or the financial capacity of the victim. The ransomware operators provide the victim with instructions on how to make the payment, including details such as the specific amount, the cryptocurrency wallet address to send the funds, and a deadline for payment. The use of cryptocurrencies facilitates quick and anonymous transactions, aligning with the urgency typically associated with ransomware attacks.

One of the key advantages for ransomware operators in demanding payments in cryptocurrency is the speed and relative ease with which transactions can be executed. Unlike traditional banking transactions that may involve intermediary institutions and compliance checks, cryptocurrency transactions occur directly between the payer and payee, allowing for rapid fund transfers. This expeditious nature of cryptocurrency transactions is crucial for ransomware operators seeking to capitalize on the time-sensitive nature of their demands and the potential reluctance of victims to involve law enforcement.

The pseudo-anonymous nature of cryptocurrency transactions, while providing a degree of privacy to users, also plays a pivotal role in the success of ransomware attacks. Cryptographic addresses, representing the destination of funds, do not inherently reveal the identity of the individuals behind them. Ransomware operators exploit this anonymity to obfuscate their financial activities, making it challenging for cybersecurity experts and law enforcement agencies to trace the flow of funds and attribute them to specific individuals or groups. This anonymity not only protects the identities of the attackers but also creates an environment where ransomware attacks can be conducted with a reduced fear of being apprehended.

The use of cryptocurrency in ransomware attacks is further compounded by the rise of privacy-focused coins, such as Monero and Zcash. These cryptocurrencies utilize advanced cryptographic techniques, such as ring signatures and zk-SNARKs, to enhance the privacy and fungibility of transactions. Privacy coins make it significantly more challenging for investigators to trace the flow of funds, providing ransomware operators with an additional layer of anonymity. The adoption of privacy coins in ransomware demands represents a strategic adaptation by malicious actors to stay ahead of evolving cybersecurity measures.

The global nature of cryptocurrency transactions adds another layer of complexity to combating ransomware. Cryptocurrencies operate on a borderless network, enabling ransomware operators to demand payments from victims located in any part of the world. This global reach complicates the jurisdictional challenges faced by law enforcement agencies and underscores the necessity for international collaboration to address the transnational nature of cybercrime. The decentralized and distributed nature of blockchain technology, the underlying infrastructure of cryptocurrencies, means that there is no central authority that can unilaterally regulate or control these transactions.

As ransomware attacks continue to proliferate, the cryptocurrency community and industry stakeholders have faced increased scrutiny regarding their role in facilitating illicit activities. Some argue that the pseudo-anonymous and decentralized nature of cryptocurrencies empowers individuals by providing financial privacy, censorship resistance, and protection from government overreach. However, the abuse of these features by ransomware operators has led to growing concerns about the potential negative impacts on the reputation and regulatory environment of the broader cryptocurrency ecosystem.

Governments and regulatory bodies have responded to the ransomware challenge by exploring ways to enhance oversight and regulation of cryptocurrency transactions. This includes initiatives to improve the transparency of cryptocurrency exchanges and wallet services, enforce Anti-Money Laundering (AML) and Know Your Customer (KYC) regulations, and collaborate with international partners to address the cross-border aspects of ransomware attacks. The goal is to strike a balance between preserving the positive aspects of cryptocurrency technology and mitigating the risks associated with its misuse for criminal activities.

While efforts to enhance regulation and collaboration are underway, the battle against ransomware requires a multi-faceted approach. Cybersecurity experts and organizations are continuously developing and deploying advanced threat detection and prevention mechanisms to identify and thwart ransomware attacks before they can cause significant damage. Furthermore, the emphasis on user education and awareness regarding best cybersecurity practices, such as regular data backups and cautious online behavior, plays a crucial role in reducing the success rate of ransomware attacks.

In conclusion, the connection between ransomware attacks and demands for payment in cryptocurrency has created a complex and challenging landscape for cybersecurity professionals, law enforcement agencies, and the cryptocurrency community. The pseudo-anonymous, borderless, and decentralized nature of cryptocurrencies provides an ideal platform for ransomware operators to carry out their illicit activities with relative impunity. As the threat landscape evolves, addressing the convergence of ransomware and cryptocurrency requires a comprehensive and collaborative approach that spans technological, regulatory, and educational domains. Balancing the benefits of cryptocurrency technology with the need for increased accountability remains a central challenge in navigating the intricate relationship between ransomware attacks and cryptocurrency payments.

Explore the challenges of tracing and recovering cryptocurrency payments.

Tracing and recovering cryptocurrency payments present formidable challenges due to the inherent characteristics of digital currencies, including their pseudonymous nature, decentralization, and the global reach of blockchain technology. Cryptocurrencies operate on decentralized networks, utilizing cryptographic techniques to secure transactions and identities. Bitcoin, the first and most well-known cryptocurrency, is often perceived as pseudonymous rather than fully anonymous. While transactions are recorded on the public blockchain, participants are identified by cryptographic addresses rather than personal information. This characteristic provides a layer of privacy for users but poses significant challenges for tracing and attributing transactions to specific individuals or entities.

One of the primary challenges in tracing cryptocurrency payments is the use of mixers and tumblers. These services allow users to mix their funds with those of others, obscuring the transaction trail and making it challenging to follow the flow of funds. Mixers and tumblers utilize complex algorithms to shuffle and anonymize transactions, breaking the link between the sender and receiver. As a result, tracing the origin or destination of funds through these services becomes an intricate task for investigators. The use of privacy-focused cryptocurrencies, such as Monero and Zcash, exacerbates this challenge by inherently providing enhanced privacy features that make it even more difficult to trace transactions on their respective blockchains.

The decentralized nature of blockchain technology contributes to the complexity of tracing cryptocurrency payments. Unlike traditional financial systems where a central authority oversees transactions, cryptocurrencies operate on a peer-to-peer network where participants validate transactions through consensus mechanisms. This decentralized architecture eliminates the need for intermediaries but complicates the task of tracking and recovering funds. Each participant in the network has access to the entire transaction history, making it more challenging for authorities to pinpoint the location or identity of malicious actors involved in illicit activities, including ransomware attacks, fraud, and money laundering.

Moreover, the global reach of cryptocurrency transactions adds another layer of difficulty to tracing and recovering payments. Cryptocurrencies facilitate cross-border transactions without the need for traditional banking infrastructure, allowing funds to move seamlessly across jurisdictions. This global aspect presents jurisdictional challenges for law enforcement agencies, as different countries may have varying regulations and legal frameworks for dealing with cryptocurrency-related crimes. The lack of a centralized authority overseeing these transactions further complicates international efforts to trace and recover funds, as coordination among multiple jurisdictions is essential but often challenging to achieve.

Addressing the challenges of tracing and recovering cryptocurrency payments requires collaboration between public and private sectors, international cooperation, and the development of innovative technological solutions. Many governments and regulatory bodies have recognized the need for enhanced oversight of the cryptocurrency ecosystem and are working to establish regulatory frameworks that strike a balance between fostering innovation and preventing illicit activities. However, achieving a globally coordinated approach remains a complex endeavor, given the diverse regulatory landscapes and varying levels of acceptance of cryptocurrencies among different nations.

The emergence of blockchain analytics firms and the increasing sophistication of their tools represent a positive development in the efforts to trace cryptocurrency payments. These firms leverage data analysis techniques to monitor and analyze blockchain transactions, providing insights into the movement of funds and the identities of users. While these tools have proven effective in certain cases, they are not foolproof, especially when dealing with privacy-focused cryptocurrencies and sophisticated mixing services. Additionally, the effectiveness of blockchain analytics tools relies on the level of transparency inherent in the blockchain of a particular cryptocurrency.

The legal and ethical considerations surrounding the use of blockchain analytics tools also present challenges. Privacy advocates argue that the increased use of these tools could infringe on individuals' right to financial privacy, as the transparent nature of blockchain transactions does not necessarily imply consent to widespread scrutiny. Striking a balance between the need for investigative tools and protecting individuals' privacy rights remains a contentious issue in the evolving landscape of cryptocurrency regulation.

In cases involving ransomware attacks, where criminals demand cryptocurrency payments in exchange for unlocking encrypted data, the challenges of tracing and recovering funds are exacerbated by the urgency and time-sensitive nature of the demands. Ransomware operators often impose tight deadlines for payment, exploiting the irreversible and pseudonymous nature of cryptocurrency transactions to create a sense of urgency for victims. The speed at which funds can be moved globally and the use of privacy-enhancing techniques make it difficult for law enforcement agencies to intervene before the funds are irreversibly transferred to the attackers.

The evolving tactics of criminals in the cryptocurrency space further complicate efforts to trace and recover funds. Some malicious actors actively seek to launder their ill-gotten gains by using a combination of mixing services, privacy coins, and other obfuscation techniques. This money laundering process aims to legitimize the source of funds and make them more challenging to trace. Additionally, criminals may leverage decentralized exchanges and peer-to-peer trading platforms that operate with minimal Know Your Customer (KYC) requirements, enabling them to convert cryptocurrency into more easily laundered forms, such as fiat currency or other cryptocurrencies.

The lack of a standardized approach to cryptocurrency regulation and anti-money laundering measures poses a significant challenge to tracing and recovering funds. While some jurisdictions have implemented robust regulatory frameworks for cryptocurrency exchanges and related services, others have been slower to adopt comprehensive measures. The absence of consistent global standards creates a fragmented landscape where criminals can exploit regulatory arbitrage, choosing jurisdictions with lax oversight to conduct their operations. Harmonizing international efforts to establish uniform regulatory standards is crucial for creating a more robust and coordinated approach to tracing and recovering cryptocurrency payments.

Technological advancements and research initiatives focused on improving the traceability of cryptocurrencies offer potential solutions to these challenges. Researchers and developers are exploring technologies like zero-knowledge proofs and privacy-preserving smart contracts to enhance privacy without sacrificing traceability. By striking a balance between privacy and traceability, these innovations aim to address the concerns surrounding the use of cryptocurrencies for illicit activities while respecting individuals' right to financial privacy

In conclusion, the challenges of tracing and recovering cryptocurrency payments underscore the intricate relationship between the pseudonymous, decentralized nature of digital currencies and the imperative to combat illicit activities. The use of privacy-focused cryptocurrencies, mixing services, and global transactions across decentralized networks complicate the efforts of law enforcement agencies and cybersecurity experts to track and attribute funds to specific individuals or entities. Achieving a comprehensive solution requires a multi-pronged approach that includes regulatory harmonization, technological innovation, international collaboration, and ongoing efforts to strike a balance between privacy and traceability in the evolving landscape of cryptocurrency use and regulation.

Highlight instances of fraudulent initial coin offerings (ICOs) and cryptocurrency scams.

The cryptocurrency space, characterized by its rapid evolution and lack of regulatory oversight in its early years, has witnessed numerous instances of fraudulent Initial Coin Offerings (ICOs) and cryptocurrency scams. One of the earliest and most notorious examples dates back to 2017 when the ICO for a project named Centra Tech raised approximately $25 million through deceptive means. The founders of Centra Tech claimed to have partnerships with major credit card companies, promoting a cryptocurrency debit card. However, it was later revealed that these partnerships were fabricated, leading to legal action by the U.S. Securities and Exchange Commission (SEC). Subsequently, the founders were charged with fraud, and the SEC obtained a court order to halt the ICO, marking one of the first instances of regulatory intervention against fraudulent ICOs.

In 2018, the case of Pincoin and iFan in Vietnam underscored the global nature of ICO scams. A company named Modern Tech orchestrated an ICO for two tokens, Pincoin and iFan, promising investors lucrative returns. The project attracted approximately 32,000 investors and raised over $660 million before the operators vanished with the funds. The incident prompted authorities in Vietnam to investigate the fraudulent scheme, leading to arrests and legal proceedings. The Pincoin and iFan scam highlighted the susceptibility of investors to deceptive ICOs, especially in regions where regulatory frameworks were still developing.

Another notable ICO scam involved the project PlexCoin, which claimed to develop a cryptocurrency that would deliver high returns to investors. In 2017, the U.S. Securities and Exchange Commission (SEC) charged the project's founder, Dominic Lacroix, and his company, PlexCorps, with violating securities laws by defrauding investors of $15 million. The SEC obtained an emergency asset freeze to prevent further fund misappropriation, and Lacroix faced legal consequences, including a permanent injunction and monetary penalties. The PlexCoin case highlighted the SEC's commitment to pursuing legal action against fraudulent ICOs and its role in protecting investors.

In 2018, the case of AriseBank brought attention to the challenges of regulating ICOs that falsely claimed to be backed by traditional banking services. AriseBank's founders, Jared Rice Sr. and Stanley Ford, falsely represented their project as the world's first decentralized bank and raised approximately $4.2 million from investors. The SEC filed charges against AriseBank, alleging that the

ICO was fraudulent and that the founders had deceived investors about the legitimacy of their operations. The legal proceedings resulted in fines and penalties against Rice and Ford, signaling regulatory efforts to address fraudulent ICOs that falsely portrayed themselves as legitimate financial institutions.

The BitConnect saga stands out as one of the most infamous cryptocurrency scams, combining elements of a Ponzi scheme with an ICO. BitConnect operated as a lending platform, promising investors daily returns on their cryptocurrency deposits. The project's native token, BCC, quickly gained popularity, attracting millions of dollars in investment. However, in early 2018, BitConnect abruptly shut down its lending and exchange platform, leading to a significant loss of funds for investors. The project's promoters faced legal action in multiple jurisdictions, with regulatory bodies labeling BitConnect as a Ponzi scheme. The incident served as a cautionary tale about the risks associated with high-yield investment programs and prompted increased scrutiny of similar projects in the cryptocurrency space.

In 2019, the PlusToken scam emerged as one of the largest Ponzi schemes in the history of cryptocurrency. Operating primarily in Asian markets, PlusToken claimed to offer high returns on cryptocurrency deposits and attracted millions of participants. The scam, estimated to have defrauded investors of over $2 billion, involved creating a complex network of wallets to obscure the flow of funds. Chinese authorities cracked down on the PlusToken operation, leading to arrests and convictions of key individuals involved. The Plus-Token scam highlighted the challenges of tracking and recovering funds in large-scale cryptocurrency frauds that span multiple jurisdictions.

In the same year, the OneCoin scam gained notoriety for its scale and international reach. OneCoin, led by Ruja Ignatova, claimed to be a legitimate cryptocurrency with its own blockchain. However, investigations revealed that OneCoin operated as a classic Ponzi scheme, with no actual blockchain or cryptocurrency behind it. The project amassed billions of dollars in investments, targeting individuals through aggressive marketing tactics. Ignatova disappeared in 2017, and legal actions were initiated against key figures associated with the scam. The OneCoin case highlighted the importance of global collaboration among law enforcement agencies to combat large-scale cryptocurrency scams that transcend borders.

The DeClouds ICO, which unfolded in 2019, demonstrated the lengths to which some fraudsters would go to deceive investors. DeClouds presented itself as a blockchain-based data storage project, promising secure and decentralized storage solutions. However, investigations later revealed that the project was a fraudulent scheme, with its founders using fake identities and fabricated credentials. The SEC intervened, obtaining a court-ordered asset freeze to halt the ICO and protect investors. The DeClouds case emphasized the importance of thorough due diligence and skepticism in the face of enticing but unsubstantiated claims made by ICO projects

The 2020 case of the Centra Tech founders concluded with legal consequences, providing a significant precedent for combating fraudulent ICOs. Co-founders Robert Farkas and Sohrab Sharma faced charges related to the deceptive sale of securities and false claims about partnerships. In 2021, both were sentenced to prison, highlighting the commitment of authorities to holding individuals accountable for fraudulent ICOs even after a significant passage of time. The Centra Tech case serves as a reminder that legal actions against individuals involved in fraudulent ICOs may unfold over an extended period.

In 2020, the SushiSwap saga brought attention to the risks associated with unaudited decentralized finance (DeFi) projects and their governance tokens. SushiSwap, a decentralized exchange (DEX) forked from Uniswap, garnered attention for its innovative features and yield farming opportunities. However, the project's pseudonymous founder, Chef Nomi, triggered controversy by selling a significant portion of the project's tokens for personal gain. The incident raised questions about the lack of accountability in certain DeFi projects and highlighted the challenges of assessing the legitimacy of projects without traditional corporate structures.

The rise of yield farming and decentralized finance projects in 2020 also saw the emergence of "rug pulls" – scams where project developers abandon a project after attracting significant investments, leaving investors with worthless tokens. Many of these projects conducted token sales or liquidity pool offerings without proper audits or transparency, relying on hype and misleading promises. As a result, investors faced substantial financial losses, and regulators increased their focus on the need for regulatory frameworks and investor protection in the rapidly growing DeFi sector.

In 2021, the case of SafeMoon brought attention to the risks associated with meme tokens and the potential for pump-and-dump schemes. SafeMoon, marketed as a "community-driven" cryptocurrency, gained popularity on social media platforms. However, concerns were raised about the lack of transparency, the sustainability of its tokenomics, and the potential for market manipulation. The incident highlighted the challenges of distinguishing legitimate projects from those driven by hype and speculative trading.

In conclusion, fraudulent ICOs and cryptocurrency scams have been pervasive throughout the evolution of the cryptocurrency space. These instances, characterized by deceptive practices, false promises, and misappropriation of funds, underscore the importance of investor education, due diligence, and regulatory oversight. As the cryptocurrency ecosystem continues to mature, regulatory bodies worldwide are intensifying efforts to establish frameworks that protect investors and maintain the integrity of the industry. The lessons learned from these notable cases contribute to an ongoing dialogue about best practices, transparency, and ethical conduct within the dynamic landscape of cryptocurrencies and blockchain technology.

Discuss the impact on investors and regulatory responses.

The impact of fraudulent Initial Coin Offerings (ICOs) and cryptocurrency scams on investors has been profound, leading to financial losses, erosion of trust, and increased scrutiny of the regulatory environment. Investors, often enticed by the promise of high returns and innovative projects, have found themselves victimized by fraudulent schemes that exploit the lack of regulatory oversight and the pseudonymous nature of cryptocurrency transactions. Financial losses incurred by investors can be substantial, ranging from individual investments to the collective losses incurred in large-scale scams. These losses not only impact individual investors but can also contribute to a broader distrust in the cryptocurrency ecosystem, affecting market sentiment and hindering the adoption of legitimate blockchain projects.

The psychological and emotional toll on investors who fall victim to cryptocurrency scams should not be underestimated. Many investors are drawn to the cryptocurrency space with the hope of participating in groundbreaking technologies and benefiting from the potential for financial gains. However, when these aspirations are shattered by fraudulent schemes, it can lead to feelings of betrayal, frustration, and disillusionment. Such negative experiences may dissuade individuals from further participation in the cryptocurrency market, limiting the growth and diversification of the investor base.

Furthermore, the impact extends beyond individual investors to the broader financial ecosystem. As fraudulent ICOs and scams gain media attention, they contribute to the stigmatization of the entire cryptocurrency industry. This negative perception may hinder the willingness of institutional investors, traditional financial institutions, and regulatory bodies to engage with and embrace the potential benefits of blockchain technology and digital assets. The lack of investor protection and the prevalence of scams become barriers to the maturation and wider acceptance of the cryptocurrency market.

In response to the challenges posed by fraudulent ICOs and cryptocurrency scams, regulatory bodies worldwide have intensified their efforts to establish frameworks that protect investors and maintain market integrity. The regulatory response has evolved over time, reflecting the dynamic nature of the cryptocurrency ecosystem and the need to balance innovation with investor protection. Regulatory approaches vary across jurisdictions, reflecting differences in legal systems, attitudes toward cryptocurrencies, and levels of technological adoption

One notable regulatory response has been the increased scrutiny of ICOs as a fundraising method. Regulatory bodies, such as the U.S. Securities and Exchange Commission (SEC), have asserted that some ICOs may involve the sale of securities, subjecting them to existing securities laws. The SEC's enforcement actions against fraudulent ICOs, including Centra Tech, PlexCoin, and others, highlight a commitment to holding individuals accountable for conducting unregistered securities offerings and engaging in fraudulent practices. These actions send a clear message that regulatory bodies are actively monitoring the cryptocurrency space and will take legal action against those who violate securities laws.

In addition to addressing fraudulent ICOs, regulatory bodies have focused on enhancing investor education and awareness. Recognizing that a well-informed investor is better equipped to navigate the risks of the cryptocurrency market, regulatory agencies have published guidelines, advisories, and educational materials. These resources aim to inform investors about the potential risks associated with ICOs, scams, and other fraudulent activities, urging them to conduct thorough due diligence before participating in cryptocurrency projects. The goal is to empower investors with the knowledge and tools needed to make informed decisions and avoid falling victim to fraudulent schemes.

Regulators have also turned their attention to cryptocurrency exchanges, recognizing them as key gatekeepers within the ecosystem. Many scams involve the trading of tokens on exchanges, making these platforms crucial points of intervention for regulatory bodies. As a result, exchanges are subject to increased scrutiny, with regulatory requirements related to anti-money laundering (AML), know your customer (KYC) procedures, and the listing of tokens. Regulatory actions, such as the imposition of fines and the revocation of licenses, have been taken against exchanges that fail to comply with these requirements or are found to be facilitating fraudulent activities

Moreover, the regulatory landscape has witnessed the emergence of specific frameworks for token sales and crowdfunding activities. Some jurisdictions have introduced regulatory sandboxes or tailored approaches that provide a regulatory framework for legitimate projects while maintaining flexibility to accommodate innovation. These frameworks aim to strike a balance between fostering blockchain-based innovation and protecting investors from fraudulent schemes. However, challenges persist in achieving global regulatory consensus, given the diverse approaches taken by different jurisdictions.

The impact on investors and regulatory responses extends to the decentralized finance (DeFi) space, which gained prominence in recent years. DeFi projects, operating on blockchain platforms and often without traditional intermediaries, present unique challenges for regulators. While DeFi has the potential to revolutionize traditional financial systems, it also introduces risks related to smart contract vulnerabilities, unaudited projects, and the absence of centralized oversight. Regulatory bodies are grappling with the need to adapt existing frameworks to cover DeFi activities while avoiding stifling innovation. Recent regulatory pronouncements and enforcement actions have signaled an increased focus on DeFi, emphasizing the importance of compliance with existing financial regulations.

The regulatory landscape has also seen a growing emphasis on global coordination and collaboration. Recognizing the transnational nature of cryptocurrency scams and the challenges posed by the borderless nature of blockchain technology, regulatory bodies are working together to share information, coordinate enforcement actions, and develop common standards. International organizations, such as the Financial Action Task Force (FATF), play a pivotal role in facilitating collaboration among regulators to address the global challenges posed by fraudulent ICOs, money laundering, and other illicit activities in the cryptocurrency space.

Despite regulatory efforts, challenges persist in creating a comprehensive and cohesive regulatory framework for the cryptocurrency industry. The evolving nature of blockchain technology, the rapid pace of innovation, and the global diversity of legal systems contribute to the complexity of regulatory responses. Achieving a delicate balance between fostering innovation and protecting investors remains an ongoing challenge, and regulatory bodies continue to adapt their approaches to address emerging issues in the cryptocurrency space.

In conclusion, the impact on investors of fraudulent ICOs and cryptocurrency scams extends beyond financial losses, encompassing emotional and psychological consequences. Regulatory responses have evolved to address these challenges, focusing on enforcement actions against fraudulent projects, investor education, scrutiny of exchanges, and the development of specific regulatory frameworks. The dynamic nature of the cryptocurrency ecosystem requires ongoing collaboration among regulators, a commitment to international coordination, and a nuanced approach that promotes innovation while safeguarding investor interests. As the cryptocurrency industry continues to mature, the interplay between investor protection and regulatory frameworks will shape the trajectory of the market and its broader acceptance in the global financial landscape.

Explore potential vulnerabilities in blockchain technology that hackers may exploit.

Blockchain technology, heralded for its decentralized and secure nature, is not immune to potential vulnerabilities that hackers may exploit. While the blockchain architecture enhances security by distributing data across a network and utilizing cryptographic techniques, certain attack vectors and vulnerabilities persist, posing challenges to the integrity and confidentiality of blockchain-based systems. One notable vulnerability is the 51% attack, where a malicious actor or group gains control of more than half of the network's computing power. This dominance allows the attacker to manipulate the blockchain, alter transaction histories, and potentially double-spend digital assets. Particularly concerning in proof-of-work (PoW) consensus algorithms, the 51% attack underscores the importance of network decentralization and the need for alternative consensus mechanisms to mitigate this vulnerability.

Smart contract vulnerabilities represent another significant threat in blockchain ecosystems. Smart contracts, self-executing programs that run on the blockchain, are susceptible to coding errors and vulnerabilities that may be exploited by attackers. The infamous DAO (Decentralized Autonomous Organization) incident in 2016 highlighted the risks associated with smart contract vulnerabilities. Exploiting a flaw in the DAO's smart contract code, an attacker drained a substantial portion of the project's funds. This incident led to a contentious hard fork in the Ethereum blockchain to reverse the exploited transactions, raising debates about the immutability of blockchains and the trade-offs between security and decentralization.

The attack vector known as the Sybil attack poses a threat to the integrity of blockchain networks, particularly in peer-to-peer systems. In a Sybil attack, a malicious actor creates multiple fake identities or nodes to control a disproportionate influence on the network. This can lead to various malicious activities, including the manipulation of consensus mechanisms, spreading misinformation, and disrupting network operations. Decentralized networks, which rely on the assumption of equal influence among nodes, are especially vulnerable to Sybil attacks, necessitating the implementation of reputation systems and other countermeasures to mitigate this risk.

Privacy concerns also emerge as potential vulnerabilities in blockchain technology, challenging the common perception of blockchains as transparent and pseudonymous. While public blockchains like Bitcoin provide transparency by recording all transactions on a public ledger, the lack of privacy features can lead to the deanonymization of users. Blockchain analysis techniques, coupled with external data sources, may expose the identities of users and their transaction histories, compromising privacy. Privacy-focused cryptocurrencies, such as Monero and Zcash, address this vulnerability by incorporating advanced cryptographic techniques to enhance transaction confidentiality, emphasizing the ongoing need for privacy-enhancing technologies in blockchain ecosystems.

In the realm of consensus mechanisms, the practicality of quantum computers poses a potential threat to the security of certain cryptographic algorithms, including those used in blockchain technology. Quantum computers, when sufficiently developed, could break widely used cryptographic schemes, such as RSA and ECC (Elliptic Curve Cryptography), jeopardizing the security of private keys and the integrity of digital signatures. Post-quantum cryptography research is underway to develop quantum-resistant algorithms, but the transition to such algorithms in blockchain networks presents a complex challenge, requiring coordination and consensus among network participants.

Governance vulnerabilities in blockchain networks can also manifest in disputes over protocol upgrades and decision-making processes. Forks, whether contentious or non-contentious, illustrate the challenges associated with reaching consensus among network participants. Contentious forks, such as the Bitcoin Cash and Ethereum hard forks, can lead to community divisions and debates over the legitimacy of competing chains. The governance structures of blockchain networks, often characterized by decentralized decision-making, face the challenge of balancing inclusivity and efficiency while mitigating the potential for contentious disputes that may undermine network stability.

Oracle vulnerabilities in decentralized applications (DApps) and smart contracts present another avenue for exploitation. Oracles are third-party services that provide external data to smart contracts, enabling them to interact with real-world information. However, the reliance on oracles introduces a potential point of failure, as malicious actors may manipulate or compromise the external data fed into smart contracts. This can lead to erroneous contract executions and financial losses. Securing oracle inputs through cryptographic verification and decentralized oracle networks is crucial for minimizing the risks associated with this vulnerability.

Supply chain vulnerabilities, particularly in supply chain management blockchains, pose risks related to the accuracy and integrity of recorded data. If malicious actors gain unauthorized access to a supply chain blockchain, they may manipulate information about the provenance and authenticity of goods. This could have far-reaching consequences, especially in industries where traceability and transparency are paramount, such as food and pharmaceuticals. Implementing robust access controls, cryptographic verification, and decentralized governance mechanisms is crucial for safeguarding supply chain blockchains against unauthorized tampering.

Another potential vulnerability lies in the interoperability of blockchain networks. As the number of blockchains and decentralized platforms grows, the need for seamless communication and value transfer between different networks becomes apparent. However, achieving interoperability introduces challenges related to standardization, security, and consensus mechanisms. Interoperability solutions, such as cross-chain bridges and interoperability protocols, must be carefully designed and implemented to prevent potential vulnerabilities that may arise during the transfer of assets and data between disparate blockchains.

The reliance on consensus mechanisms, whether proof-of-work (PoW), proof-of-stake (PoS), or other variations, introduces environmental vulnerabilities. In PoW-based blockchains, the energy consumption associated with mining has raised concerns about sustainability and the environmental impact of blockchain technology. This vulnerability has prompted the exploration of alternative consensus mechanisms, such as PoS, delegated PoS, and variations like proof-of-burn, to reduce the ecological footprint of blockchain networks. Striking a balance between security, energy efficiency, and decentralization remains a challenge in addressing environmental vulnerabilities associated with consensus mechanisms.

In conclusion, while blockchain technology provides enhanced security through decentralization and cryptographic techniques, it is not immune to potential vulnerabilities that hackers may exploit. From smart contract vulnerabilities and privacy concerns to Sybil attacks, quantum computing threats, and governance challenges, addressing these vulnerabilities requires a multi-faceted approach. Continuous research, innovation, and collaboration within the blockchain community are essential to developing robust solutions that enhance the security, scalability, and sustainability of blockchain ecosystems. As the technology evolves, the ability to mitigate potential vulnerabilities will play a crucial role in determining the resilience and long-term success of blockchain applications across various industries.

Discuss the ongoing efforts to enhance the security of blockchain networks.

Ongoing efforts to enhance the security of blockchain networks reflect the dynamic nature of the cryptocurrency and blockchain space, where innovation and adaptation are essential to address emerging threats. One of the fundamental strategies employed to bolster blockchain security involves continuous advancements in consensus mechanisms. The limitations and environmental concerns associated with proof-of-work (PoW) have led to the exploration and adoption of alternative consensus mechanisms, such as proof-of-stake (PoS) and delegated PoS. PoS, which relies on validators staking their cryptocurrency as collateral, reduces the energy consumption of blockchain networks while maintaining security. Innovations in consensus mechanisms aim to strike a balance between decentralization, security, and environmental sustainability, fostering the evolution of blockchain networks towards more efficient and resilient architectures.

Smart contract security remains a focal point in ongoing security efforts, given the critical role of smart contracts in decentralized applications (DApps) and blockchain ecosystems. The Ethereum ecosystem, a prominent platform for deploying smart contracts, has witnessed various initiatives to improve smart contract security. Formal verification techniques, which involve mathematically proving the correctness of smart contract code, are gaining traction as a proactive measure to identify and mitigate vulnerabilities before deployment. Additionally, the development of specialized auditing firms and tools dedicated to smart contract security assessments provides a valuable layer of scrutiny, enhancing the resilience of blockchain-based applications against potential exploits and vulnerabilities.

Privacy-focused cryptocurrencies and privacy enhancements in existing blockchains are at the forefront of ongoing security initiatives. The inherent transparency of public blockchains, while promoting accountability, raises privacy concerns. Advances in privacy-preserving technologies, such as zero-knowledge proofs and ring signatures, have been integrated into cryptocurrencies like Monero and Zcash to enhance transaction confidentiality. Moreover, blockchain projects are exploring the implementation of privacy features, such as confidential transactions, to protect user data while maintaining the integrity of the blockchain. Balancing privacy and transparency is a delicate task, and ongoing efforts seek to establish standards and best practices that align with evolving regulatory expectations.

The threat of quantum computing to traditional cryptographic algorithms has prompted ongoing research and development of quantum-resistant cryptography. While large-scale quantum computers capable of breaking widely used encryption methods are not yet a reality, the proactive nature of blockchain security efforts aims to future-proof systems against this potential threat. Post-quantum cryptographic algorithms, resistant to quantum attacks, are being explored and integrated into blockchain networks. The transition to quantum-resistant algorithms requires careful consideration of backward compatibility and consensus among network participants, emphasizing the collaborative nature of ongoing security enhancements in the blockchain space.

Interoperability solutions represent a critical aspect of ongoing security efforts, particularly as blockchain networks proliferate and diversify. Projects like Polkadot, Cosmos, and others aim to facilitate interoperability between different blockchains, enabling seamless communication and value transfer. The development of standardized protocols, cross-chain bridges, and interoperability frameworks addresses the potential vulnerabilities associated with isolated blockchain networks. Interoperability not only enhances the functionality of blockchain ecosystems but also fosters a collaborative approach to security, where networks can benefit from shared resources and insights.

Governance models within blockchain networks are undergoing continuous refinement to address potential vulnerabilities related to decision-making processes and protocol upgrades. The challenges associated with contentious and non-contentious forks underscore the importance of transparent and inclusive governance structures. Ongoing efforts focus on implementing mechanisms for decentralized decision-making, community voting, and dispute resolution. Additionally, the exploration of on-chain governance, where participants influence protocol changes directly through voting mechanisms, contributes to the evolution of more resilient and adaptable governance models within blockchain networks.

Efforts to secure oracle inputs in decentralized applications (DApps) and smart contracts are actively addressing vulnerabilities associated with external data feeds. Oracles, which provide real-world information to smart contracts, are susceptible to manipulation by malicious actors. The development of decentralized oracle networks, cryptographic verification mechanisms, and secure data transmission protocols enhances the reliability of oracles, mitigating the risks of erroneous contract executions and data manipulation. As blockchain networks expand their use cases to include decentralized finance (DeFi) and other applications relying on external data, securing oracles becomes paramount for maintaining the integrity of blockchain-based systems.

Environmental considerations continue to shape ongoing security efforts, particularly in response to the energy consumption associated with proof-of-work (PoW) consensus mechanisms. Transitioning to more energy-efficient consensus mechanisms, such as proof-of-stake (PoS) or delegated PoS, represents a proactive response to environmental concerns. Furthermore, innovations in consensus mechanisms, such as proof-of-burn and delegated PoS variations, aim to reduce the ecological footprint of blockchain networks without compromising security. Sustainable blockchain development emphasizes the importance of aligning security practices with environmental responsibility, ensuring the long-term viability of blockchain technology.

Supply chain security is a critical focus area within ongoing blockchain security efforts, especially in industries where traceability and transparency are paramount. Integrating blockchain technology into supply chain management enhances the accuracy and integrity of recorded data, addressing vulnerabilities related to data tampering and counterfeiting. Initiatives to secure supply chain blockchains involve the use of cryptographic verification, immutable records, and decentralized data storage. Collaboration between stakeholders, including manufacturers, distributors, and regulators, contributes to the development of secure and transparent supply chain ecosystems leveraging blockchain technology.

In addressing potential vulnerabilities related to network decentralization, ongoing efforts emphasize the development of alternative consensus mechanisms that mitigate the risks associated with the 51% attack. Innovations such as delegated proof-of-stake (DPoS), practical Byzantine fault tolerance (PBFT), and variations of PoS aim to distribute influence more evenly among network participants, reducing the likelihood of a single entity gaining majority control. The continuous exploration of consensus mechanisms aligns with the evolving understanding of network security requirements and the dynamic landscape of blockchain ecosystems.

Education and awareness initiatives play a crucial role in ongoing security efforts within the blockchain space. The rapidly evolving nature of blockchain technology requires stakeholders, including developers, users, and regulators, to stay informed about emerging threats and best practices. Educational programs, workshops, and community engagement contribute to a collective understanding of security challenges and empower participants to adopt secure practices in blockchain development and usage. Promoting a culture of security consciousness fosters a resilient and proactive approach to addressing potential vulnerabilities in blockchain networks.

In conclusion, ongoing efforts to enhance the security of blockchain networks encompass a diverse array of strategies and innovations. From advancements in consensus mechanisms and smart contract security to the exploration of privacy-preserving technologies, quantum-resistant cryptography, and interoperability solutions, the blockchain community is actively addressing potential vulnerabilities with a forward-looking perspective. The collaborative nature of these efforts, involving developers, researchers, regulators, and users, underscores the commitment to building secure and sustainable blockchain ecosystems. As the technology continues to evolve, ongoing security initiatives will play a pivotal role in shaping the future of blockchain adoption across diverse industries and applications.

Chapter 5: Advanced Persistent Threats (APTs)

Define Advanced Persistent Threats and their characteristics.

Advanced Persistent Threats (APTs) represent a sophisticated and prolonged form of cyber threat, characterized by the strategic, targeted, and persistent nature of the attacks. APTs are orchestrated by well-funded and highly skilled threat actors, often state-sponsored groups, organized crime syndicates, or advanced cybercriminal organizations, with the primary objective of compromising specific targets for espionage, data theft, or disruption. One defining characteristic of APTs is their focus on long-term infiltration and covert operations, allowing attackers to remain undetected within a target's network for extended periods, sometimes spanning months or even years. This strategic approach contrasts with opportunistic and less persistent cyber threats, reflecting a level of determination and patience unique to APTs.

The life cycle of an APT typically unfolds in multiple stages, each meticulously planned and executed by the threat actors. The initial stage involves reconnaissance, where attackers gather information about the target, including its network architecture, vulnerabilities, and potential points of entry. This reconnaissance phase often leverages social engineering, open-source intelligence (OSINT), and other covert methods to gain insights into the target's operations. APTs excel in tailoring their attacks based on the specific characteristics and vulnerabilities discovered during this reconnaissance, making their campaigns highly customized and difficult to defend against using traditional security measures.

The second stage of an APT involves the delivery of a tailored and often sophisticated malware or malicious code to the target's network. This may be achieved through various means, including spear-phishing emails, watering hole attacks, or the exploitation of software vulnerabilities. The malware used in APTs is designed to be evasive, polymorphic, and adaptable, enabling it to bypass traditional security measures and remain undetected by antivirus solutions. Encryption, obfuscation, and anti-analysis techniques are commonly employed to enhance the stealth and resilience of APT malware.

Once the malware is successfully deployed, APTs progress to the third stage – exploitation. In this phase, the attackers exploit the compromised systems to establish a foothold within the target's network. This often involves privilege escalation, where the attackers seek to gain administrative access to maximize their control and maintain persistence. APTs frequently exploit zero-day vulnerabilities or leverage previously unknown vulnerabilities to ensure that their attacks are not hindered by existing security patches or measures. The exploitation phase highlights the advanced technical capabilities of APT actors, enabling them to navigate complex network environments and evade detection.

The fourth stage, known as installation, involves the establishment of backdoors, command-and-control (C2) infrastructure, and other mechanisms that facilitate ongoing communication and control between the attackers and the compromised systems. APTs prioritize resilience and adaptability in their infrastructure to withstand countermeasures implemented by the target organization. The installation phase sets the stage for continuous monitoring, data exfiltration, and the execution of further malicious activities within the compromised network.

The fifth stage, often the longest and most critical, is the command-and-control phase. APT actors maintain persistent control over the compromised systems, enabling them to manipulate, exfiltrate, or manipulate data as needed. This phase is characterized by the use of advanced techniques to evade detection, such as living-off-the-land tactics, where attackers leverage legitimate tools and protocols already present in the target's environment. APTs may also employ techniques like domain generation algorithms (DGAs) to dynamically generate C2 domain names, making it challenging for defenders to block or attribute malicious activity.

The exfiltration phase, the sixth stage, involves the unauthorized extraction of sensitive data from the compromised network. APTs carefully select and exfiltrate information based on their objectives, which may include intellectual property, classified information, financial data, or personally identifiable information (PII). The exfiltration process is conducted discreetly to minimize the likelihood of detection, often leveraging encrypted channels and concealing data within seemingly legitimate network traffic. APT actors prioritize data theft without raising alarm bells, underscoring the importance of their stealth and persistence.

Post-exploitation activities form the seventh stage, where APTs take steps to maintain access, cover their tracks, and prepare for future operations. This involves the removal of any traces of the attack, such as log entries and artifacts, to hinder forensic analysis and attribution efforts. APT actors may also engage in lateral movement within the network, exploring additional targets or expanding their access to enhance their operational capabilities. This phase reflects the ongoing nature of APT campaigns, with threat actors adapting their tactics to the evolving security landscape.

The eighth and final stage involves the retreat or withdrawal of APT actors from the compromised environment. This withdrawal may be triggered by the achievement of the attackers' objectives, the exposure of their activities, or the implementation of effective countermeasures by the target organization. The retreat phase highlights the dynamic nature of APT campaigns, where threat actors continuously assess risks, adapt to defensive measures, and adjust their tactics to maximize their chances of long-term success.

Key characteristics of APTs include their stealth, sophistication, and adaptability. APTs employ evasion techniques, such as polymorphic malware and encryption, to evade traditional security solutions. The use of zero-day vulnerabilities and previously unknown exploits underscores the advanced technical capabilities of APT actors. Moreover, APTs often exhibit a keen understanding of the target's infrastructure, operations, and personnel, leveraging this knowledge to tailor their attacks and increase their chances of success. The attribution of APTs is challenging due to the use of false flags, proxy servers, and other techniques to obfuscate the origin of the attacks, making it difficult for defenders and investigators to identify the responsible entities accurately.

To counter APTs, organizations implement a comprehensive cybersecurity strategy that combines advanced threat detection technologies, threat intelligence, user training, and proactive incident response capabilities. Ongoing research and collaboration within the cybersecurity community are essential to staying ahead of evolving APT tactics and techniques. As APTs continue to pose a significant threat to governments, critical infrastructure, and organizations globally, the collective efforts of cybersecurity professionals and the continuous refinement of defensive measures are crucial to mitigating the impact of these persistent and sophisticated cyber threats.

Discuss the long-term nature of APT campaigns.

The long-term nature of Advanced Persistent Threat (APT) campaigns is a defining characteristic that sets them apart from traditional, opportunistic cyber attacks. APTs exhibit a strategic, patient, and persistent approach that involves a sustained and often covert presence within a target's network over an extended period, sometimes spanning months or even years. This prolonged engagement allows threat actors to carefully plan and execute their operations, navigate complex network environments, and achieve their objectives without triggering immediate detection. The extended timeframe of

APT campaigns is driven by various factors, each contributing to the unique and sophisticated nature of these cyber threats.

One key aspect contributing to the long-term nature of APT campaigns is the meticulous reconnaissance conducted by threat actors during the initial stages of the attack lifecycle. APTs invest significant time and resources in gathering intelligence about the target organization, its network architecture, personnel, and potential vulnerabilities. This reconnaissance phase enables threat actors to tailor their attacks to the specific characteristics of the target, increasing the likelihood of success while minimizing the risk of detection. The information gleaned during reconnaissance serves as the foundation for the subsequent stages of the APT campaign, highlighting the strategic planning inherent in these cyber operations.

The deliberate and methodical delivery of malware represents another factor contributing to the protracted duration of APT campaigns. Unlike rapid, opportunistic attacks that may seek immediate financial gains, APTs prioritize stealth and evasion, often utilizing sophisticated malware that is designed to remain undetected by traditional security measures. The development and deployment of such advanced malware involve careful consideration of the target's defenses, the need for evasion techniques, and the creation of adaptable code that can evolve over time. The patient delivery of this tailored malware allows APT actors to establish a foothold within the target's network without raising suspicions, laying the groundwork for sustained operations.

Once inside the target environment, APTs focus on exploitation and privilege escalation to solidify their presence. The careful navigation of the network, identification of critical assets, and the establishment of persistent access points contribute to the longevity of APT campaigns. Threat actors employ advanced techniques, such as lateral movement within the network, to explore additional targets or gain access to high-value systems. This phase reflects the commitment of APT actors to maintaining access and expanding their operational capabilities over an extended period. The strategic positioning within the network enhances their ability to manipulate, exfiltrate, or manipulate data without immediate detection.

A crucial factor influencing the duration of APT campaigns is the continuous evolution of the threat landscape and the adaptive nature of APT actors. As cybersecurity defenses improve and organizations enhance their security postures, APTs respond by developing new tactics, techniques, and procedures (TTPs) to overcome emerging challenges. This ongoing adaptation allows APTs to remain effective and avoid obsolescence, emphasizing the dynamic and resilient nature of these cyber threats. The ability of APT actors to incorporate the latest vulnerabilities, zero-day exploits, and evasion techniques into their operations extends the lifespan of APT campaigns, making them an enduring challenge for defenders.

The command-and-control (C2) phase of APT campaigns contributes significantly to their long-term nature. APT actors establish sophisticated communication channels, often utilizing encrypted and covert methods to maintain persistent control over compromised systems. The decentralized and adaptable nature of the C2 infrastructure allows threat actors to communicate with compromised endpoints, receive commands, and exfiltrate data while minimizing the risk of detection. The strategic placement of C2 infrastructure within the target's network, coupled with living-off-the-land tactics that leverage legitimate tools, enables APTs to operate clandestinely and extend their campaigns over an extended timeframe.

The exfiltration phase of APT campaigns further underscores their long-term nature, as threat actors carefully select and extract sensitive data over an extended period. APT actors prioritize discretion, using encryption and covert channels to exfiltrate information without triggering alerts. The patient extraction of valuable data aligns with the overarching goals of APT campaigns, which often involve the theft of intellectual property, classified information, financial data, or other high-value assets. The extended exfiltration process allows APTs to maximize the impact of their operations while minimizing the risk of detection, contributing to the persistent and stealthy nature of these cyber threats.

Post-exploitation activities, where APT actors cover their tracks, remove traces of the attack, and prepare for future operations, also play a role in the extended duration of APT campaigns. The careful consideration of forensic analysis and attribution risks demonstrates the strategic mindset of APT actors. By eliminating evidence of their presence and maintaining a low profile, APTs increase their chances of remaining undetected and operational within the target environment for an extended period. The continuous refinement of their tactics, combined with a proactive approach to countermeasures, reflects the ongoing commitment of APT actors to achieving their objectives over the long term.

The withdrawal or retreat phase of APT campaigns may occur once the threat actors have accomplished their goals, their activities are exposed, or effective countermeasures are implemented by the target organization. This phase highlights the dynamic and adaptive nature of APT campaigns, where threat actors assess risks, adjust tactics, and strategically withdraw from the compromised environment. The decision to retreat is often informed by a careful evaluation of the evolving threat landscape, the potential for attribution, and the sustainability of their operations. The withdrawal phase underscores that APT campaigns are not only persistent but also responsive to changes in the cybersecurity landscape.

The long-term nature of APT campaigns is further accentuated by the challenges associated with attribution. APT actors employ various techniques to obfuscate their origins, including the use of false flags, proxy servers, and the compromise of intermediary systems. Attribution difficulties make it challenging for defenders and investigators to accurately identify the responsible entities behind APT campaigns. This lack of clear attribution contributes to the sustained operational capabilities of APT actors, as the absence of concrete evidence makes it harder for the international community to respond effectively to state-sponsored APTs.

In conclusion, the long-term nature of Advanced Persistent Threat campaigns is a multifaceted phenomenon shaped by strategic planning, patient execution, continuous adaptation, and a persistent commitment to achieving specific objectives. APT actors leverage sophisticated tactics, advanced malware, and an in-depth understanding of their targets to establish and maintain a covert presence within compromised networks for extended periods. The evolving threat landscape, coupled with the adaptive nature of APTs, underscores the enduring challenge these campaigns pose to cybersecurity professionals and organizations globally. As defenders continue to enhance their capabilities, the proactive and patient approach of APT actors ensures that these campaigns remain a prominent and formidable force in the cybersecurity landscape.

Explore notable APT campaigns, such as Stuxnet and Operation Aurora.

Notable Advanced Persistent Threat (APT) campaigns, such as Stuxnet and Operation Aurora, have left an indelible mark on the landscape of cybersecurity, showcasing the capabilities of state-sponsored actors and advanced cybercriminal groups. Stuxnet, discovered in 2010, stands out as one of the most sophisticated and unprecedented APT campaigns in history. Widely attributed to a joint effort by the United States and Israel, Stuxnet was designed with a specific target in mind—the Iranian nuclear program. This highly sophisticated worm employed multiple zero-day vulnerabilities, allowing it to propagate through USB drives and network shares, evading traditional security measures. What set Stuxnet apart was its capacity to manipulate programmable logic controllers (PLCs) used in supervisory control and data acquisition (SCADA) systems. Specifically crafted to damage Iran's uranium-enrichment centrifuges, Stuxnet showcased a level of complexity and precision rarely seen in cyber operations. This groundbreaking APT campaign marked a paradigm shift, demonstrating that cyber capabilities could be harnessed for geopolitical objectives with tangible real-world impact.

Operation Aurora, detected in 2009, was another landmark APT campaign that shook the cybersecurity community. Attributed to Chinese state-sponsored actors, Operation Aurora targeted major technology companies, including Google, Adobe, and Juniper Networks. The campaign began with sophisticated spear-phishing emails, exploiting vulnerabilities in Internet Explorer to gain initial access. Once inside the target networks, the attackers utilized a combination of zero-day exploits and advanced malware to conduct cyber espionage, exfiltrating intellectual property and sensitive information. The scale and audacity of Operation Aurora underscored the growing prominence of nation-state cyber threats, revealing the potential for APTs to compromise highly influential organizations and pilfer intellectual property for economic or strategic advantage. Operation Aurora fueled discussions on the role of cyber capabilities in statecraft and the need for robust defenses against nation-state-sponsored cyber threats.

Equally noteworthy is the APT campaign known as Duqu, discovered in 2011, which exhibited clear connections to Stuxnet. Duqu shared similar code and characteristics with Stuxnet but operated as an information-stealing malware rather than a destructive one. Duqu's primary function was to gather intelligence on industrial control systems and critical infrastructure. The modular and adaptive nature of Duqu allowed it to remain undetected for an extended period. This APT campaign reinforced the notion that sophisticated threat actors often repurpose and build upon previously successful tools and techniques, emphasizing the importance of understanding the evolving tactics employed by APT groups.

The Ocean Buffalo campaign, also known as APT30, is notable for its extensive and prolonged cyber-espionage operations against Southeast Asian governments and organizations. Active since at least 2005 and attributed to Chinese state-sponsored actors, APT30 focused on collecting geopolitical intelligence, particularly related to territorial disputes in the South China Sea. The campaign showcased a diverse set of tools and tactics, including the use of custom malware, spear-phishing, and strategic web compromises. The sustained nature of the Ocean Buffalo campaign highlighted the persistent efforts of state-sponsored APTs to gather intelligence over the long term, influencing regional dynamics and asserting dominance in geopolitical hotspots.

More recently, the APT campaign known as NotPetya, initially discovered in 2017, gained prominence for its widespread impact and disruptive capabilities. Though initially disguised as ransomware, NotPetya was later revealed to be a destructive cyber weapon designed to cause widespread disruption. The campaign originated from a compromised software update for a Ukrainian accounting software, spreading globally and affecting organizations in various sectors. While its initial delivery vector involved a supply chain compromise, NotPetya demonstrated the potential for APTs to cause significant collateral damage beyond their intended targets. The campaign underscored the need for organizations to prioritize cyber resilience and incident response capabilities to mitigate the impact of destructive APTs.

APT28, also known as Fancy Bear, is a Russian state-sponsored APT group that has gained notoriety for its involvement in various high-profile cyber operations. Notably linked to the Russian military intelligence agency GRU, APT28 has been implicated in cyber-espionage campaigns targeting government entities, military organizations, and political groups. The group gained widespread attention for its alleged interference in the 2016 U.S. presidential election, as well as its involvement in cyber operations against NATO member states. APT28's use of advanced phishing techniques, zero-day exploits, and malware, combined with its persistent targeting of geopolitical adversaries, exemplifies the strategic and long-term nature of state-sponsored APT campaigns.

The Lazarus Group, associated with North Korea, has been involved in a series of APT campaigns with diverse objectives, including cyber espionage, financial theft, and disruption. Notably, the Lazarus Group was linked to the 2014 Sony Pictures hack, where it allegedly sought to retaliate against the release of a film depicting the fictional assassination of North Korea's leader. The group has also been implicated in financial heists targeting banks and cryptocurrency exchanges, showcasing the versatility of APT groups in pursuing both geopolitical and financial objectives. Lazarus Group's ability to operate across different domains and maintain a long-term presence in various campaigns exemplifies the multifaceted nature of APT activities.

The APT group known as SandWorm, discovered in 2014, has been attributed to Russian state-sponsored actors and gained attention for its involvement in cyber-espionage campaigns against governments and critical infrastructure entities. SandWorm has been linked to the deployment of a zero-day vulnerability in Microsoft Windows, emphasizing the group's capability to exploit unknown vulnerabilities for strategic objectives. The campaign highlighted the significance of software vulnerabilities as potent tools in the arsenal of APT groups, prompting increased emphasis on vulnerability management and patching as essential cybersecurity practices.

These notable APT campaigns collectively underscore the evolving and enduring nature of cyber threats orchestrated by state-sponsored actors and advanced cybercriminal groups. Stuxnet and Operation Aurora, as pioneering APT campaigns, set the stage for subsequent operations that showcased increased sophistication, versatility, and strategic objectives. From cyber-espionage to destructive attacks and financial theft, APTs have demonstrated a broad range of capabilities, emphasizing the need for a comprehensive and adaptive cybersecurity posture. As the cybersecurity landscape continues to evolve, understanding the characteristics and motivations of APT groups remains crucial for defenders seeking to safeguard critical infrastructure, sensitive information, and geopolitical stability in an increasingly interconnected and digitized world.

Discuss the motivations and targets of these sophisticated attacks.

The motivations and targets of sophisticated cyber attacks, particularly those orchestrated by Advanced Persistent Threat (APT) groups, are multifaceted and often reflect the complex intersection of geopolitics, espionage, financial gain, and ideological objectives. Understanding the diverse motives behind these attacks is crucial for developing effective cybersecurity strategies and mitigating the impact on targeted entities.

Geopolitical Motivations:

State-sponsored APT groups frequently engage in cyber operations driven by geopolitical motives. These attacks aim to advance the strategic interests of nation-states, influencing global affairs and gaining a competitive edge. Notable examples include the Stuxnet campaign, attributed to the United States and Israel, which targeted Iran's nuclear program as a means of disrupting its nuclear ambitions. Geopolitically motivated attacks may involve cyber-espionage to gather intelligence on adversaries, influence elections, or assert dominance in regional conflicts. The motivations in these cases are rooted in the desire for strategic advantage, national security, and the protection of geopolitical interests.

Economic Motivations:

Cyber attacks with economic motivations are often driven by the pursuit of financial gain, intellectual property theft, or disruption of competitors. APT campaigns such as Operation Aurora, attributed to Chinese state-sponsored actors, exemplify this motivation. Operation Aurora targeted major technology companies to steal intellectual property and gain a competitive advantage in economic sectors such as information technology and telecommunications. Economic espionage through cyber means can provide attackers with access to valuable trade secrets, research and development data, and proprietary technologies, enabling them to leapfrog competitors and enhance their economic standing.

Ideological and Political Motivations:

Certain cyber attacks are motivated by ideological or political objectives, seeking to promote a specific agenda, challenge perceived injustices, or advance a particular ideology. Hacktivist groups, driven by political or social causes, often employ disruptive tactics to raise awareness or protest against perceived wrongdoings. The motivations of these attacks may include political activism, protest against government policies, or advocacy for social justice. Notorious hacktivist groups like Anonymous have engaged in cyber operations to protest against censorship, corruption, and human rights violations, showcasing how cyber tools can be wielded as a means of ideological expression.

Military and Defense Objectives:

APT campaigns with military and defense objectives aim to gain a tactical advantage in conflict scenarios by leveraging cyber capabilities. State-sponsored APT groups may target military infrastructure, defense contractors, or government agencies to gather intelligence, disrupt command and control systems, or compromise critical military assets. The motivations in these cases are closely tied to the desire for military superiority, strategic insight into adversary capabilities, and the ability to cripple or neutralize military infrastructure in the event of hostilities.

Criminal Motivations:

Sophisticated cyber attacks are not limited to state-sponsored actors; cybercriminal organizations also leverage advanced techniques for financial gain. Cybercrime APT groups often target financial institutions, cryptocurrency exchanges, and businesses with the aim of stealing funds, conducting ransomware attacks, or engaging in fraudulent activities. Notable examples include the Lazarus Group, which has been linked to financial heists targeting banks and cryptocurrency exchanges. The financial motivations behind these attacks highlight the lucrative opportunities that cybercrime presents for well-organized and technically proficient groups.

Critical Infrastructure and National Security:

Sophisticated cyber attacks frequently target critical infrastructure sectors, such as energy, transportation, and healthcare, with the potential to cause widespread disruption and damage. The motivations behind these attacks may include compromising national security, exerting control or influence over adversaries, or creating chaos and panic. APT groups may exploit vulnerabilities in industrial control systems (ICS) to disrupt operations, compromise essential services, or cause physical damage. The targeting of critical infrastructure reflects the intersection of geopolitical, military, and ideological motivations, with the potential for far-reaching consequences.

Supply Chain Exploitation:

Sophisticated attackers often target the supply chain as a means of compromising trusted entities and gaining access to high-value targets. Supply chain attacks involve infiltrating trusted vendors, service providers, or software developers to compromise the integrity of products or services. Notable examples include the NotPetya campaign, which originated from a compromised software update for a Ukrainian accounting software, affecting organizations globally. The motivations behind supply chain attacks may include the desire to compromise a broader set of targets, evade traditional defenses, or conduct large-scale disruptive operations.

Espionage and Intelligence Gathering:

One of the primary motivations behind APT campaigns is cyber-espionage, driven by the pursuit of intelligence on political, military, economic, or technological matters. APT groups engage in targeted attacks to gather sensitive information, monitor the activities of adversaries, and gain insights into decision-making processes. The motivations for cyber-espionage are rooted in the quest for strategic advantage, situational awareness, and the ability to inform policymaking. APT groups often employ advanced tactics, such as spear-phishing and zero-day exploits, to infiltrate high-value targets and conduct covert intelligence-gathering operations.

Global Influence and Coercion:

Sophisticated cyber attacks can be motivated by the desire to exert global influence, coerce adversaries, or shape international narratives. State-sponsored APT groups may target media organizations, political entities, or influencers to manipulate information, spread propaganda, or undermine trust in democratic processes. The motivations behind these attacks include the pursuit of soft power, the shaping of public opinion, and the ability to influence global events. Cyber operations that aim to influence perceptions and narratives underscore the evolving nature of information warfare in the digital age.

Technological Advancement and Innovation:

In some cases, sophisticated cyber attacks may be motivated by the pursuit of technological advancement and innovation. APT groups may target research institutions, technology companies, or government agencies to gain access to cutting-edge research, development plans, or emerging technologies. The motivations behind these attacks are rooted in the desire to leapfrog technological advancements, accelerate innovation, or gain a competitive edge in strategic sectors. The theft of intellectual property for technological advancement highlights the broader implications of cyber attacks on innovation and progress.

In conclusion, the motivations and targets of sophisticated cyber attacks are diverse and dynamic, reflecting a complex interplay of geopolitical, economic, ideological, and strategic factors. State-sponsored APT groups, cybercriminal organizations, and hacktivist entities leverage advanced techniques to achieve their objectives, ranging from intelligence gathering and economic espionage to disruptive operations and ideological expression. The evolving landscape of cyber threats underscores the need for organizations, governments, and the cybersecurity community to adopt adaptive and comprehensive defense strategies that address the multifaceted nature of sophisticated cyber attacks in an interconnected and digital world.

Discuss the difficulties in attributing APTs to specific threat actors.

Attributing Advanced Persistent Threats (APTs) to specific threat actors is an intricate and challenging task, marked by numerous complexities and uncertainties. The nature of APT operations, often characterized by sophisticated tactics, techniques, and procedures (TTPs), makes the attribution process inherently elusive. The difficulties in pinpointing the origin of APTs arise from a combination of factors, including the use of false flags, the exploitation of third-party infrastructure, the evolving landscape of cyber threats, and the advanced capabilities of threat actors.

One significant challenge in attribution stems from the deliberate use of false flags by APT groups. False flag operations involve tactics designed to mislead investigators and attribution efforts by planting misleading indicators or characteristics that point to a different origin or actor. APT groups may mimic the TTPs of other threat actors, use tools associated with different campaigns, or manipulate digital artifacts to create a deceptive trail. This intentional obfuscation complicates the attribution process, as researchers and analysts must carefully differentiate between genuine indicators and deceptive elements to accurately identify the responsible entity.

The use of proxy servers and compromised infrastructure further obscures the origins of APT campaigns. Threat actors often leverage intermediary systems to conduct their operations, routing traffic through multiple servers to conceal their true location and identity. This technique, known as "living off the land," involves using legitimate infrastructure and tools present in the target environment to blend in with normal network activity. By exploiting compromised servers or using anonymization services, APT groups can effectively anonymize their activities, making it challenging for investigators to trace the source of the attacks back to the original perpetrators.

Attribution difficulties are exacerbated by the global and interconnected nature of the internet. APT actors frequently exploit the geopolitical landscape to launch attacks from jurisdictions with lax cyber regulations or those that provide plausible deniability. The use of compromised infrastructure scattered across different countries adds layers of complexity to the attribution process, as the true origin of the attacks may be concealed behind a web of anonymized connections and diverse hosting providers. The transnational nature of cyber threats poses a challenge to legal and diplomatic efforts to hold threat actors accountable, as jurisdictional boundaries complicate law enforcement actions.

The dynamic evolution of APT tactics and techniques further complicates attribution efforts. APT groups continually adapt their methodologies in response to advancements in cybersecurity defenses, changes in geopolitical tensions, and improvements in forensic analysis techniques. This agility allows threat actors to stay one step ahead of defenders, modifying their tools, infrastructure, and procedures to avoid detection and attribution. The constant evolution of APT capabilities requires cybersecurity professionals to maintain a deep understanding of emerging threats, making it challenging to attribute attacks based solely on historical or signature-based approaches.

Attribution challenges also arise from the widespread availability of hacking tools and malware in the underground market. APT groups may reuse or repurpose publicly available tools to conduct their operations, blurring the lines between sophisticated state-sponsored campaigns and cybercriminal activities. This commoditization of cyber tools enables less skilled actors to adopt advanced techniques, further muddying the attribution waters. Additionally, the use of open-source tools and malware developed by multiple threat actors complicates efforts to attribute specific attacks to a single entity, as multiple actors may have access to and deploy the same tools independently.

The lack of a universally accepted framework for attribution standards contributes to the complexities in attributing APTs. Unlike traditional criminal investigations where forensic evidence and legal standards guide attribution, the inherently anonymous and cross-border nature of cyber operations presents unique challenges. Attribution in cyberspace often involves a combination of technical analysis, intelligence assessments, and geopolitical context. Varying degrees of confidence in attribution may exist, and public disclosures by governments and private entities may differ in their assessments, leading to inconsistencies and debates within the cybersecurity community.

Attribution challenges are further compounded by the possibility of false positives and the difficulty in distinguishing between different APT groups. The use of shared infrastructure, tools, and techniques across multiple campaigns can lead to misattribution if analysts rely solely on technical indicators without considering broader contextual factors. APT groups may intentionally adopt similar

TTPs to create confusion, making it challenging to discern whether observed similarities are indicative of a shared origin or deliberate deception. The risk of misattribution underscores the need for a comprehensive and multidimensional approach that considers technical, behavioral, and geopolitical factors in the attribution process.

In some cases, APT actors strategically target third-party entities or intermediaries to launch attacks, further complicating attribution. By compromising the infrastructure of other organizations, threat actors can obscure their activities, making it appear as though the attacks originated from entities unrelated to the actual perpetrators. This tactic introduces a layer of complexity in tracing the source of APT campaigns, as investigators must unravel the intricacies of the compromised infrastructure and identify the true actors behind the attacks.

The inherent asymmetry in cyberspace, where offensive capabilities often outpace defensive measures, adds to the challenges of attribution. APT groups exploit this imbalance by continually innovating and leveraging advanced techniques, making it difficult for defenders to keep pace. The agility and sophistication of APTs contribute to an environment where attribution is not only complex but also time-sensitive. Delayed attribution may limit the effectiveness of response efforts, allowing threat actors to cover their tracks, disband, or adapt their tactics in response to public disclosures.

Despite these challenges, advancements in threat intelligence, collaborative information sharing within the cybersecurity community, and the development of attribution frameworks have improved the accuracy and reliability of attribution efforts. Threat intelligence feeds, shared indicators of compromise (IOCs), and collaboration between cybersecurity researchers and organizations contribute to a more comprehensive understanding of APT activities. International cooperation, such as joint attributions by multiple countries or intelligence agencies, can enhance the credibility and impact of attribution efforts, sending a clear message to threat actors that their actions are being closely monitored and scrutinized.

In conclusion, attributing APTs to specific threat actors remains a formidable challenge due to the deliberate use of false flags, the exploitation of third-party infrastructure, the dynamic nature of cyber threats, and the complexities of the global internet. The interconnected and anonymous nature of cyberspace, coupled with the lack of standardized attribution frameworks, underscores the need for a multifaceted approach that combines technical analysis with geopolitical context and collaborative efforts within the cybersecurity community. While attribution difficulties persist, ongoing advancements in threat intelligence and international cooperation contribute to a more nuanced understanding of APT activities, enabling defenders to develop proactive strategies and enhance the resilience of critical systems in the face of sophisticated cyber threats.

Explore the role of false flags and misdirection in APT campaigns.

The use of false flags and misdirection represents a sophisticated and strategic dimension within Advanced Persistent Threat (APT) campaigns, adding layers of complexity to the attribution process and complicating efforts to identify the true origin of cyber attacks. False flags involve deliberate efforts by threat actors to plant misleading indicators, characteristics, or attributions within their operations, creating a deceptive trail that leads investigators away from their actual identity and motivations. Misdirection, closely related to false flags, involves diverting attention, obscuring true intentions, and strategically manipulating the narrative surrounding APT campaigns. The role of false flags and misdirection in APT operations is multifaceted, encompassing strategic objectives such as anonymity, misattribution, psychological impact, and the creation of plausible deniability.

Anonymity stands out as a primary motivation for the incorporation of false flags and misdirection in APT campaigns. Threat actors, whether state-sponsored entities, cybercriminal organizations, or hacktivist groups, seek to operate covertly and conceal their true identity to avoid detection and attribution. By deploying false flags, APT actors intentionally introduce misleading elements that attribute their activities to other entities or mimic the tactics of different threat groups. This intentional obfuscation serves as a smokescreen, making it challenging for cybersecurity researchers, incident responders, and intelligence analysts to accurately identify the responsible actors behind the attacks. The pursuit of anonymity through false flags aligns with the broader strategic goal of APT groups to maintain a persistent and covert presence within target environments.

Misattribution, closely tied to anonymity, is another key role played by false flags and misdirection in APT campaigns. Threat actors leverage deceptive techniques to lead investigators astray, creating confusion and fostering uncertainty about the true origin of the attacks. By mimicking the tactics, techniques, and procedures (TTPs) of other APT groups or introducing false indicators that point to a different actor, APTs introduce ambiguity into the attribution process. The intentional creation of misattribution introduces doubt, forcing analysts to carefully navigate the intricate web of deceptive elements to uncover the actual perpetrators. This deliberate misdirection complicates the task of accurately attributing cyber attacks and highlights the cat-and-mouse game between APT groups and the cybersecurity community.

The psychological impact of false flags and misdirection in APT campaigns extends beyond technical considerations to influence the perceptions and reactions of the targeted entities, the cybersecurity community, and the broader public. APT actors understand that the mere suggestion of multiple possible threat actors can instill doubt, erode confidence in attribution assessments, and create a sense of insecurity. The psychological impact is particularly pronounced in cases where APT groups deliberately adopt the persona or TTPs of other well-known threat actors, leading to speculation, debates, and conflicting assessments within the cybersecurity community. This psychological warfare dimension underscores the strategic thinking behind false flags and misdirection, as threat actors seek to exploit uncertainty for their advantage.

The creation of plausible deniability is a strategic objective that aligns with the use of false flags and misdirection in APT campaigns. State-sponsored APT groups, in particular, may deploy cyber operations to achieve geopolitical objectives while maintaining a level of deniability to avoid diplomatic consequences or international scrutiny. False flags provide a mechanism for APT actors to deflect blame, create confusion about attribution, and distance themselves from the consequences of their actions. This intentional ambiguity allows state sponsors to deny involvement, shift responsibility to other entities, or exploit the lack of concrete evidence linking them to the cyber operations. Plausible deniability becomes a powerful tool in the hands of APT actors, enabling them to conduct operations with reduced fear of retaliation or diplomatic fallout.

The intentional mimicry of TTPs associated with other APT groups represents a nuanced aspect of false flags and misdirection. APT actors carefully study the tactics employed by rival threat groups or unrelated actors and selectively incorporate elements of these techniques into their own operations. This strategic borrowing serves dual purposes: it confounds attribution efforts by introducing familiar but misleading patterns, and it leverages the reputation or notoriety of other threat actors to divert attention. Cybersecurity researchers may initially associate observed TTPs with a known APT group, only to discover later that the similarities were deliberately introduced as part of a false flag operation. This intentional mirroring of tactics exemplifies the adaptability and creativity of APT actors in shaping the narrative around their activities.

The manipulation of digital artifacts, such as malware code, command-and-control infrastructure, and tool signatures, plays a crucial role in the implementation of false flags and misdirection. APT actors may intentionally modify or reuse code snippets from other malware families, employ generic tools available in the public domain, or adjust their infrastructure to resemble that of different threat actors. These manipulations serve to blur the lines between APT campaigns, making it challenging for defenders to rely solely on technical indicators for attribution. The deliberate manipulation of digital artifacts adds a layer of complexity to the attribution process, forcing analysts to critically assess the authenticity of observed patterns and discern intentional deception from legitimate traces of APT activity.

The strategic use of misdirection extends to the exploitation of geopolitical tensions and regional conflicts. APT actors may capitalize on existing hostilities or ongoing disputes to attribute their activities to rival nation-states or adversaries. By framing their operations within the context of geopolitical rivalries, APT groups can divert attention from their true motives and objectives. This geopolitical misdirection not only complicates attribution efforts but also contributes to the broader narrative of cyber operations as tools of statecraft in the international arena. The deliberate alignment of APT campaigns with geopolitical dynamics reflects the broader influence that cyber operations exert on global politics.

In conclusion, the role of false flags and misdirection in APT campaigns is multifaceted, encompassing anonymity, misattribution, psychological impact, plausible deniability, mimicry of TTPs, manipulation of digital artifacts, and exploitation of geopolitical tensions. APT actors, whether state-sponsored or cybercriminal, strategically employ these techniques to navigate the complex landscape of cybersecurity defenses, sow uncertainty among defenders, and achieve their objectives with reduced risk of attribution. The cat-and-mouse game between APT groups and the cybersecurity community underscores the ongoing challenges in accurately identifying and attributing cyber attacks in a field where deception and misdirection are integral components of the adversary playbook.

Break down the stages of an APT attack, including reconnaissance, initial compromise, persistence, and exfiltration.

The stages of an Advanced Persistent Threat (APT) attack unfold in a strategic and methodical manner, reflecting the sophisticated nature of these campaigns designed for long-term presence and stealth. The APT lifecycle typically comprises several distinct stages, each serving a specific purpose in achieving the threat actor's objectives. The stages include reconnaissance, initial compromise, lateral movement, persistence, and exfiltration. Understanding these stages is crucial for developing effective cybersecurity strategies and mitigating the impact of APTs.

The first stage of an APT attack is reconnaissance, where threat actors gather information about the target organization. This phase involves extensive research to identify potential vulnerabilities, key personnel, and the organization's technological infrastructure. Threat actors may leverage open-source intelligence, social engineering, and other techniques to collect data on the target's employees, technologies in use, and network architecture. Reconnaissance is a critical precursor to subsequent stages, enabling threat actors to tailor their attack strategies and increase the likelihood of a successful compromise.

Following reconnaissance, the initial compromise marks the entry point of the APT into the target environment. Threat actors deploy various tactics, such as spear-phishing emails, watering hole attacks, or exploiting unpatched vulnerabilities, to gain a foothold. Social engineering plays a significant role in this stage, as attackers craft convincing lures to trick employees into opening malicious attachments or clicking on malicious links. The initial compromise often involves the use of sophisticated malware designed to evade detection and establish a covert presence within the target network. Successful execution of this stage grants the threat actor access to the organization's systems, initiating the broader APT campaign.

Once inside the network, threat actors focus on lateral movement, seeking to expand their influence and escalate privileges within the compromised environment. This stage involves navigating through the organization's systems, compromising additional hosts, and exploring avenues to move deeper into the network. APT groups leverage advanced tools and techniques to remain undetected, exploiting vulnerabilities and weaknesses to extend their reach. Lateral movement may involve the use of compromised credentials, privilege escalation exploits, or the exploitation of trust relationships between different network segments. The goal is to establish a comprehensive understanding of the network's layout and identify high-value assets.

Persistence is a crucial aspect of APT campaigns, ensuring that threat actors maintain a long-term and covert presence within the compromised environment. To achieve persistence, APT groups employ various techniques to establish backdoors, install persistent malware, or manipulate system configurations. Rootkits and stealthy malware are often used to evade traditional security measures and maintain persistence even after system reboots. Persistence is critical for threat actors to weather system updates, security patches, and other changes within the target environment, allowing them to continue their operations undetected over an extended period.

Exfiltration is the final stage of the APT attack lifecycle, where threat actors seek to siphon off sensitive data from the compromised environment. This stage is the culmination of the attacker's efforts to achieve their specific objectives, whether they are focused on stealing intellectual property, gaining access to classified information, or compromising sensitive data for financial gain. Threat actors employ covert channels, encryption, and other evasion techniques to transfer exfiltrated data outside the target network without raising suspicions. The exfiltration process is carefully orchestrated to avoid detection, and threat actors may use compromised endpoints or external servers as staging points for data exfiltration.

Throughout the APT attack lifecycle, threat actors continuously adapt their tactics, techniques, and procedures (TTPs) to evade detection and maintain stealth. APT campaigns are characterized by a persistent and patient approach, with threat actors often remaining dormant for extended periods to avoid raising alarm bells. The use of custom malware, zero-day exploits, and sophisticated evasion techniques underscores the advanced capabilities of APT groups. Detecting and mitigating APTs require a multi-faceted approach that combines advanced threat intelligence, behavioral analysis, and proactive security measures to identify and respond to the various stages of the attack lifecycle.

The detection and mitigation of APTs pose significant challenges for organizations, as threat actors continuously evolve their strategies to bypass traditional security defenses. Behavioral analytics, anomaly detection, and threat hunting play crucial roles in identifying the subtle and nuanced indicators of APT activity. Proactive measures, such as regular security audits, penetration testing, and employee training on social engineering awareness, can bolster an organization's defenses against APT attacks. Additionally, maintaining up-to-date patching and robust incident response plans can enhance an organization's ability to detect and respond to APT campaigns in a timely manner.

In conclusion, the stages of an APT attack encompass reconnaissance, initial compromise, lateral movement, persistence, and exfiltration. These stages reflect the meticulous planning and strategic execution characteristic of APT campaigns. By understanding the lifecycle of APT attacks, organizations can better prepare for and respond to the evolving tactics employed by threat actors seeking to infiltrate, persist within, and extract valuable information from target environments. The persistent and adaptive nature of APTs underscores the importance of a comprehensive cybersecurity strategy that combines advanced threat detection, proactive defense measures, and robust incident response capabilities.

Discuss the meticulous planning and execution involved.

The meticulous planning and execution of sophisticated cyber attacks, particularly in the context of Advanced Persistent Threats (APTs), embody a strategic and calculated approach by threat actors seeking to infiltrate, persist within, and extract valuable information from target environments. APT campaigns are characterized by a high level of sophistication, often involving well-resourced and patient adversaries, such as nation-states, organized cybercriminal groups, or highly skilled hacktivist organizations. The success of APTs hinges on meticulous planning that encompasses multiple dimensions, including target selection, reconnaissance, tool development, social engineering, evasion tactics, and the orchestration of a coordinated attack lifecycle.

The first phase of meticulous planning involves target selection, a critical decision that defines the strategic objectives of the APT campaign. Threat actors carefully identify and evaluate potential targets based on geopolitical, economic, military, or ideological considerations. Nation-states, for instance, may target entities aligned with their geopolitical adversaries or those possessing valuable intelligence or technological assets. Cybercriminal groups may focus on financial institutions, critical infrastructure, or organizations holding lucrative data. The selection process reflects the broader objectives of the threat actors, whether they seek political influence, economic gain, or the compromise of specific individuals or organizations.

Reconnaissance plays a pivotal role in the planning stage, serving as the foundation for subsequent attack activities. Threat actors conduct extensive research to gather information about the chosen target, its employees, technological infrastructure, and vulnerabilities. This reconnaissance phase involves the collection of open-source intelligence, social engineering tactics, and the identification of potential entry points into the target network. Advanced threat actors may leverage publicly available information, social media profiles, and domain registrations to construct a detailed profile of the target, enabling them to tailor their attack strategies for maximum effectiveness.

Once target selection and reconnaissance are complete, threat actors proceed to the development and customization of sophisticated tools and malware. This stage of meticulous planning involves creating or adapting malicious software that can bypass security defenses, remain undetected within the target environment, and achieve the specific objectives of the campaign. Advanced malware may include polymorphic code, rootkits, or zero-day exploits designed to exploit unknown vulnerabilities. Customization is a key aspect, as APT actors tailor their tools to evade signature-based detection mechanisms and blend seamlessly into the target's ecosystem.

Social engineering emerges as a critical component of APT planning, enabling threat actors to exploit human vulnerabilities within the target organization. Meticulously crafted spear-phishing emails, fraudulent websites, and other deceptive techniques are employed to trick employees into divulging sensitive information, clicking on malicious links, or unwittingly executing malware. Social engineering tactics often leverage information gathered during the reconnaissance phase to create convincing lures, increasing the likelihood of successful initial compromise. The artful manipulation of human behavior underscores the psychological dimension of APT planning, as threat actors exploit trust, curiosity, and urgency to achieve their objectives.

The meticulous planning of APT campaigns extends to the orchestration of a coordinated attack lifecycle, involving distinct stages such as initial compromise, lateral movement, persistence, and exfiltration. The careful sequencing of these stages reflects a strategic understanding of the target environment and the need for long-term presence without triggering alarm bells. The initial compromise marks the entry point into the target network, often facilitated by exploiting vulnerabilities, deploying custom malware, and leveraging social engineering. The lateral movement phase involves navigating through the organization's systems, compromising additional hosts, and identifying high-value assets. This stage requires a deep understanding of the target's network architecture, trust relationships, and potential points of vulnerability.

Persistence is a key objective of APT planning, emphasizing the need for threat actors to maintain a covert and long-term presence within the compromised environment. Achieving persistence involves establishing backdoors, installing persistent malware, and manipulating system configurations to ensure ongoing access. Threat actors employ advanced techniques to evade detection, such as utilizing rootkits, employing anti-forensic measures, and adapting to changes within the target environment. Persistence is crucial for weathering security updates, patch deployments, and other changes that might otherwise disrupt APT operations.

Exfiltration, the final stage of the APT attack lifecycle, is meticulously planned to ensure the covert extraction of sensitive data without raising suspicions. Threat actors leverage encrypted communication channels, covert channels, or compromised external servers to transfer exfiltrated data outside the target network. The exfiltration process is carefully timed to avoid detection, often occurring gradually over an extended period to minimize the risk of discovery.

Meticulous planning in the exfiltration phase ensures that APT actors achieve their specific objectives, whether they involve stealing intellectual property, acquiring classified information, or compromising sensitive data for financial gain.

The adaptability and agility of APT actors are crucial aspects of meticulous planning, allowing threat actors to adjust their tactics, techniques, and procedures (TTPs) in response to evolving cybersecurity defenses. APT campaigns are characterized by continuous innovation, with threat actors incorporating new tools, zero-day exploits, and evasion techniques to stay ahead of defenders. This dynamic approach requires meticulous planning at each stage of the attack lifecycle, ensuring that APT actors can adapt to changes in the threat landscape, exploit emerging vulnerabilities, and remain effective over extended periods.

Mitigating the impact of APTs necessitates a proactive and multidimensional defense strategy that considers the meticulous planning and execution tactics employed by threat actors. Behavioral analytics, anomaly detection, threat intelligence, and continuous monitoring play essential roles in identifying the subtle indicators of APT activity. Robust cybersecurity practices, including regular security audits, employee training, and vulnerability management, are crucial for disrupting the meticulous planning of APT campaigns. Collaboration within the cybersecurity community and information sharing about emerging threats contribute to a collective defense posture against APTs, enabling organizations to enhance their resilience in the face of persistent and sophisticated cyber adversaries.

Explore the industries and sectors commonly targeted by APT groups.

Advanced Persistent Threat (APT) groups, sophisticated and well-organized cyber adversaries, have strategically honed their focus on a plethora of industries and sectors, leaving an indelible mark on the digital landscape. Among the prime targets, government entities stand at the forefront. APT groups often direct their efforts toward governmental organizations, driven by a desire to access classified information, manipulate geopolitical dynamics, or even disrupt critical infrastructure. The energy sector, encompassing oil and gas facilities and power grids, is another bullseye for APT groups seeking to exploit vulnerabilities for financial gain or as a means of exerting influence. Simultaneously, the financial industry finds itself in the crosshairs, with APT groups aiming to pilfer sensitive financial data, conduct economic espionage, or disrupt financial systems for political purposes.

The healthcare sector, entrusted with a treasure trove of personal and medical data, becomes a natural target for APT groups seeking to exploit and monetize such information or disrupt healthcare operations. Similarly, the technology sector, a hub of innovation and intellectual property, falls victim to APT campaigns seeking to gain a competitive edge, steal cutting-edge research, or compromise supply chain integrity. APT actors also extend their reach to the defense industry, engaging in cyber-espionage to gain insights into military capabilities, strategic plans, and defense technologies.

Critical infrastructure, spanning transportation systems, water supplies, and telecommunications networks, represents yet another battleground. APT groups recognize the potential havoc that can be wreaked by disrupting these essential services, leading to cascading effects on societies at large. Additionally, the education sector emerges as a target due to its repository of valuable research data, personal information, and intellectual property. APT groups, driven by diverse motives, may seek to infiltrate academic institutions for both economic and geopolitical advantages.

The industrial sector, inclusive of manufacturing and production facilities, encounters APT threats that aim to sabotage operations, steal proprietary manufacturing processes, or compromise the integrity of the supply chain. Meanwhile, the aerospace industry attracts APT attention due to its strategic importance, with adversaries aiming to gain access to sensitive data related to aircraft designs, defense contracts, and technological advancements. Moreover, the media and entertainment sector faces APT campaigns that seek to manipulate narratives, compromise content distribution networks, or even engage in acts of cyber warfare to suppress freedom of information.

Within the realm of intellectual property and research, APT groups continually target research and development efforts across various sectors, aiming to gain an edge by pilfering innovative ideas and breakthroughs. In the retail sector, the theft of customer data for financial gain is a common motive, as APT groups exploit vulnerabilities in e-commerce platforms or point-of-sale systems. Finally, the hospitality industry becomes a focal point for cyber adversaries seeking to compromise customer data, payment information, or loyalty program details.

In navigating this complex landscape, organizations across diverse sectors must remain vigilant and fortified against the persistent and evolving threats posed by APT groups. The cyber arms race persists, and understanding the motives and methods of these adversaries is imperative for bolstering cybersecurity defenses and safeguarding the integrity of critical systems and sensitive information.

Discuss the geopolitical motivations behind APT campaigns.

Geopolitical motivations underscore the intricate web of Advanced Persistent Threat (APT) campaigns, weaving a narrative that extends far beyond mere cyber intrusions. These campaigns, orchestrated by nation-states or state-sponsored entities, often serve as digital instruments to further geopolitical objectives. The relentless pursuit of power, influence, and strategic advantages on the global stage propels these cyber actors into action. Central to their motives is the desire to gather intelligence, a cornerstone of geopolitical maneuvering. APT campaigns, driven by the need for situational awareness, target governmental entities to access classified information, diplomatic communications, and military intelligence. This clandestine information provides a nuanced understanding of adversaries and allies alike, enabling adept nations to shape their geopolitical strategies with a distinct advantage.

Economic espionage represents another critical facet of APT campaigns' geopolitical motivations. Nations engage in cyber operations to pilfer intellectual property, trade secrets, and cutting-edge research from foreign competitors. This calculated theft bolsters domestic industries, fostering economic growth and technological prowess. APT groups, acting as extensions of national interests, infiltrate sectors like technology, manufacturing, and research, aiming to secure a competitive edge in the global economic arena. The stolen intellectual capital not only accelerates domestic innovation but also hampers the economic prospects of targeted nations, leading to a skewed balance of power in the geopolitical landscape.

The use of APT campaigns as geopolitical tools extends beyond mere intelligence gathering and economic advantage. Cyberspace becomes a battleground for shaping narratives and perceptions, influencing public opinion, and even destabilizing political rivals. Disinformation campaigns, often intertwined with APT operations, aim to manipulate social and political discourse, fostering division within target nations. By sowing seeds of discord, APT groups can weaken the fabric of societies, ultimately impacting political stability and diplomatic relations. The weaponization of information in cyberspace becomes a potent geopolitical strategy, amplifying the impact of traditional statecraft.

Furthermore, the strategic targeting of critical infrastructure in foreign nations serves as a coercive geopolitical tool. APT groups leverage their capabilities to compromise essential services such as energy grids, transportation systems, and telecommunications networks. By wielding the threat of disruptive cyber attacks, nations seek to influence the behavior of others, coercing them into alignment with their geopolitical objectives. This calculated use of cyber capabilities blurs the lines between traditional and digital warfare, with the potential to exert significant influence without resorting to overt military actions.

In the realm of regional conflicts and territorial disputes, APT campaigns become instruments of asymmetric warfare. State-sponsored cyber actors may target neighboring nations to gather intelligence on military capabilities, disrupt communications, or even disable defense systems. These actions, often masked behind layers of anonymity, allow nations to pursue their geopolitical objectives without triggering direct military confrontations. The strategic advantage gained in cyberspace can reshape the balance of power in contested regions, serving as a force multiplier in geopolitical maneuvering.

The attribution challenge in cyberspace adds a layer of complexity to APT campaigns' geopolitical motivations. The ability to conduct operations anonymously provides a degree of deniability, allowing nations to pursue their interests covertly. This lack of accountability fosters a sense of impunity, emboldening APT actors to engage in aggressive cyber activities without fear of immediate repercussions. The asymmetric nature of cyber operations enables smaller nations to wield significant influence, challenging the traditional power dynamics seen in conventional geopolitics.

In conclusion, the geopolitical motivations behind APT campaigns are multifaceted and deeply intertwined with the broader strategies of nation-states. From intelligence gathering and economic advantage to shaping narratives and coercive diplomacy, APT groups serve as instrumental tools in the pursuit of geopolitical objectives. As the digital realm continues to play an increasingly central role in global affairs, understanding and mitigating the impact of APT campaigns become imperative for nations seeking to safeguard their sovereignty and security in an interconnected world.

Chapter 6: The Underground Economy

Define the concept of the dark web and the underground economy.

The dark web, a clandestine corner of the internet hidden from conventional search engines, represents a realm shrouded in secrecy and anonymity. Operating on overlay networks that require specific software, configurations, or authorization for access, the dark web enables users to engage in activities beyond the scope of the visible internet. It fosters an environment where privacy and discretion are prioritized, providing a haven for those seeking to operate beyond the watchful eyes of law enforcement and surveillance. One of the defining features of the dark web is its use of encrypted communication protocols such as Tor (The Onion Router), which anonymizes users by routing their internet traffic through a series of volunteer-operated servers, making it challenging to trace their online activities.

Within the recesses of the dark web, a thriving underground economy emerges as a parallel marketplace, operating beyond legal and regulatory frameworks. This clandestine economy encompasses a spectrum of illicit goods and services, often facilitated by cryptocurrencies like Bitcoin, which offer a degree of financial anonymity. The underground economy's multifaceted nature spans a range of activities, including the sale of stolen data, hacking tools, drugs, counterfeit currency, forged documents, and even malicious software and services for cybercriminal purposes. The dark web provides a platform where buyers and sellers can engage in transactions with a semblance of security, shielded by the layers of encryption and anonymity protocols.

The trade in stolen data is a prominent facet of the dark web's underground economy. Cybercriminals exploit vulnerabilities in digital systems to pilfer sensitive information, ranging from personal credentials and financial data to intellectual property and trade secrets. This purloined data is then traded or sold on dark web marketplaces, where buyers may include identity thieves, fraudsters, or other cybercriminals seeking to exploit the information for financial gain. The anonymity afforded by the dark web facilitates these transactions, making it a hub for the illicit trade of data that fuels various forms of cybercrime.

The sale of drugs on the dark web has garnered significant attention, with anonymous marketplaces offering a platform for drug dealers to reach a global clientele. Cryptocurrencies provide a discreet method of payment, and the decentralized nature of these transactions makes it challenging for law enforcement agencies to track and apprehend those involved. The Silk Road, an infamous dark web marketplace that was seized and shut down by law enforcement in 2013, serves as a stark example of the scale and scope of the drug trade on the dark web, underscoring the challenges authorities face in combating such illicit activities.

Counterfeit currency and forged documents find a lucrative market within the dark web's underground economy. Criminal enterprises produce and distribute fake passports, driver's licenses, credit cards, and even counterfeit currency notes. These forged documents can be used for a myriad of illegal activities, including identity theft, human trafficking, and financial fraud. The dark web acts as a conduit for these transactions, providing a platform where sellers and buyers can connect discreetly, shielded by the layers of encryption that characterize this hidden corner of the internet.

The proliferation of hacking tools and services on the dark web amplifies the scope of cyber threats faced by individuals, organizations, and even governments. Malicious software, ransomware, and other cyber weapons are readily available for purchase, empowering both seasoned cybercriminals and aspiring hackers with the means to compromise digital systems. The dark web serves as a marketplace where hackers can monetize their skills, offering services such as Distributed Denial of Service (DDoS) attacks, password cracking, and even the sale of exploit kits that target software vulnerabilities. This commodification of cybercrime tools contributes to the democratization of cyber threats, allowing actors with varying levels of technical expertise to engage in illicit activities.

While the dark web's underground economy is often associated with illicit and criminal activities, it is essential to acknowledge that not all transactions within this realm are inherently malicious. The dark web also provides a platform for individuals living under repressive regimes to communicate securely, access uncensored information, and engage in activities that promote privacy and freedom of expression. Whistleblowers, journalists, and activists operating in environments where freedom of speech is restricted may leverage the anonymity of the dark web to share information without fear of reprisal.

In conclusion, the dark web and its associated underground economy constitute a complex and multifaceted ecosystem, characterized by anonymity, encryption, and illicit transactions. It serves as a hub for cybercriminal activities, ranging from the trade of stolen data to the sale of drugs, hacking tools, and forged documents. While the dark web presents challenges for law enforcement and cybersecurity efforts, it also plays a role in facilitating privacy and freedom of expression for those facing oppressive conditions. Understanding the dynamics of the dark web is crucial for policymakers, law enforcement agencies, and cybersecurity professionals seeking to mitigate the risks posed by this hidden realm of the internet.

Discuss the anonymity and encryption methods used in the underground.

The underground, particularly within the realms of the dark web and illicit online activities, places a premium on anonymity and encryption, fostering an environment where privacy and discretion are paramount. One of the foundational tools enabling this clandestine atmosphere is The Onion Router (Tor). Tor, a decentralized network that directs internet traffic through a series of volunteer-operated servers, employs layers of encryption to obfuscate users' online activities. By bouncing communications between nodes, Tor ensures that the source and destination of the traffic remain concealed, offering a level of anonymity that goes beyond the capabilities of standard internet browsers. This technology serves as a gateway to the dark web, allowing users to access websites with the ".onion" domain suffix, where transactions and interactions occur shielded from the prying eyes of conventional search engines and surveillance.

Cryptocurrencies, with Bitcoin being a prime example, play a pivotal role in securing financial transactions within the underground economy. The decentralized and pseudonymous nature of cryptocurrencies provides a layer of financial anonymity for users engaging in illicit transactions. Bitcoin, in particular, employs cryptographic techniques to secure transactions and control the creation of new units, allowing users to conduct financial activities without the need for traditional banking intermediaries. The use of cryptocurrency mixers or tumblers further complicates the tracing of transactions by combining multiple transactions into a single pool, making it challenging to link specific funds to individual users. The adoption of cryptocurrencies in the underground enhances the overall cloak of anonymity, as financial transactions become increasingly detached from the traditional banking system.

Virtual Private Networks (VPNs) represent another cornerstone of anonymity within the underground. By encrypting internet traffic and routing it through servers located in different geographic locations, VPNs conceal users' IP addresses and geographical origins. This makes it difficult for third parties to trace online activities back to specific individuals or locations. In the underground, VPNs serve as an additional layer of protection for users seeking to mask their identities while accessing the dark web, engaging in cybercriminal activities, or evading geographically restricted content. However, it is important to note that while VPNs provide a degree of anonymity, their efficacy depends on the trustworthiness of the VPN service provider, as they have the potential to access users' data.

End-to-end encryption is a fundamental technology employed to secure communications and transactions within the underground. Messaging platforms and email services that implement end-to-end encryption ensure that only the intended recipients can decipher the messages. Even if intercepted during transmission, the encrypted content remains indecipherable without the corresponding decryption keys. This technology is particularly crucial for maintaining the confidentiality of communications among cybercriminals, as it prevents third-party entities, including law enforcement, from gaining access to the content of messages or transactions. Popular messaging applications like Signal and Telegram, known for their commitment to privacy and security, have gained traction within the underground due to their robust implementation of end-to-end encryption.

For those engaging in cyber activities, the use of Virtual Machines (VMs) provides a layer of defense against forensic analysis and detection. VMs allow users to create isolated environments within their physical devices, where various operating systems and applications can run independently. This compartmentalization helps in obscuring the underlying hardware and software configurations of the host machine, making it more challenging for forensic experts to gather information about the user's identity or the specific tools and techniques employed. The ability to discard or reset VMs further facilitates the disposal of potentially incriminating evidence, contributing to the overall anonymity of cyber actors within the underground.

Privacy-focused operating systems, such as Tails (The Amnesic Incognito Live System), are designed to leave minimal digital footprints. Tails operates as a live system that can be booted from a USB drive or DVD, leaving no traces on the host machine. It routes all internet traffic through the Tor network by default, providing users with a secure and anonymous environment for online activities. The use of Tails is prevalent among those in the underground seeking to minimize the risk of forensic analysis or surveillance, as it prioritizes privacy and anonymity by design.

In conclusion, the underground leverages a myriad of tools and technologies to cultivate an environment where anonymity and encryption are fundamental. From the use of Tor to navigate the dark web to the adoption of cryptocurrencies, VPNs, end-to-end encryption, and privacy-focused operating systems, these tools collectively form the backbone of the clandestine activities within the digital underground. The pursuit of privacy and discretion is a driving force shaping the technological landscape of the underground, presenting ongoing challenges for law enforcement and cybersecurity professionals seeking to counteract illicit activities within this hidden realm. Understanding the intricacies of these anonymity and encryption methods is essential for those tasked with navigating the complex terrain of the digital underground and mitigating the associated risks.

Explore markets where cybercriminals buy and sell stolen data, hacking tools, and other illicit goods.

In the expansive and clandestine realm of the cybercriminal underground, markets dedicated to the trade of stolen data, hacking tools, and various illicit goods have flourished, creating a shadow economy that operates beyond the purview of legal and ethical norms. These underground markets serve as digital bazaars where cybercriminals converge to exchange a wide array of commodities, fueling an ecosystem of criminal activities. Stolen data, a prized currency within these markets, is often traded for financial gain or used as a tool for further cyber exploitation. Personal information, ranging from login credentials and credit card details to social security numbers, becomes a commodity that cybercriminals buy and sell, creating a robust market fueled by the continuous breaches of databases, websites, and online platforms.

One of the primary categories of data traded on these markets is login credentials. Compromised usernames and passwords from various sources, including data breaches and phishing attacks, find their way into these illicit marketplaces. Cybercriminals purchase these credentials with the intention of unauthorized access to user accounts, whether for financial fraud, identity theft, or further exploitation. The widespread reuse of passwords across multiple online platforms amplifies the value of such data, making it a lucrative asset for those engaged in cybercrime. These markets serve as a one-stop shop for cybercriminals seeking to acquire credentials for various purposes, from accessing financial accounts to compromising corporate systems.

Credit card information, often referred to as "carding" in the underground lexicon, represents another lucrative commodity within these markets. Stolen credit card details are traded for various purposes, including unauthorized transactions, online purchases, or the creation of counterfeit cards. The value of credit card data is influenced by factors such as the card's type, expiration date, and the additional information known as Card Verification Value (CVV). Cryptocurrencies play a pivotal role in these transactions, providing a degree of anonymity for both buyers and sellers in the illicit trade of financial information.

Beyond personal data, the trade of sensitive corporate information is prevalent within underground markets. Corporate espionage takes on a digital form as cybercriminals target organizations to pilfer intellectual property, trade secrets, and proprietary information. This stolen corporate data may include product designs, research and development plans, or strategic business insights. The buyers, often competitors or entities with a vested interest in gaining a competitive edge, acquire this information to shortcut the innovation process or undermine the market position of targeted companies. The value of such corporate data within these markets underscores the significant economic ramifications of cyber espionage.

Hacking tools and services represent a distinct category within these underground markets, catering to individuals with varying levels of technical expertise. Malware, ransomware, exploit kits, and other malicious software are offered for sale or rent, enabling even those with limited technical skills to engage in cybercriminal activities. The commodification of hacking tools democratizes cyber threats, allowing a broader range of actors to conduct attacks ranging from simple phishing campaigns to sophisticated cyber intrusions. These tools may be accompanied by support services, such as tutorials and customer support, further lowering the barrier to entry for aspiring cybercriminals.

The underground markets also facilitate the trade of so-called "zero-day exploits" – previously unknown vulnerabilities in software or hardware. These exploits, which exploit security weaknesses before vendors have had the opportunity to patch them, are highly sought after by cybercriminals and even nation-state actors. The ability to purchase or sell zero-day exploits provides a lucrative avenue for those seeking to compromise systems for various purposes, including espionage, cyber warfare, or financial gain. The anonymity of these transactions within underground markets adds an additional layer of complexity to the efforts of security researchers and law enforcement agencies attempting to thwart potential attacks.

In addition to digital commodities, physical goods and services find a place within the cybercriminal underground. Counterfeit passports, driver's licenses, and other forged documents are available for purchase, catering to those seeking false identities for illegal activities. Firearms, drugs, and other contraband also make their way into these markets, forming a nexus where cybercriminal activities intersect with the broader spectrum of criminal enterprises. The integration of physical and digital goods within these markets highlights the adaptability and resilience of the cybercriminal ecosystem.

Cryptocurrency markets within the underground further enable illicit transactions by providing a decentralized and pseudonymous means of conducting financial activities. Bitcoin, Monero, and other privacy-focused cryptocurrencies serve as the primary mediums of exchange, offering a level of anonymity that traditional banking systems lack. Cryptocurrencies facilitate transactions not only for the purchase of stolen data and hacking tools but also for other illicit goods and services, creating a financial infrastructure that operates in tandem with the digital underground.

The structure of these markets is often reminiscent of legitimate e-commerce platforms, complete with user reviews, ratings, and customer support. This level of professionalism within the cybercriminal underground mirrors the dynamics of legitimate markets, fostering an environment that instills a degree of trust among participants. Marketplaces operate on the principle of escrow services, where a trusted third party holds the cryptocurrency until the buyer confirms receipt of the purchased goods or services. This system reduces the risk of fraud within these transactions and contributes to the overall efficiency of the underground markets.

Law enforcement agencies and cybersecurity professionals continually grapple with the challenges posed by these underground markets. The anonymous nature of transactions, the use of encryption technologies, and the agility of cybercriminals to adapt to evolving security measures make it difficult to dismantle these illicit ecosystems. Cooperation between international law enforcement agencies, sharing threat intelligence, and disrupting the financial infrastructure supporting these markets are essential components of efforts to combat cybercrime. Additionally, raising awareness about cybersecurity best practices and implementing robust security measures at organizational and individual levels are crucial in mitigating the impact of stolen data and hacking tools circulating within these underground markets.

In conclusion, the cybercriminal underground serves as a thriving marketplace where stolen data, hacking tools, and various illicit goods change hands, fueling a shadow economy that operates beyond the reach of legal oversight. The trade of personal and corporate data, coupled with the commodification of hacking tools, highlights the intricate web of cybercriminal activities within these markets. As technology advances, the cybercriminal ecosystem continues to evolve, presenting ongoing challenges for those tasked with maintaining the security and integrity of digital systems. Understanding the dynamics of these underground markets is essential for developing effective strategies to counteract cybercrime and protect individuals, organizations, and society at large from the pervasive threats emanating from this hidden realm.

Discuss the range of products available on these platforms.

Within the expansive and clandestine realms of cybercriminal marketplaces, a staggering array of products is available, creating a flourishing underground economy where the digital underworld converges to engage in illicit transactions. Stolen data, a commodity of immense value within these markets, encompasses a diverse range of personal information. Login credentials, a staple product, are often harvested through phishing attacks, data breaches, or malware infections. These credentials, comprising usernames and passwords, unlock access to a myriad of online accounts, ranging from email and social media to banking and e-commerce platforms. Buyers in these markets seek to exploit these credentials for unauthorized access, leading to a variety of malicious activities such as identity theft, financial fraud, and further cyber exploitation.

Credit card information, commonly referred to as "carding" within the cybercriminal lexicon, represents another high-demand product on these platforms. Stolen credit card details, including card numbers, expiration dates, and Card Verification Values (CVVs), enable cybercriminals to conduct unauthorized transactions, make online purchases, or engage in fraudulent activities. The trade of credit card information is fueled by the widespread reuse of passwords and the enduring vulnerabilities present in online payment systems. Cryptocurrencies, with their decentralized and pseudonymous nature, play a pivotal role in facilitating transactions for these illicit financial products, offering a layer of anonymity for both buyers and sellers.

Beyond individual data, corporate information is a prized commodity within these underground markets. Cybercriminals actively engage in corporate espionage, targeting organizations to pilfer intellectual property, trade secrets, and strategic business insights. Stolen corporate data includes product designs, research and development plans, financial records, and proprietary information. The buyers of such data often include competitors or entities seeking a competitive advantage in the marketplace. The underground markets become a conduit for the transfer of corporate secrets, creating an environment where economic espionage is a thriving enterprise, shaping the competitive landscape of industries.

Hacking tools and services form a distinct category within these underground marketplaces, catering to individuals with varying levels of technical expertise. Malicious software, commonly referred to as malware, is available for purchase or rent, enabling even those with limited technical skills to engage in cybercriminal activities. Ransomware, a particularly pernicious form of malware that encrypts a victim's files and demands payment for their release, can be acquired on these platforms. Exploit kits, tools that leverage vulnerabilities in software or hardware, are also readily available, allowing cybercriminals to compromise systems and networks. The commodification of hacking tools democratizes cyber threats, lowering the entry barriers for aspiring criminals and amplifying the overall cyber risk landscape.

The sale of zero-day exploits, previously unknown vulnerabilities in software or hardware, is a sophisticated and sought-after product within these markets. Cybercriminals, as well as nation-state actors, actively seek these exploits to compromise systems before vendors have the opportunity to release patches. The availability of zero-day exploits provides a powerful weapon for those with malicious intent, enabling them to launch targeted attacks with a higher likelihood of success. The anonymity and decentralization of these transactions within the underground markets contribute to the challenge of pre-emptively mitigating the risks associated with these undisclosed vulnerabilities.

The underground markets also facilitate the trade of physical goods and services, blurring the lines between the digital and physical realms of criminal enterprise. Counterfeit passports, driver's licenses, and other forged documents are available for purchase, catering to those seeking false identities for illicit activities. Firearms, drugs, and other contraband make their way into these markets, creating a nexus where cybercriminal activities intersect with the broader spectrum of criminal enterprises. The integration of physical and digital goods within these markets underscores the adaptability and resilience of the cybercriminal ecosystem, as it extends its reach into traditional criminal domains.

Cryptocurrency markets within the underground further enable illicit transactions by providing a decentralized and pseudonymous means of conducting financial activities. Bitcoin, Monero, and other privacy-focused cryptocurrencies serve as the primary mediums of exchange, offering a level of anonymity that traditional banking systems lack. Cryptocurrencies facilitate transactions not only for the purchase of stolen data and hacking tools but also for other illicit goods and services, creating a financial infrastructure that operates in tandem with the digital underground. The decentralized nature of cryptocurrency transactions complicates efforts by law enforcement agencies to trace and apprehend those involved in illicit activities.

The structure of these underground markets mirrors that of legitimate e-commerce platforms, complete with user reviews, ratings, and customer support. This level of professionalism fosters an environment that instills a degree of trust among participants, despite the inherently illegal nature of the transactions. Marketplaces operate on the principle of escrow services, where a trusted third party holds the cryptocurrency until the buyer confirms receipt of the purchased goods or services. This system reduces the risk of fraud within these transactions and contributes to the overall efficiency of the underground markets.

In conclusion, the range of products available on cybercriminal platforms within the underground is extensive and diverse, reflecting the sophistication and adaptability of the digital criminal ecosystem. Stolen data, hacking tools, corporate secrets, physical goods, and even the means of financial transactions are all commodified within these shadowy marketplaces. The anonymity, professionalism, and accessibility of these platforms contribute to the resilience of the cybercriminal underground, posing ongoing challenges for law enforcement agencies, cybersecurity professionals, and society at large. Understanding the dynamics of these products within the underground markets is essential for developing effective strategies to counteract cybercrime and protect individuals, organizations, and critical infrastructures from the pervasive threats emanating from this hidden realm.

Discuss the predominant use of cryptocurrency for transactions in the underground economy.

Cryptocurrency, led by pioneers like Bitcoin and followed by a myriad of alternatives including Monero and Ethereum, has emerged as the predominant medium of exchange within the clandestine and complex realm of the underground economy. This digital form of currency, characterized by its decentralized nature and cryptographic security, has revolutionized the landscape of illicit transactions, offering a level of anonymity and efficiency that traditional financial systems struggle to match. The primary allure of cryptocurrency within the underground lies in its ability to provide a veil of pseudonymity for both buyers and sellers, fostering an environment where cybercriminals, hackers, and individuals engaged in various illicit activities can conduct financial transactions without the risk of immediate identification.

Bitcoin, as the pioneering cryptocurrency, took center stage in the early adoption of digital currencies within the underground economy. Its decentralized nature, facilitated by blockchain technology, allows users to transact without the need for intermediaries such as banks. This aspect not only reduces transaction costs but also enables a degree of financial autonomy, crucial for those operating in the shadows. Bitcoin transactions are recorded on a public ledger, the blockchain, which adds a layer of transparency to the network. However, the pseudonymous nature of Bitcoin addresses, which act as identifiers for users, allows a level of obfuscation, making it challenging to directly link transactions to real-world identities.

The use of Bitcoin within the underground is not confined to a specific type of illicit activity; rather, it spans a wide spectrum. Stolen data, such as login credentials and credit card information, is frequently traded for Bitcoin in these markets. Cybercriminals leverage the cryptocurrency's anonymity to receive payments for their products or services, ranging from hacking tools and malware to ransomware-as-a-service. The ability to monetize cybercrime through Bitcoin transactions facilitates a thriving ecosystem of malicious actors, driving the relentless pursuit of new attack vectors and techniques.

Cryptocurrency markets within the underground extend beyond digital products and services, encompassing the trade of physical goods such as drugs, counterfeit passports, and even firearms. The decentralized and pseudonymous nature of Bitcoin transactions provides a layer of protection for buyers and sellers engaged in the illicit trade of physical items. The potential for anonymity in financial transactions becomes particularly attractive for those involved in traditional criminal enterprises, as the integration of cryptocurrency within these markets enables a seamless crossover between the digital and physical realms of criminality.

Monero, designed with a specific emphasis on privacy and anonymity, has gained prominence within the underground economy as an alternative to Bitcoin. Monero transactions are crafted to be untraceable, employing advanced cryptographic techniques such as ring signatures and stealth addresses. Ring signatures amalgamate multiple transactions, obscuring the actual transaction within a group, while stealth addresses create unique, one-time addresses for each transaction, preventing the linkage of multiple transactions to a single user. The inherent privacy features of Monero make it an attractive choice for cybercriminals seeking enhanced anonymity, especially when engaged in activities such as the purchase of hacking tools, the trade of stolen data, or the facilitation of ransomware payments.

The evolution of Ethereum has introduced smart contract functionality to the world of cryptocurrencies, opening new avenues within the underground economy. Smart contracts are self-executing contracts with the terms of the agreement directly written into code. In the underground, these contracts are employed for a variety of purposes, including escrow services and the automation of specific transactions. Ethereum's programmable nature allows cybercriminals to innovate and create decentralized applications (DApps) tailored to their specific needs. However, the public and transparent nature of the Ethereum blockchain presents challenges to complete anonymity, as transaction histories are traceable, albeit with more complexity than traditional financial systems.

The integration of privacy-focused cryptocurrencies like Monero and Zcash within the underground reflects an ongoing cat-and-mouse game between those seeking enhanced anonymity and the efforts of law enforcement and cybersecurity professionals. As the authorities deploy sophisticated tools and techniques to trace cryptocurrency transactions, cybercriminals respond by adopting more privacy-centric alternatives. This dynamic adaptation underscores the agility and resilience of the underground economy, as it constantly evolves to stay one step ahead of those seeking to disrupt its operations.

Cryptocurrency tumblers or mixers represent yet another layer of privacy for those engaging in transactions within the underground. These services mix multiple transactions, obfuscating the origin and destination of funds. Users deposit their cryptocurrencies into a pool, and the mixer then redistributes the funds in a way that makes it challenging to trace individual transactions. While tumblers can introduce an additional layer of anonymity, they also serve as a point of vulnerability for law enforcement efforts, as they may focus on identifying and dismantling these mixing services to disrupt the flow of illicit funds.

The decentralized nature of cryptocurrency markets within the underground poses significant challenges for law enforcement agencies attempting to combat cybercrime. Traditional regulatory frameworks struggle to keep pace with the rapid evolution of digital currencies and their applications within the criminal underworld. The international nature of cryptocurrency transactions further complicates jurisdictional efforts to regulate and monitor these activities effectively. Efforts to address these challenges include the development of regulatory frameworks, collaboration between international law enforcement agencies, and advancements in blockchain analytics to trace and attribute illicit transactions.

In conclusion, the predominant use of cryptocurrency for transactions within the underground economy has reshaped the landscape of cybercrime, providing a medium that combines decentralization, pseudonymity, and efficiency. Bitcoin remains a staple within these markets, offering a level of transparency tempered by pseudonymity. Privacy-focused cryptocurrencies like Monero and Zcash address the shortcomings of Bitcoin by prioritizing anonymity, catering to those who seek enhanced privacy within their transactions. The decentralized and borderless nature of cryptocurrency transactions complicates the regulatory landscape and presents ongoing challenges for those tasked with mitigating the impact of cybercrime. As the underground economy continues to evolve, the role of cryptocurrency within it is likely to remain a central and dynamic feature, shaping the future of illicit transactions in the digital realm.

Explore the challenges of tracking and regulating these transactions.

The challenges of tracking and regulating transactions within the realm of cryptocurrencies, especially in the context of the underground economy, are multifaceted and present a complex web of obstacles for law enforcement agencies, regulatory bodies, and cybersecurity professionals. The decentralized and pseudonymous nature of cryptocurrency transactions, exemplified by the likes of Bitcoin and privacy-focused alternatives such as Monero, introduces a layer of anonymity that traditional financial systems struggle to replicate. This characteristic becomes a double-edged sword, offering a level of privacy that is attractive to users seeking to engage in illicit activities within the underground while simultaneously presenting challenges for those attempting to monitor and regulate these transactions.

One of the primary challenges lies in the pseudonymous nature of cryptocurrency transactions. While the use of blockchain technology ensures transparency in terms of transaction history, the actual identities of users involved in these transactions are often obscured by cryptographic addresses. Bitcoin addresses, for example, are alphanumeric strings that act as identifiers for users but lack direct ties to real-world identities. This pseudonymity makes it inherently difficult to attribute transactions to specific individuals, hindering the efforts of law enforcement agencies to identify and apprehend cybercriminals engaged in illicit activities within the underground.

The global and decentralized nature of cryptocurrency transactions further exacerbates the challenges of tracking and regulation. Traditional financial systems operate within established regulatory frameworks governed by national and international authorities. Cryptocurrencies, on the other hand, transcend borders and operate outside the jurisdiction of any single regulatory body. This lack of a centralized authority poses difficulties for regulatory bodies attempting to establish comprehensive frameworks to govern cryptocurrency transactions. The absence of a unified regulatory approach allows the underground economy to leverage the international nature of cryptocurrencies, making it challenging for authorities to coordinate efforts and enforce regulations effectively.

Privacy-focused cryptocurrencies, designed specifically to enhance user anonymity, add an additional layer of complexity to tracking and regulation efforts. Monero, for instance, employs advanced cryptographic techniques such as ring signatures and stealth addresses to obfuscate transaction details, making it challenging for blockchain analytics tools to trace the flow of funds. The use of privacy coins within the underground amplifies the difficulty of attributing transactions to specific individuals or entities, limiting the efficacy of traditional investigative methods. As these privacy-focused technologies evolve, regulators and law enforcement agencies face an ongoing arms race to develop tools and techniques that can pierce through the enhanced layers of anonymity.

Cryptocurrency tumblers or mixers, services designed to anonymize transactions by mixing multiple transactions together, further complicate tracking efforts. Users seeking additional privacy within their transactions may leverage these services to obscure the origin and destination of funds. Tumblers introduce an additional layer of obfuscation, as the mixing process makes it challenging to trace the movement of individual funds through the blockchain. The decentralized and automated nature of these services creates hurdles for regulatory bodies attempting to identify and regulate entities offering tumbling services within the underground economy.

The adaptability and innovation within the underground ecosystem pose ongoing challenges for regulatory bodies. As law enforcement agencies and regulatory bodies develop tools and strategies to track and regulate cryptocurrency transactions, the cybercriminal underworld responds with countermeasures and new techniques. This dynamic and evolving landscape demands a high level of agility and innovation from those responsible for regulating and monitoring financial transactions within the digital realm. The rapid emergence of new cryptocurrencies, privacy-centric technologies, and decentralized financial systems further underscores the need for continuous adaptation and collaboration among international regulatory bodies.

The lack of standardization in cryptocurrency regulation across jurisdictions amplifies the challenges faced by regulatory bodies. Each country or region may adopt different approaches to cryptocurrency regulation, ranging from embracing it as a legitimate form of currency to outright bans. The absence of a harmonized global regulatory framework creates opportunities for illicit actors within the underground economy to exploit regulatory gaps and jurisdictional variations. Cybercriminals can strategically operate in regions with lax regulations, leveraging the fragmented nature of cryptocurrency governance to their advantage.

Attempts to regulate cryptocurrency transactions must contend with the tension between privacy and security. While privacy is a fundamental aspect of cryptocurrency design, it also provides a shield for those engaged in illegal activities within the underground. Balancing the need for user privacy with the imperative to prevent and investigate cybercrime poses a nuanced challenge for regulatory bodies. Striking the right balance requires a comprehensive understanding of the technological intricacies of cryptocurrencies, as well as collaboration between industry stakeholders, cybersecurity experts, and policymakers.

Blockchain analytics, tools developed to trace and analyze transactions on public blockchains, offer a potential solution for tracking cryptocurrency transactions. These tools leverage the transparent nature of blockchain ledgers to identify patterns, trace fund flows, and attribute transactions to specific addresses. However, their efficacy is limited, especially when dealing with privacy-focused cryptocurrencies and sophisticated mixing services. Moreover, the use of decentralized and peer-to-peer exchanges, which operate outside traditional financial systems, provides alternative avenues for users to convert cryptocurrencies into traditional fiat currencies without passing through regulated exchanges, further complicating tracking efforts.

The lack of know-your-customer (KYC) and anti-money laundering (AML) procedures on certain cryptocurrency exchanges contributes to the challenges of regulating transactions. Some exchanges operate without stringent identification requirements, allowing users to trade cryptocurrencies without verifying their identities. This lax approach to KYC and AML measures facilitates the anonymity sought by those engaging in illicit activities within the underground. Regulatory efforts to mandate and enforce KYC and AML procedures face resistance from proponents of privacy within the cryptocurrency community, highlighting the inherent tension between privacy rights and the need for financial accountability.

Cryptocurrency-related fraud, including Ponzi schemes, initial coin offering (ICO) scams, and other forms of financial deception, further complicates regulatory efforts. Illicit actors within the underground exploit the hype and lack of regulatory oversight surrounding certain cryptocurrency projects to defraud unsuspecting investors. The global and decentralized nature of cryptocurrency markets makes it challenging for regulators to intervene and recover funds once fraud has occurred. These fraudulent activities not only harm individual investors but also contribute to a negative perception of the entire cryptocurrency ecosystem, warranting regulatory responses to protect investors and maintain market integrity.

In conclusion, the challenges of tracking and regulating cryptocurrency transactions within the underground economy are intricate and multifaceted. The pseudonymous nature of transactions, global decentralized operations, privacy-centric technologies, and the adaptability of the cybercriminal underworld collectively create an environment where traditional regulatory frameworks struggle to keep pace. The evolving landscape demands continuous collaboration between international regulatory bodies, law enforcement agencies, and industry stakeholders. Striking a balance between privacy rights, security imperatives, and financial accountability remains a complex task, requiring a nuanced approach that considers the unique characteristics of cryptocurrencies and their applications within the digital realm. As the regulatory landscape continues to evolve, the ongoing challenge is to develop effective strategies that mitigate the risks associated with illicit cryptocurrency transactions while preserving the legitimate and innovative aspects of this burgeoning financial ecosystem.

Explore services offered in the underground, including hacking-for-hire and DDoS attacks.

The underground ecosystem thrives on a diverse array of services that cater to the illicit needs of cybercriminals, hackers, and various malicious actors. Hacking-for-hire services represent a prominent facet of this clandestine marketplace, offering a menu of skills and expertise for those seeking to exploit vulnerabilities or gain unauthorized access to systems. These services often range from relatively simple tasks, such as email account compromise or social media hacking, to more sophisticated endeavors like network intrusions or corporate espionage. The availability of hacking-for-hire services democratizes cyber threats, enabling individuals with varying levels of technical proficiency to enlist the assistance of skilled hackers for nefarious purposes.

Distributed Denial of Service (DDoS) attacks stand out as another prevalent service within the underground economy. These attacks involve overwhelming a target's online services, rendering them inaccessible to legitimate users. The underground markets offer DDoS-for-hire services, where individuals or organizations can rent the services of botnets—networks of compromised computers—to launch large-scale and coordinated DDoS attacks. These attacks can be employed for various purposes, including extortion, revenge, or as a smokescreen to distract from other malicious activities. The availability of DDoS-for-hire services amplifies the scale and impact of such attacks, as they become accessible to even those without extensive technical knowledge.

Crypting services play a crucial role in the underground by providing a means to obfuscate and encrypt malicious software, making it more challenging for antivirus programs and security solutions to detect and analyze. Malware authors and distributors leverage crypters to "crypt" their malicious payloads, allowing them to evade traditional security measures. These services often offer a range of customization options, allowing cybercriminals to tailor the level of obfuscation to suit their specific needs. The use of crypting services

exemplifies the ongoing arms race between cybersecurity professionals and those seeking to exploit vulnerabilities within digital systems.

Ransomware-as-a-Service (RaaS) platforms have gained notoriety within the underground economy, providing a turnkey solution
for individuals with limited technical expertise to launch ransomware attacks. RaaS offerings typically include the ransomware
payload, a user-friendly management interface, and sometimes even
customer support. Affiliates can leverage these platforms to distribute ransomware, with a portion of the ransom payments going to
the developers of the RaaS, fostering a criminal ecosystem that operates on a profit-sharing model. The commodification of ransomware
through these services has contributed to the proliferation of such
attacks, targeting individuals, businesses, and even critical infrastructure.

Credential stuffing services cater to cybercriminals seeking to
capitalize on the reuse of passwords across multiple online platforms.
These services automate the process of attempting login credentials
obtained from data breaches on various websites, exploiting the common practice of users utilizing the same passwords across different
accounts. Cybercriminals leverage credential stuffing to gain unauthorized access to accounts, leading to identity theft, financial fraud,
and the potential compromise of sensitive information. The prevalence of credential stuffing underscores the importance of strong and
unique passwords as a foundational element of cybersecurity.

Social engineering services offer a range of manipulative techniques designed to exploit human psychology and deceive individuals into divulging sensitive information or taking specific actions.
Phishing campaigns, spear-phishing, and business email compromise
(BEC) fall under the umbrella of social engineering, with services
providing tailored approaches to target specific individuals, organizations, or industries. The underground markets facilitate the exchange of phishing kits, custom-designed email templates, and even

access to compromised email accounts, streamlining the process for cybercriminals looking to launch effective social engineering attacks.

The trade of stolen data represents a cornerstone of the underground economy, where various types of personal and corporate information are bought and sold for financial gain. Login credentials, credit card details, personally identifiable information (PII), and even healthcare records are commodified within these markets. Cybercriminals leverage this data for a spectrum of malicious activities, including identity theft, financial fraud, and the compromise of online accounts. The accessibility and variety of stolen data within the underground contribute to a thriving ecosystem where cybercriminals can quickly monetize their efforts.

Carding services focus on the illicit trade of credit card information, leveraging stolen or skimmed card details for financial gain. These services offer not only the raw data but also tutorials on how to use the information for unauthorized transactions. The underground markets serve as hubs for the exchange of credit card data, with prices varying based on factors such as card type, expiration date, and additional information like Card Verification Value (CVV). Cryptocurrencies play a pivotal role in facilitating transactions for these illicit financial products, offering a layer of anonymity for both buyers and sellers within the underground economy.

Physical goods and services are not excluded from the offerings within the underground markets. Counterfeit passports, driver's licenses, and other forged documents are available for purchase, catering to those seeking false identities for illegal activities. Firearms, drugs, and other contraband also find their way into these markets, creating a nexus where cybercriminal activities intersect with traditional criminal enterprises. The integration of physical and digital goods within these markets underscores the adaptability and resilience of the cybercriminal ecosystem.

Escrow services function as a trust-building mechanism within the underground economy, providing a secure way for buyers and sellers to engage in transactions without mutual trust. These services act as intermediaries, holding cryptocurrency payments in escrow until both parties fulfill their obligations. This mechanism reduces the risk of fraud within transactions, as funds are released only when both parties confirm the completion of the agreed-upon exchange. The use of escrow services adds a layer of professionalism to the underground markets, mirroring the dynamics of legitimate e-commerce platforms.

The evolution of underground markets has also seen the emergence of services related to the exploitation of software vulnerabilities. Zero-day exploits, previously unknown vulnerabilities in software or hardware, are actively traded within the underground. Cybercriminals and even nation-state actors seek these exploits to compromise systems before vendors release patches. The underground markets offer a platform for buying and selling these valuable tools, contributing to the ongoing challenge of securing digital systems against advanced and persistent threats.

In conclusion, the services offered within the underground economy span a broad spectrum, providing a comprehensive toolkit for cybercriminals seeking to exploit vulnerabilities, compromise systems, and monetize their efforts. Hacking-for-hire, DDoS attacks, crypting services, RaaS platforms, credential stuffing, social engineering, the trade of stolen data, carding services, and even the convergence of physical and digital goods all contribute to a thriving ecosystem. The adaptability, sophistication, and accessibility of these services underscore the ongoing challenges faced by law enforcement agencies, regulatory bodies, and cybersecurity professionals in mitigating the impact of cybercrime and securing the digital landscape against evolving threats. Understanding the intricacies of these services is essential for developing effective strategies to counteract the pervasive threats emanating from the hidden and complex realm of the underground economy.

Discuss the motivations of individuals providing such services.

The motivations driving individuals to provide illicit services within the underground economy are diverse and complex, shaped by a combination of personal, economic, and societal factors. At the heart of these motivations lies a convergence of opportunism, skill, and, in some cases, a disconnection from traditional ethical norms. One of the primary motivators is the pursuit of financial gain. The underground economy offers a lucrative avenue for individuals to monetize their technical skills, whether in hacking, coding, or exploiting vulnerabilities. The allure of quick and substantial financial rewards often attracts individuals who perceive an opportunity to capitalize on their expertise, sometimes at the expense of others. The prospect of financial gain is particularly enticing for those facing economic hardships, creating a pathway to supplement income or establish an alternative revenue stream.

For some, engagement in the underground economy is driven by ideological or anti-establishment sentiments. These individuals may view themselves as digital activists or hacktivists, leveraging their skills to advance a particular cause, challenge perceived injustices, or disrupt entities they oppose. This ideological motivation is often rooted in a desire for societal or political change, using cyber tools and tactics as a means of expressing dissent or resistance. The digital landscape becomes a battleground for individuals seeking to make a statement, drawing attention to issues they believe warrant public awareness or change.

The pursuit of notoriety and recognition also serves as a powerful motivator within the underground ecosystem. Individuals providing hacking-for-hire services or engaging in high-profile cyber attacks may seek acknowledgment for their technical prowess and capabilities. The digital realm offers a platform where skills are showcased and reputations are built, leading to a sense of prestige and recognition within the underground community. This desire for acknowledgment can be intertwined with ego, as individuals compete for status and validation among their peers, establishing a hierarchy based on technical prowess and the scale of their exploits.

The ever-evolving landscape of technology and cybersecurity fuels a motivation based on intellectual challenge. For some, the allure lies in testing their skills against sophisticated security measures, overcoming barriers, and staying ahead of defenders. The constant cat-and-mouse game between cybercriminals and security professionals provides an intellectual stimulation that appeals to those with a passion for technology and problem-solving. The thrill of outsmarting security systems, discovering novel vulnerabilities, and crafting sophisticated exploits becomes a driving force for individuals seeking intellectual gratification within the underground.

In certain instances, individuals may be motivated by a lack of ethical constraints or moral inhibitions, allowing them to engage in activities that would be considered unacceptable or criminal in conventional contexts. The anonymity provided by the digital realm often enables individuals to distance themselves from the real-world consequences of their actions, leading to a detachment from the ethical considerations that might deter similar behavior in offline environments. This moral disconnection can be exacerbated by a perceived sense of impunity within the underground, where the challenges of attribution and prosecution contribute to a perception of minimal consequences.

A sense of rebellion against authority or established norms is a recurring theme in the motivations of those providing illicit services. Some individuals may harbor resentment or dissatisfaction with societal structures, institutions, or perceived injustices. Engaging in cybercrime within the underground becomes a form of rebellion, allowing them to subvert established systems and challenge the status quo. The anonymity provided by the digital realm empowers individuals to act as digital outlaws, evading traditional forms of authority and expressing their dissent through disruptive and illicit activities.

The evolving landscape of cyber threats and the increasing sophistication of attacks have led to the emergence of cyber mercenaries and contractors. These individuals may not be driven by personal ideologies or ethical detachment but rather view their skills as a commodity to be sold to the highest bidder. Governments, criminal organizations, or private entities may enlist the services of these cyber mercenaries for a range of purposes, including cyber espionage, information warfare, or corporate espionage. The motivations in such cases are often driven by financial incentives, with individuals viewing their expertise as a marketable skill in the burgeoning cyber arms trade.

The underground ecosystem provides a community and a sense of belonging for individuals who may feel alienated or marginalized in conventional society. The camaraderie among like-minded individuals who share similar skills, interests, or motivations fosters a subculture within the digital underground. This sense of community can become a powerful motivator, providing a social network where individuals find acceptance, recognition, and a shared identity. The tight-knit nature of the underground community often contributes to a culture of secrecy and loyalty, where individuals may be more inclined to engage in illicit activities to maintain their standing within this digital subculture.

The gamification of cybercrime, where individuals compete to achieve specific goals or objectives, introduces another layer of motivation within the underground. Whether it's achieving the highest number of compromised accounts, successfully executing a high-profile attack, or developing novel malware, the competitive aspect turns cybercrime into a game for some individuals. The pursuit of virtual achievements, recognition within the underground community, and the thrill of the game contribute to a mindset where cybercriminal activities become a form of digital sport.

Psychological factors, such as a desire for power and control, also play a role in motivating individuals within the underground. The ability to manipulate systems, compromise networks, and exert influence over digital landscapes provides a sense of empowerment for those seeking control in a rapidly changing and interconnected world. The digital realm becomes a playground where individuals can assert their dominance and impact, fostering a motivation rooted in the pursuit of power and the thrill of exerting influence.

In conclusion, the motivations of individuals providing illicit services within the underground economy are multifaceted and shaped by a combination of economic, ideological, psychological, and societal factors. Financial gain, ideological beliefs, a desire for notoriety, intellectual challenge, moral disconnection, rebellion against authority, the pursuit of belonging, the gamification of cybercrime, the allure of power and control—all contribute to the complex tapestry of motivations. Understanding these motivations is essential for developing effective strategies to deter and combat cybercrime, as it allows for a more nuanced approach that addresses the root causes driving individuals toward illicit activities in the digital realm.

Trace the evolution of online forums where cybercriminals communicate and collaborate.

The evolution of online forums where cybercriminals communicate and collaborate is a dynamic narrative that mirrors the broader advancements in technology, changes in cyber threats, and the constant cat-and-mouse game between cybercriminals and law enforcement. The earliest instances of cybercriminal collaboration can be traced back to the nascent days of the internet, where hackers and phreakers engaged in discussions on bulletin board systems (BBS). These early forums, characterized by text-based interfaces and limited interactivity, provided a platform for individuals to share information, exchange hacking techniques, and discuss the emerging landscape of digital exploits.

As the internet continued to grow and evolve, so did the forums where cybercriminals congregated. The transition from BBS to more sophisticated web-based forums marked a significant shift in the accessibility and scale of these platforms. In the late 1990s and early 2000s, hacking forums such as "HackThisSite" and "HackForums" gained popularity, serving as hubs for individuals interested in hacking, programming, and cybersecurity. These forums facilitated the exchange of knowledge, tools, and even the coordination of collaborative hacking endeavors.

The advent of the deep web and dark web further transformed the landscape of cybercriminal forums. The deep web, which comprises parts of the internet not indexed by search engines, became a haven for cybercriminal discussions and collaboration. The dark web, a subset of the deep web that requires specific tools like Tor for access, provided an even more clandestine environment where users could engage in illicit activities with a higher degree of anonymity. Forums like "CarderPlanet" and "DarkMarket" gained prominence, specializing in the trade of stolen data, credit card information, and hacking tools.

One of the watershed moments in the evolution of cybercriminal forums was the rise of "CardingWorld" in the mid-2000s. This forum, dedicated to carding and credit card fraud, became a focal point for cybercriminals involved in financial crimes. The forum's success highlighted the specialization within the cybercriminal ecosystem, with dedicated platforms catering to specific illicit activities. CardingWorld's prominence also underscored the international nature of cybercrime, as users from around the world collaborated on schemes ranging from credit card fraud to identity theft.

The closure of high-profile cybercriminal forums by law enforcement, such as the takedown of "CarderPlanet" in 2004, prompted the emergence of more resilient and decentralized platforms. The decentralization of cybercriminal forums became a strategic response to mitigate the risks of law enforcement intervention. Rather than relying on a single centralized forum, cybercriminals began using a distributed network of forums, making it more challenging for authorities to dismantle the entire ecosystem. These decentralized forums, often hosted on multiple servers and domains, showcased the adaptability of cybercriminals in response to external threats.

The maturation of cybercriminal forums in the mid-2000s also saw the emergence of more sophisticated and exclusive platforms. Forums like "L33tCrew" and "Digital Gangster" operated as closed communities, requiring invitations or vetting processes for membership. This exclusivity fostered a sense of trust and reduced the risk of infiltration by law enforcement. The closed nature of these forums also contributed to a more specialized and focused collaboration among members, often engaged in high-level hacking, data breaches, and the development of advanced malware.

The evolution of cybercriminal forums continued into the 2010s with the emergence of the "darknet" and the Silk Road marketplace. While not a traditional forum, Silk Road exemplified the convergence of cybercrime and the underground economy. Operating on the Tor network, Silk Road facilitated the anonymous trade of illicit goods and services, primarily drugs. The success of Silk Road demonstrated the potential for decentralized platforms to facilitate not only cybercrime discussions but also the actual trade of physical and digital contraband.

The closure of Silk Road in 2013 by law enforcement underscored the risks associated with operating such platforms, leading to increased scrutiny and proactive efforts by authorities to combat cybercrime forums. This period also witnessed the rise of encrypted messaging platforms, such as Telegram and Signal, as alternative communication channels for cybercriminals. These platforms offered end-to-end encryption, adding an extra layer of security for communication and collaboration. Telegram, in particular, gained popularity for hosting private groups where cybercriminals could share information, coordinate attacks, and trade illicit goods.

In recent years, the evolution of cybercriminal forums has witnessed a resurgence in more traditional forum formats alongside the continued use of encrypted messaging apps. Platforms like "Exploit" and "Nulled" cater to a diverse range of cybercriminal activities, including the sale of hacking tools, malware, and the exchange of stolen data. The broader adoption of cryptocurrencies, such as Bitcoin and Monero, as a means of payment within these forums has further enhanced the anonymity and resilience of the underground ecosystem.

The commodification of cybercrime has led to the emergence of cybercrime-as-a-service (CaaS) platforms, where individuals can purchase hacking services, ransomware, or even rent a botnet for DDoS attacks. The availability of these services on specialized forums, often with user reviews and ratings, mirrors the dynamics of legitimate e-commerce platforms. The commercialization of cybercrime has expanded the reach of malicious activities, allowing less technically proficient individuals to engage in cyber threats with relative ease.

In conclusion, the evolution of online forums where cybercriminals communicate and collaborate reflects a complex interplay of technological advancements, law enforcement interventions, and the adaptability of cybercriminals. From the early days of text-based BBS to the decentralized and encrypted platforms of the dark web, these forums have become integral to the cybercriminal ecosystem. The specialization, decentralization, and international collaboration within these forums highlight the resilience and sophistication of the underground economy. As technology continues to advance, the trajectory of cybercriminal forums will likely continue to evolve, presenting ongoing challenges for law enforcement, cybersecurity professionals, and society at large. Understanding this evolution is crucial for developing effective strategies to mitigate the impact of cybercrime and secure the digital landscape against emerging threats.

Discuss the role of these forums in knowledge sharing and skill development.

Cybercriminal forums play a multifaceted and paradoxical role in knowledge sharing and skill development within the underground ecosystem. These digital platforms, often hidden in the recesses of the internet, serve as virtual meeting places where individuals with varying levels of technical expertise converge to exchange information, collaborate on illicit activities, and enhance their skills in the realm of cybercrime. The nature of these forums facilitates a dynamic and reciprocal process of learning, where both novices and seasoned cybercriminals contribute to the collective pool of knowledge.

One of the fundamental functions of cybercriminal forums is the dissemination of knowledge related to hacking techniques, vulnerabilities, and tools. Novice members, often referred to as "script kiddies," can access a wealth of tutorials, guides, and educational materials that break down complex hacking methods into more digestible steps. These resources range from basic tutorials on password cracking and website defacement to more advanced guides on malware development and network exploitation. The open sharing of this knowledge lowers the entry barriers for individuals seeking to enter the world of cybercrime, democratizing access to information that was once considered exclusive to a select few.

The forums also foster a sense of community-driven mentorship, where more experienced cybercriminals willingly share their insights and expertise with those seeking to enhance their skills. This mentorship dynamic allows newcomers to benefit from the practical experiences and lessons learned by seasoned individuals. Experienced members often provide guidance on effective evasion techniques, discuss the latest trends in cybersecurity, and offer troubleshooting assistance for those encountering technical challenges. The collaborative nature of these interactions serves as a conduit for skill development, enabling less-experienced members to rapidly acquire and apply knowledge that might otherwise be difficult to access.

Skill development within cybercriminal forums is not limited to theoretical knowledge but extends to hands-on training through the sharing of tools and software. Underground forums act as repositories for a wide array of hacking tools, malware, and exploit kits, freely distributed or available for purchase. Members can access and experiment with these tools, gaining practical experience in deploying attacks, analyzing vulnerabilities, and understanding the intricacies of different attack vectors. The practical exposure facilitated by these forums transforms theoretical knowledge into tangible skills, allowing members to hone their abilities through real-world application.

The collaborative nature of these forums extends beyond individual skill development to collective problem-solving. Members often engage in discussions and forums to troubleshoot technical issues, brainstorm innovative approaches to circumvent security measures, or collectively analyze the aftermath of a successful attack. This collaborative problem-solving not only enhances the skill set of individual participants but also contributes to the evolution and innovation of cyber threats. The forums become incubators for creativity and experimentation, pushing the boundaries of what is possible within the realm of cybercrime.

The diverse range of expertise within cybercriminal forums allows for specialization and the development of niche skills. Members often gravitate towards specific areas of interest, such as web application security, malware analysis, or social engineering. Specialization within these forums results in the creation of sub-communities or dedicated sections focusing on particular aspects of cybercrime. This specialization not only facilitates in-depth knowledge sharing within niche domains but also encourages members to refine and perfect their skills in specific areas of interest.

However, the knowledge-sharing dynamics within cybercriminal forums are not solely altruistic, as members actively engage in a form of reciprocity. Individuals who share valuable knowledge, tools, or insights may receive recognition, status, or even financial rewards from the community. This incentive structure encourages active participation and contributions, creating a self-sustaining ecosystem where knowledge flows freely in exchange for social or economic benefits. The reciprocal nature of knowledge sharing within these forums fosters a sense of camaraderie and mutual support among members.

The evolution of cyber threats and security measures necessitates continuous learning and adaptation within the cybercriminal community. As security technologies advance, forums become spaces where members discuss and dissect emerging trends in cybersecurity. Discussions may revolve around the latest security protocols, vulnerabilities, or countermeasures implemented by organizations and governments. This exchange of information allows cybercriminals to stay abreast of the ever-changing landscape, adapting their tactics and techniques to circumvent evolving security measures.

The knowledge-sharing aspect of these forums also extends to discussions about the legal landscape, potential risks, and evasion strategies. Members often share insights into the legal consequences of various cybercriminal activities, providing guidance on jurisdictions with lax enforcement or lenient cybercrime laws. Discussions on evasion strategies may include tips on maintaining anonymity, using virtual private networks (VPNs), or leveraging encrypted communication tools to minimize the risk of law enforcement detection.

This knowledge-sharing related to the legal and evasion aspects of cybercrime reflects the strategic and calculated nature of activities within the underground ecosystem.

The underground forums serve as repositories for threat intelligence, with members actively discussing and disseminating information related to vulnerabilities, exploits, and potential targets. This collective intelligence gathering allows cybercriminals to prioritize their efforts, focusing on high-value targets or exploiting newly discovered vulnerabilities before they are patched. The forums become hubs for the exchange of zero-day exploits, previously unknown vulnerabilities, and techniques for evading detection, enabling members to stay ahead of security professionals and law enforcement agencies.

While knowledge sharing and skill development are central aspects of cybercriminal forums, these platforms also contribute to the commercialization of cybercrime. The underground economy facilitated by these forums involves the buying and selling of hacking services, stolen data, and malware. The commercialization aspect introduces a transactional element, where individuals may offer their expertise for financial gain or purchase tools and services to expedite their malicious activities. The availability of cybercrime-as-a-service (CaaS) platforms within these forums further commodifies specific skill sets, enabling individuals to rent botnets, purchase ransomware, or hire hackers for targeted attacks.

In conclusion, cybercriminal forums play a pivotal role in knowledge sharing and skill development within the underground ecosystem. These platforms serve as virtual spaces where individuals with varying levels of technical expertise converge to exchange information, collaborate on illicit activities, and enhance their skills in the realm of cybercrime. The dynamics of mentorship, hands-on training, collective problem-solving, specialization, and reciprocity contribute to the continuous evolution of skills and tactics within the cybercriminal community. Understanding the intricate interplay of these factors is essential for cybersecurity professionals and law enforcement agencies aiming to develop effective strategies to counteract cyber threats and secure the digital landscape against evolving challenges.

Chapter 7: The Cat-and-Mouse Game of Cybersecurity

Define the dynamic nature of the cybersecurity landscape.

The cybersecurity landscape is inherently dynamic, characterized by a perpetual state of evolution, adaptation, and complexity. This dynamism arises from the interplay of technological advancements, emerging threat vectors, geopolitical influences, and the continuous efforts of both defenders and adversaries to outmaneuver each other. At its core, the dynamic nature of cybersecurity reflects the rapid pace at which technology evolves, introducing new opportunities and challenges that reshape the digital terrain. The relentless march of innovation in computing, networking, and information technologies provides both the tools for progress and the vulnerabilities that adversaries exploit, creating a constantly shifting battleground for cybersecurity professionals.

Technological innovation, a driving force behind the dynamic nature of cybersecurity, continually expands the attack surface. As organizations adopt cloud computing, the Internet of Things (IoT), artificial intelligence (AI), and other transformative technologies, the complexity and diversity of potential targets for cyber threats increase exponentially. Each innovation introduces new vectors for exploitation, and cyber adversaries are quick to capitalize on these opportunities. The expanding attack surface challenges defenders to adapt their security measures to safeguard an ever-growing array of devices, applications, and interconnected systems.

The evolution of threat vectors is a key contributor to the dynamic nature of cybersecurity. Cyber adversaries are adept at adapting their tactics to exploit the latest vulnerabilities and circumvent traditional security measures. The rapid proliferation of sophisticated malware, ransomware, and other malicious tools illustrates the agility of cyber threats. Attackers exploit not only technical vulnerabilities but also human factors through social engineering and phishing attacks, capitalizing on the weakest link in the cybersecurity chain—human behavior. Defenders must continually refine their strategies to anticipate and mitigate evolving threat vectors, often engaging in a constant game of cat and mouse with cybercriminals.

Geopolitical dynamics inject an additional layer of complexity into the cybersecurity landscape. Nation-state actors, hacktivist groups, and cybercriminal organizations operate within a geopolitical context that influences their motives, targets, and techniques. State-sponsored cyber attacks, cyber espionage, and politically motivated hacking incidents underscore the interconnectedness of cyberspace with global politics. The geopolitical dimension introduces a strategic element to cybersecurity, where the actions of nation-states can have cascading effects on the digital security of organizations and individuals. The attribution of cyber attacks to specific actors becomes a complex challenge, further complicating the response to cyber threats.

The interconnectedness of the digital ecosystem amplifies the dynamic nature of cybersecurity. The proliferation of digital platforms, online services, and interconnected networks creates a web of dependencies that transcends geographical boundaries. An incident in one part of the world can have ripple effects across the global digital infrastructure. The interconnected nature of cyberspace facilitates the rapid spread of cyber threats, making them borderless and challenging traditional notions of jurisdiction in addressing cybercrime. As organizations and individuals become more interconnected, the impact of cybersecurity incidents extends beyond technical considerations to encompass economic, social, and geopolitical dimensions.

The threat landscape is further influenced by the commodification of cybercrime. Cybercriminals operate within an underground economy where tools, services, and stolen data are traded as commodities. The commercialization of cyber threats introduces a profit motive, leading to the emergence of cybercrime-as-a-service (CaaS) platforms. Criminal actors can rent botnets, purchase exploit kits, and even hire skilled hackers for specific tasks. This economic dimension transforms cybercrime into a dynamic marketplace where adversaries continually innovate to maximize their financial gains. The commodification of cyber threats not only fuels the evolution of malicious tools but also incentivizes attackers to develop more sophisticated and targeted approaches.

The dynamic nature of cybersecurity is further compounded by the challenges posed by the sheer volume of data generated and processed in the digital age. The explosion of big data, fueled by the interconnectedness of devices and the digitization of various facets of life, presents both opportunities and challenges for cybersecurity. The vast amounts of data generated provide valuable insights for threat detection and analysis, but they also create a daunting task of distinguishing meaningful signals from noise. Cybersecurity professionals grapple with the complexities of analyzing massive datasets in real-time to identify anomalous activities and potential security incidents.

The rapid evolution of the regulatory landscape contributes to the dynamic nature of cybersecurity. Governments and regulatory bodies worldwide are responding to the escalating cyber threats by enacting new laws and regulations aimed at enhancing cybersecurity measures. Compliance requirements, such as the General Data Protection Regulation (GDPR) and the California Consumer Privacy Act (CCPA), compel organizations to implement robust security measures to protect sensitive data. The changing regulatory environment necessitates ongoing adjustments to cybersecurity strategies, as organizations must navigate complex and evolving legal frameworks while maintaining effective security postures.

Human factors introduce a dynamic and unpredictable element into the cybersecurity landscape. Insider threats, whether intentional or unintentional, can pose significant risks to organizations. The actions of employees, contractors, or other individuals with access to systems and sensitive information can result in security incidents. The human element encompasses not only potential insider threats but also the broader challenge of cybersecurity awareness and education. As technology evolves, ensuring that individuals are informed and vigilant about cyber threats becomes a critical aspect of maintaining a resilient cybersecurity posture.

The dynamic nature of cybersecurity is further underscored by the continuous advancements in defensive technologies and strategies. Security professionals employ a range of tools, including antivirus software, intrusion detection systems, firewalls, and endpoint protection solutions, to defend against cyber threats. However, the rapid evolution of the threat landscape necessitates constant innovation in defensive measures. The rise of advanced threat detection technologies, threat intelligence platforms, and machine learning-driven security solutions reflects the ongoing efforts to stay ahead of sophisticated adversaries.

Incident response and recovery play a crucial role in navigating the dynamic cybersecurity landscape. Organizations must be prepared to respond swiftly and effectively to security incidents, minimizing the impact and preventing further damage. The continuous refinement of incident response plans, the conduct of regular security drills, and the integration of threat intelligence into response strategies are essential components of a proactive cybersecurity approach. The ability to adapt and learn from each incident contributes to the resilience of organizations in the face of evolving cyber threats.

In conclusion, the dynamic nature of the cybersecurity landscape arises from the interplay of technological innovation, evolving threat vectors, geopolitical influences, interconnectedness, commodification of cybercrime, big data challenges, regulatory changes, human factors, and advancements in defensive technologies. Cybersecurity is a perpetual journey where defenders must continuously adapt to the evolving digital terrain. Embracing a proactive and agile mindset, staying informed about emerging threats, and fostering collaboration within the cybersecurity community are essential for navigating the complexities and uncertainties of the dynamic cybersecurity landscape.

Discuss the constant evolution of cyber threats.

The constant evolution of cyber threats is an ever-shifting landscape, shaped by a myriad of factors that range from technological advancements and criminal innovation to geopolitical tensions and the evolving nature of the digital ecosystem. At the core of this dynamic evolution is the relentless pace of technological progress, where each innovation presents both opportunities and challenges for cyber adversaries. The perpetual race between defenders and attackers is fueled by the constant exploration of new attack vectors, exploitation techniques, and tools that capitalize on the vulnerabilities introduced by emerging technologies. This technological arms race defines the evolution of cyber threats, creating a landscape that demands constant vigilance, adaptation, and innovation from those tasked with defending against malicious actors.

The advent of the Internet of Things (IoT) has emerged as a significant catalyst in the evolution of cyber threats. The proliferation of interconnected devices, ranging from smart home appliances to industrial sensors, has expanded the attack surface exponentially. Cybercriminals leverage the vulnerabilities inherent in poorly secured IoT devices to launch attacks that can range from distributed denial-of-service (DDoS) assaults to infiltrating critical infrastructure. The sheer diversity of IoT devices, often with limited security measures in place, provides ample opportunities for attackers to exploit weaknesses and orchestrate large-scale, coordinated attacks. The evolution of IoT-related threats underscores the importance of addressing security considerations at the design and implementation stages of these interconnected systems.

The rise of artificial intelligence (AI) and machine learning introduces a double-edged sword into the cyber threat landscape. While these technologies empower defenders with advanced threat detection and analysis capabilities, they also offer new avenues for cybercriminals to refine and automate their attack methodologies. Adversarial machine learning techniques, where attackers manipulate AI algorithms to evade detection, represent a growing concern. Additionally, the use of AI in crafting more convincing phishing attacks, generating realistic deepfake content, and automating malware creation exemplifies how cyber threats evolve in tandem with the very technologies intended to enhance cybersecurity.

Cryptocurrency, particularly the decentralized nature of blockchain technology, has transformed the landscape of cyber threats, providing both challenges and opportunities for malicious actors. The use of cryptocurrencies, such as Bitcoin, for ransom payments has fueled the proliferation of ransomware attacks, where attackers encrypt data and demand payment in untraceable digital currencies. The anonymity and pseudo-anonymity offered by cryptocurrencies facilitate illicit transactions on the dark web, enabling the trade of hacking tools, stolen data, and other cybercrime commodities. The evolution of cyber threats in the realm of cryptocurrency extends beyond financial motivations to encompass the exploitation of blockchain vulnerabilities, such as smart contract flaws and decentralized finance (DeFi) vulnerabilities.

Nation-state actors and advanced persistent threats (APTs) contribute significantly to the evolving landscape of cyber threats. State-sponsored cyber espionage, cyber warfare, and politically motivated attacks introduce a level of sophistication that poses formidable challenges for defenders. APT groups, often backed by nation-states, engage in long-term, targeted campaigns that leverage advanced techniques to compromise high-value targets, including government agencies, critical infrastructure, and multinational corporations. The dynamic nature of these threats involves constant innovation in tactics, techniques, and procedures (TTPs), as APT actors adapt to changing geopolitical dynamics and defensive measures implemented by their adversaries.

The underground economy, facilitated by the dark web and various cybercrime-as-a-service (CaaS) platforms, plays a pivotal role in the evolution of cyber threats. The commodification of hacking tools, malware, and cybercriminal services provides less technically proficient individuals with the means to launch sophisticated attacks. The underground ecosystem operates as a marketplace where cybercriminals can purchase ransomware-as-a-service, distributed denial-of-service (DDoS) attacks, or even hire skilled hackers for specific tasks. This commercialization aspect transforms cyber threats into accessible commodities, fostering a competitive environment where innovation is driven by financial incentives and profit-sharing models.

The evolution of cyber threats is intricately connected to the rapidly changing tactics employed by ransomware operators. While ransomware itself is not a new phenomenon, the tactics, techniques, and targets have evolved significantly over time. Modern ransomware attacks often involve data exfiltration before encryption, leading to the additional threat of data leakage and extortion. Ransomware-as-a-service (RaaS) platforms have democratized the distribution of ransomware, allowing even individuals with minimal technical skills to engage in these lucrative attacks. The emergence of double-extortion tactics, where attackers threaten to release sensitive data unless a ransom is paid, adds a layer of complexity and urgency to the response efforts of targeted organizations.

The exploitation of supply chain vulnerabilities has become a prevalent tactic in the arsenal of cyber threats. Cybercriminals recognize the interconnected nature of the digital supply chain, targeting software vendors, service providers, and third-party partners to compromise high-profile targets indirectly. Supply chain attacks often involve the insertion of malicious code into legitimate software updates or the compromise of hardware components, enabling attackers to infiltrate trusted environments with greater stealth. Notable incidents, such as the SolarWinds supply chain attack, underscore the sophistication and impact of these evolving threat vectors, prompting organizations to reassess and enhance their supply chain security measures.

The ongoing evolution of cyber threats is fueled by the persistent challenge of exploiting human factors. Social engineering, phishing attacks, and other manipulative tactics that target human behavior remain highly effective means of gaining unauthorized access to systems and sensitive information. Cyber adversaries continually refine their social engineering techniques, leveraging psychological manipulation, context-aware spear-phishing, and impersonation tactics to deceive individuals. The constant adaptation of these tactics to exploit current events, global crises, or individual vulnerabilities underscores the importance of cybersecurity awareness and education as a critical defense mechanism against evolving human-centric threats.

The dynamic nature of cyber threats is evident in the increasing prevalence of state-sponsored cyber attacks on critical infrastructure. Nation-states recognize the strategic advantage of targeting essential systems such as energy grids, water supplies, and transportation networks. The evolving landscape of cyber threats includes the potential for destructive attacks on critical infrastructure, with the capacity to disrupt essential services and inflict significant economic and societal consequences. The sophistication and persistence of state-sponsored actors in this arena necessitate a concerted effort to bolster the resilience and security of critical infrastructure against evolving cyber threats.

The expansion of attack surfaces to the cloud introduces a new frontier in the evolution of cyber threats. As organizations migrate their data, applications, and infrastructure to cloud environments, cyber adversaries adapt their tactics to exploit vulnerabilities in cloud configurations and services. Misconfigurations, insecure application programming interfaces (APIs), and inadequate access controls become points of entry for attackers seeking to compromise cloud-based assets. The dynamic nature of cloud environments, characterized by rapid scalability and frequent updates, demands continuous monitoring, robust identity and access management, and a proactive security posture to mitigate the evolving risks associated with cloud-based cyber threats.

In conclusion, the constant evolution of cyber threats reflects the intricate interplay of technological innovation, geopolitical dynamics, the commodification of cybercrime, the persistence of state-sponsored actors, supply chain vulnerabilities, human factors, and the expanding attack surface. The cybersecurity landscape is not static; it is a dynamic and ever-shifting terrain that demands continuous adaptation and innovation from defenders. Cyber threats evolve in response to advancements in technology, changes in adversary tactics, and the shifting geopolitical landscape, requiring a holistic and proactive approach to cybersecurity that encompasses technology, education, collaboration, and strategic foresight. Understanding the multifaceted nature of these evolving threats is essential for organizations, cybersecurity professionals, and policymakers seeking to develop effective strategies to safeguard the digital landscape against an ever-changing array of cyber risks.

Explore the factors that give hackers an advantage in the ongoing cyber warfare.

Hackers maintain a strategic advantage in the ongoing cyber warfare, a multidimensional conflict marked by constant technological evolution, asymmetric power dynamics, and the agility of malicious actors to exploit vulnerabilities in the digital realm. One of the primary factors contributing to the hackers' advantage lies in the rapid pace of technological innovation. As technology advances, introducing new functionalities, devices, and infrastructures, it simultaneously introduces potential vulnerabilities that hackers can exploit. The complexity and interconnectedness of modern systems provide a vast attack surface, offering malicious actors numerous entry points and vectors to infiltrate networks, compromise data, and disrupt critical operations. The rapid adoption of emerging technologies, such as the Internet of Things (IoT), artificial intelligence (AI), and cloud computing, amplifies the challenges faced by defenders, as securing these technologies requires constant adaptation to evolving threats.

The asymmetry of cyber warfare further tilts the advantage toward hackers. Cybercriminals and state-sponsored actors operate within an environment that often lacks clear rules of engagement, attribution challenges, and the ability to conceal their identities. This asymmetry is particularly pronounced when considering the resources at the disposal of well-funded adversaries compared to those of defenders, who must navigate constrained budgets and resource limitations. The agility and flexibility of hackers, unburdened by bureaucratic processes and legal constraints, enable them to rapidly adjust tactics, techniques, and procedures in response to defensive measures, contributing to a persistent imbalance in the cyber domain.

A crucial factor contributing to the hackers' advantage is the dynamic and decentralized nature of the cyber threat landscape. Cybercriminals often operate in loosely affiliated networks, sharing knowledge, tools, and resources on underground forums and the dark web. This decentralization allows for a diffusion of responsibility and specialization, as individual actors or groups can focus on specific aspects of cybercrime, from developing sophisticated malware to executing targeted social engineering attacks. The collective intelligence and collaboration within the hacker community foster an environment where knowledge is rapidly disseminated, and tactics quickly evolve, creating challenges for defenders who must contend with a diverse array of threats.

The anonymity afforded to hackers in the digital realm further amplifies their advantage. Tools like virtual private networks (VPNs), anonymizing browsers, and cryptocurrencies provide a layer of concealment that shields attackers from easy identification and attribution. The ability to operate behind a veil of anonymity not only emboldens hackers but also complicates the efforts of law enforcement and cybersecurity professionals to trace and apprehend them. The lack of a universally accepted framework for international cooperation on cybercrime exacerbates the challenge, allowing hackers to exploit jurisdictional gaps and evade consequences.

Another factor that contributes to the hackers' advantage is the thriving underground economy. The commercialization of cybercrime, facilitated by the dark web and various cybercrime-as-a-service (CaaS) platforms, allows less technically proficient individuals to access sophisticated hacking tools, malware, and services. The underground market operates as a dynamic marketplace where actors can buy and sell exploits, ransomware, and stolen data, creating a robust ecosystem that fuels the ongoing evolution of cyber threats. This commodification lowers the barrier to entry, enabling a broader range of adversaries to participate in cyber warfare without the need for deep technical expertise.

The exploitation of supply chain vulnerabilities represents a strategic advantage for hackers, allowing them to compromise high-profile targets indirectly. By targeting software vendors, service providers, or third-party partners, hackers can infiltrate trusted environments with greater stealth and persistence. Supply chain attacks often involve the compromise of software updates or the insertion of malicious code into legitimate hardware components, providing a vector for persistent and sophisticated threats. The ripple effects of a successful supply chain attack can be extensive, affecting multiple organizations downstream and showcasing the difficulty defenders face in securing interconnected and interdependent digital supply chains.

The psychological dimension of cyber warfare also plays a crucial role in providing hackers with an advantage. Social engineering tactics, including phishing, spear-phishing, and pretexting, leverage human vulnerabilities to gain unauthorized access to systems and sensitive information. Exploiting psychological factors, such as trust, urgency, or curiosity, hackers can manipulate individuals into divulging credentials, clicking on malicious links, or unwittingly facilitating a cyber attack. Human factors represent a persistent and challenging aspect of cybersecurity, as even well-designed technical defenses can be circumvented through the exploitation of human psychology.

The evolving nature of cyber threats, characterized by polymorphic malware, zero-day exploits, and advanced persistent threats (APTs), contributes to the advantage held by hackers. Polymorphic malware, capable of dynamically changing its code to evade signature-based detection, poses challenges for traditional antivirus solutions. Zero-day exploits, targeting previously unknown vulnerabilities, allow attackers to initiate attacks before defenders can develop and deploy patches. APTs, often associated with nation-state actors, engage in prolonged and targeted campaigns, leveraging advanced techniques to infiltrate and persist within targeted environments. The sophistication and diversity of these evolving threats require defenders to maintain a high level of situational awareness and invest in advanced threat detection capabilities.

The global nature of cyberspace, coupled with the lack of universally accepted norms and treaties governing cyber warfare, contributes to the hackers' advantage. Nation-states, hacktivist groups, and cybercriminal organizations operate within a landscape marked by ambiguity and the absence of clear rules of engagement. The lack of a universally agreed-upon framework for attributing cyber attacks and responding to cyber threats results in a strategic advantage for hackers, who can exploit the absence of enforceable norms to act with relative impunity. The international community's struggle to establish clear guidelines for responsible state behavior in cyberspace further complicates efforts to deter malicious actors.

The speed at which hackers can exploit vulnerabilities compared to the pace of developing and deploying effective defensive measures creates a temporal advantage for malicious actors. As organizations strive to identify and remediate vulnerabilities, hackers can capitalize on the window of opportunity presented by the lag between the discovery of a vulnerability and its mitigation. This temporal asymmetry places defenders in a constant reactive mode, responding to emerging threats rather than proactively preventing them. The challenge of achieving real-time threat detection and response becomes paramount in mitigating the hackers' advantage in exploiting vulnerabilities.

In conclusion, a confluence of factors contributes to the advantage held by hackers in the ongoing cyber warfare. The rapid pace of technological innovation, the asymmetry of power dynamics, the dynamic and decentralized nature of the cyber threat landscape, the anonymity afforded to hackers, the thriving underground economy, the exploitation of supply chain vulnerabilities, the psychological dimension of cyber warfare, the evolving nature of cyber threats, the global nature of cyberspace, and the temporal advantage in exploiting vulnerabilities collectively create an environment where hackers can operate with agility and adaptability. Effectively addressing these factors requires a holistic and multidimensional approach that encompasses technological innovation, international cooperation, regulatory frameworks, public-private partnerships, and the continuous development of advanced cybersecurity capabilities. Only by understanding and mitigating these factors can defenders begin to level the playing field and enhance resilience against the evolving challenges posed by malicious actors in the complex landscape of cyber warfare.

Discuss the rapid adaptation of hacking techniques.

The rapid adaptation of hacking techniques constitutes a hallmark of the ever-evolving landscape of cybersecurity. Malicious actors continually refine and innovate their methodologies to exploit vulnerabilities, circumvent defenses, and achieve their objectives in an increasingly interconnected and technologically advanced environment. One of the key drivers of this rapid adaptation is the dynamic nature of technology itself. As organizations embrace new technologies and methodologies, hackers adeptly pivot to exploit emerging attack surfaces and vulnerabilities. The perpetual introduction of novel software, hardware, and communication protocols presents a rich landscape for innovation in hacking techniques, requiring cybersecurity professionals to remain vigilant and proactive in identifying and mitigating evolving threats.

Polymorphic malware exemplifies the hackers' ability to rapidly adapt their techniques to evade traditional security measures. Polymorphic malware dynamically alters its code and characteristics with each instance, making it challenging for signature-based antivirus solutions to detect and block. This adaptive quality allows hackers to bypass static defenses, such as signature-based detection, by ensuring that each iteration of the malware appears unique. The use of polymorphic techniques underscores the importance of dynamic and behavior-based detection methods, as cybersecurity professionals strive to keep pace with the mutating nature of malicious code.

Zero-day exploits represent another facet of the rapid adaptation of hacking techniques. Zero-day vulnerabilities are those for which no official patch or fix is available, providing attackers with an opportunity to exploit security gaps before defenders can develop and deploy effective countermeasures. The discovery and weaponization of zero-day vulnerabilities are highly sought-after capabilities in the hacker community, as they allow for targeted and stealthy attacks. The underground economy, where hackers buy and sell information about zero-day vulnerabilities, further accelerates the pace at which these exploits are weaponized, emphasizing the need for organizations to employ proactive vulnerability management and threat intelligence strategies.

Advanced Persistent Threats (APTs) embody a sophisticated and persistent form of cyber attack that showcases the rapid adaptation of hacking techniques. APT actors, often state-sponsored or highly organized groups, employ a combination of social engineering, zero-day exploits, and advanced malware to infiltrate and maintain long-term access to targeted systems. The ability of APTs to adapt their tactics, techniques, and procedures (TTPs) in response to defensive measures challenges cybersecurity professionals to deploy comprehensive defense-in-depth strategies. APTs often exhibit patience, studying their targets, and evolving their approaches over time, making detection and mitigation a complex and ongoing challenge.

Social engineering tactics underscore the human-centric aspect of hacking techniques, exploiting psychological manipulation to deceive individuals and gain unauthorized access to systems. Phishing, spear-phishing, and pretexting are common social engineering techniques that hackers adapt to suit evolving circumstances. The use of social engineering often leverages current events, personalized information, or psychological triggers to increase the likelihood of success. As individuals become more aware of traditional phishing methods, hackers innovate by crafting more convincing and tailored attacks, requiring a continuous emphasis on cybersecurity awareness, education, and training.

The rapid adaptation of hacking techniques is further exemplified by the evolution of ransomware attacks. While ransomware itself is not a new phenomenon, the tactics employed by ransomware operators have become increasingly sophisticated and targeted. Ransomware-as-a-Service (RaaS) platforms enable less technically proficient individuals to engage in ransomware attacks, contributing to the proliferation of these incidents. The introduction of double-extortion tactics, where attackers threaten to release sensitive data in addition to encrypting it, showcases the constant innovation in the ransomware landscape. The ability to adapt extortion methods and target high-profile victims highlights the agility of ransomware operators, necessitating a multifaceted approach to defense that includes robust backup strategies, user training, and advanced threat detection.

Supply chain attacks represent a strategic adaptation of hacking techniques, where attackers exploit vulnerabilities in software vendors, service providers, or third-party partners to compromise high-profile targets indirectly. By compromising the supply chain, hackers can infiltrate trusted environments with greater stealth and persistence. The SolarWinds supply chain attack, which impacted numerous organizations, exemplifies the sophistication and impact of this evolving tactic. Defending against supply chain attacks requires a comprehensive approach that includes rigorous vetting of third-party vendors, continuous monitoring of the digital supply chain, and the implementation of secure development practices to mitigate the risk of software and hardware tampering.

The use of artificial intelligence (AI) and machine learning (ML) introduces a transformative dimension to hacking techniques. Hackers leverage AI and ML algorithms to enhance the sophistication of their attacks, enabling automated and adaptive capabilities. Adversarial machine learning represents an evolving threat, where attackers manipulate AI algorithms to evade detection or produce misleading results. The incorporation of AI-driven techniques in phishing attacks, malware creation, and even deepfake content generation highlights the dynamic and disruptive potential of AI in the hands of malicious actors. The defense against AI-enhanced hacking techniques involves the development of counter-AI measures, such as adversarial training and anomaly detection, to thwart evolving attack methodologies.

The thriving underground economy, facilitated by the dark web and cybercrime-as-a-service (CaaS) platforms, contributes to the rapid adaptation of hacking techniques. In this shadowy marketplace, hackers exchange information, tools, and services, accelerating the spread of innovative attack methods. CaaS platforms allow less technically proficient individuals to access advanced hacking tools and malware, contributing to the democratization of cybercrime. The commercialization of hacking techniques transforms cyber threats into commodities, with the potential for even non-technical actors to engage in sophisticated attacks by purchasing ready-made solutions. This commodification highlights the need for defenders to continually update their understanding of emerging threats and employ advanced threat intelligence to stay ahead of evolving tactics.

The use of encryption and anonymity tools presents a dual-edged sword in the adaptation of hacking techniques. While encryption is a fundamental component of secure communications, malicious actors exploit it to conceal their activities and evade detection. The use of virtual private networks (VPNs), anonymizing browsers, and cryptocurrencies further complicates the efforts of cybersecurity professionals and law enforcement to trace and attribute cyber attacks. The constant innovation in encryption methods and anonymity technologies emphasizes the ongoing challenge of striking a balance between privacy and security in the digital realm.

The geopolitical landscape introduces a strategic dimension to the rapid adaptation of hacking techniques. Nation-state actors engage in cyber espionage, cyber warfare, and politically motivated attacks, leveraging advanced techniques to achieve their objectives. The attribution challenge in cyberspace allows state-sponsored actors to operate with relative impunity, rapidly adapting their tactics to exploit changing geopolitical dynamics. The use of false flags, misdirection, and proxy entities adds layers of complexity to the attribution process, contributing to the strategic advantage of nation-state hackers. The geopolitical context introduces an element of statecraft into hacking techniques, requiring defenders to consider not only the technical aspects of cyber threats but also the broader political and strategic implications.

In conclusion, the rapid adaptation of hacking techniques is a dynamic and multifaceted phenomenon driven by the relentless pace of technological innovation, the asymmetry of power dynamics, the dynamic and decentralized nature of the cyber threat landscape, the anonymity and encryption tools at the disposal of hackers, the thriving underground economy, and the interplay of human psychology. The constant evolution of hacking techniques demands a proactive and adaptive approach to cybersecurity that encompasses advanced threat detection, continuous monitoring, employee training, secure development practices, and international collaboration. As hackers continue to innovate and exploit emerging opportunities, defenders must remain vigilant, agile, and committed to staying ahead of the curve in the ongoing cat-and-mouse game of cybersecurity.

Highlight advancements in cybersecurity technologies and strategies.

Advancements in cybersecurity technologies and strategies represent a critical response to the ever-evolving threat landscape, characterized by sophisticated cyber attacks, rapid technological innovation, and the increasing interconnectivity of digital ecosystems. One significant advancement is the adoption of artificial intelligence (AI) and machine learning (ML) in cybersecurity. AI-powered tools enhance threat detection capabilities by analyzing vast datasets to identify patterns, anomalies, and potential security incidents. Machine learning algorithms can adapt and evolve, improving their ability to recognize new and emerging threats without relying on predefined signatures. This proactive approach allows organizations to stay ahead of rapidly evolving attack techniques, providing a more robust defense against sophisticated cyber threats.

Another notable advancement is the evolution of endpoint detection and response (EDR) solutions. Traditional antivirus solutions are often signature-based and struggle to keep up with polymorphic malware and other advanced threats. EDR solutions, on the other hand, focus on real-time monitoring and analysis of endpoint activities. These solutions leverage behavioral analytics, threat intelligence, and machine learning to detect and respond to anomalous activities indicative of a potential security incident. EDR tools empower organizations to quickly identify and mitigate cyber threats at the endpoint level, reducing the risk of successful attacks.

Cloud security has emerged as a critical area of focus, given the widespread adoption of cloud computing. Advanced cloud security solutions provide robust protection for data and applications hosted in cloud environments. Security-as-a-Service (SecaaS) offerings, such as cloud-based firewalls, secure web gateways, and cloud access security brokers (CASBs), help organizations extend their security perimeter to the cloud. These technologies enable better visibility, control, and compliance in cloud environments, addressing the unique challenges associated with securing data and workloads in the cloud.

The integration of threat intelligence into cybersecurity strategies has become increasingly sophisticated. Threat intelligence platforms aggregate and analyze data from various sources, providing organizations with actionable insights into emerging threats and attack trends. Automated threat intelligence sharing allows for real-time collaboration among organizations, enabling a collective defense against cyber threats. The contextual information provided by threat intelligence enhances incident response capabilities, enabling organizations to prioritize and remediate security incidents more effectively.

In response to the growing threat of ransomware attacks, the development of advanced anti-ransomware solutions has become a pivotal focus within cybersecurity. These solutions employ behavioral analysis, machine learning, and heuristic techniques to detect and mitigate ransomware threats before they can encrypt critical data. Some solutions also incorporate data protection mechanisms, such as backup and recovery features, to ensure organizations can restore their systems and data in the event of a successful ransomware attack.

Network security has seen significant advancements with the implementation of software-defined networking (SDN) and network function virtualization (NFV). SDN allows for dynamic and centralized control of network resources, facilitating more agile and responsive security measures. NFV enables the virtualization of network functions, allowing security services to be deployed flexibly and scaled based on demand. These technologies enhance network visibility, segmentation, and control, making it more challenging for attackers to move laterally within the network.

Identity and access management (IAM) technologies have evolved to address the complexities of modern IT environments. Adaptive authentication, multi-factor authentication (MFA), and biometric authentication methods enhance the security of user access. Identity governance and administration (IGA) solutions automate the management of user identities, access permissions, and compliance. The Zero Trust security model, which assumes no implicit trust within or outside an organization, has gained prominence, emphasizing continuous verification and least privilege access.

In response to the increasing sophistication of phishing attacks, email security solutions have advanced to provide more robust protection against email-borne threats. Advanced threat protection (ATP) solutions leverage machine learning to analyze email content, attachments, and user behavior, identifying and blocking malicious emails. Email authentication standards, such as Domain-based Message Authentication, Reporting, and Conformance (DMARC), enhance email security by preventing domain spoofing and phishing attempts.

Security orchestration, automation, and response (SOAR) platforms have become integral components of cybersecurity strategies. SOAR platforms streamline and automate incident response processes, enabling organizations to respond rapidly to security incidents. These platforms integrate with various security tools, orchestrate incident response workflows, and leverage automation to execute predefined response actions. SOAR solutions enhance the efficiency of cybersecurity teams, allowing them to focus on more complex tasks while automating repetitive and time-consuming activities.

The concept of deception technology has gained traction as a proactive cybersecurity strategy. Deception technologies create decoy systems, files, or credentials that appear enticing to attackers. If an attacker interacts with these decoys, security teams are alerted, enabling them to detect and respond to threats in their early stages. Deception technology provides a valuable layer of deception and misdirection, making it more challenging for attackers to navigate and understand an organization's real IT environment.

Container security has become a critical consideration in the era of containerized applications and microservices architecture. Container orchestration platforms, such as Kubernetes, have introduced security features to protect containerized workloads. Container security solutions provide runtime protection, vulnerability scanning, and configuration management for containers, ensuring that security is an integral part of the DevOps lifecycle.

Threat hunting has emerged as a proactive cybersecurity strategy to identify and eliminate threats that may evade automated detection. Threat hunting involves actively searching for signs of malicious activity within an organization's network and endpoints. Threat hunters leverage advanced analytics, threat intelligence, and expertise to identify subtle indicators of compromise and uncover hidden threats. The integration of threat hunting into cybersecurity operations enhances the organization's ability to detect and respond to sophisticated adversaries.

Quantum-safe cryptography has gained attention as a response to the potential threat posed by quantum computers to traditional cryptographic algorithms. Quantum computers have the potential to break widely used encryption algorithms, necessitating the development and adoption of quantum-resistant cryptographic methods. Quantum-safe cryptography aims to ensure that cryptographic systems remain secure even in the era of quantum computing, providing a long-term solution for protecting sensitive data.

The continuous evolution of cybersecurity technologies and strategies is complemented by the growing emphasis on cybersecurity hygiene and culture. Organizations recognize the importance of cultivating a security-aware culture among employees, fostering a sense of shared responsibility for cybersecurity. Security awareness training programs educate employees about the latest threats, phishing tactics, and best practices for maintaining a secure digital environment. The human element is considered a crucial component in the overall cybersecurity posture, with organizations investing in ongoing training and awareness initiatives.

In conclusion, advancements in cybersecurity technologies and strategies reflect a dynamic response to the evolving threat landscape. From the integration of artificial intelligence and machine learning to the evolution of endpoint security, cloud security, and threat intelligence, organizations are embracing innovative solutions to enhance their cybersecurity posture. The proactive adoption of advanced technologies, coupled with a focus on identity and access management, email security, and security orchestration, automation, and response, showcases a multifaceted approach to cybersecurity. As the cybersecurity landscape continues to evolve, organizations must remain agile, adaptive, and committed to staying ahead of emerging threats through a combination of technology, strategy, and human-centric approaches.

Discuss the role of artificial intelligence and machine learning in threat detection.

The role of artificial intelligence (AI) and machine learning (ML) in threat detection represents a paradigm shift in cybersecurity, empowering organizations to enhance their capabilities in identifying and mitigating cyber threats. AI and ML technologies leverage advanced algorithms to analyze vast amounts of data, discern patterns, and identify anomalies indicative of potential security incidents. One of the primary applications of AI and ML in threat detection lies in the realm of behavioral analytics. These technologies enable the creation of baseline behavioral profiles for users, devices, and systems within an organization. By continuously monitoring and analyzing deviations from these baselines, AI-powered systems can identify unusual or suspicious activities that may indicate a security threat. This proactive approach allows for the early detection of threats, even those that do not exhibit known patterns or signatures.

Machine learning algorithms play a crucial role in the evolution of signature-based threat detection. Traditional signature-based methods rely on predefined patterns or signatures of known threats to identify malicious activities. However, these approaches struggle to keep pace with the rapidly evolving nature of cyber threats, particularly with the rise of polymorphic malware and zero-day exploits. ML algorithms, on the other hand, can dynamically adapt and learn from new data, allowing them to identify and categorize threats without relying solely on predetermined signatures. This adaptability enables organizations to detect and respond to emerging threats in real-time, mitigating the limitations associated with static signature databases.

AI and ML technologies are instrumental in the evolution of anomaly detection, providing organizations with a more robust and adaptive approach to identifying unusual activities that may indicate security incidents. Anomaly detection involves identifying deviations from normal behavior within a system or network. Machine learning models can be trained to recognize normal patterns and behaviors, allowing them to detect deviations that may signify potential threats. This method is particularly effective in uncovering insider threats, advanced persistent threats (APTs), and other stealthy attacks that may go unnoticed by traditional security mechanisms. The ability to adapt to changing environments and evolving attack techniques makes anomaly detection a valuable component of modern threat detection strategies.

The integration of threat intelligence feeds into AI and ML systems enhances the contextual understanding of security events. Threat intelligence provides real-time information about known threats, indicators of compromise (IoCs), and emerging attack trends. By leveraging AI and ML algorithms, organizations can analyze and correlate threat intelligence data with their internal security telemetry, enriching the context of security events. This integration enables more accurate and informed decision-making in threat detection, allowing organizations to prioritize and respond to incidents based on their potential impact and relevance. The fusion of threat intelligence with AI-driven analysis creates a more comprehensive and dynamic defense against a wide range of cyber threats.

AI-driven network traffic analysis represents a transformative capability in threat detection, particularly in the realm of advanced persistent threats (APTs) and sophisticated attacks that aim to operate stealthily within a network. Machine learning models can analyze network traffic patterns, identify anomalous behavior, and uncover indicators of compromise that may signify a targeted attack. The ability to correlate diverse network activities and discern subtle anomalies enables organizations to detect malicious activities that may evade traditional signature-based methods. This proactive approach to network traffic analysis aligns with the need for continuous monitoring and rapid response to emerging threats within complex and dynamic network environments.

Endpoint security has been significantly bolstered by the integration of AI and ML technologies, providing organizations with the means to detect and respond to threats at the individual device level. AI-driven endpoint detection and response (EDR) solutions analyze the behavior of endpoints, such as desktops, laptops, and servers, in real-time. By employing machine learning models, these solutions can identify suspicious activities, detect malware, and respond to security incidents autonomously. The continuous monitoring and adaptive nature of AI-powered EDR solutions enhance the organization's ability to identify and contain threats before they escalate. This level of sophistication is crucial in addressing the growing complexity of endpoint security challenges in today's diverse and decentralized computing environments.

AI and ML are instrumental in the evolution of malware detection and classification. Traditional signature-based approaches struggle to keep pace with the sheer volume and diversity of malware variants. AI-powered malware detection employs behavioral analysis and heuristics to identify malicious activities, even when specific signatures are not known. Machine learning models can learn from the characteristics of known malware and identify previously unseen variants based on their behavior. The ability to detect polymorphic malware, which dynamically changes its code to evade signature-based detection, exemplifies the efficacy of AI and ML in addressing the challenges posed by the evolving landscape of cyber threats.

The role of AI and ML in enhancing email security cannot be overstated, especially in the context of phishing attacks, business email compromise (BEC), and other email-borne threats. AI-driven email security solutions analyze the content, context, and sender behavior to identify phishing attempts and malicious emails. Machine learning algorithms can recognize patterns associated with phishing tactics, such as suspicious links, social engineering techniques, and impersonation attempts. The adaptive nature of AI allows these solutions to evolve and adapt to new and emerging email threats, providing a dynamic defense against a constantly changing threat landscape. The integration of AI-driven email security complements traditional security measures, offering a layered defense that is critical in mitigating the risks associated with email-based attacks.

Natural language processing (NLP) and sentiment analysis, both driven by AI and ML, play a role in detecting threats within unstructured data sources, such as text-based communications. These technologies enable the analysis of text for indicators of malicious intent, sentiment, or contextual anomalies. In the context of insider threat detection, for example, NLP can be employed to analyze employee communications and identify language patterns or behaviors indicative of potential security risks. The ability to extract meaningful insights from unstructured data sources enhances the organization's ability to identify and respond to emerging threats that may manifest in various forms of digital communication.

The evolution of AI and ML technologies extends to the realm of deception and threat hunting. Deception technologies leverage

AI-driven tactics to create decoy systems, files, or credentials within an organization's environment. These decoys appear enticing to attackers and, when interacted with, trigger alerts that indicate potential security incidents. Machine learning models enhance the sophistication of deception techniques, allowing organizations to dynamically adapt their deceptive environment based on evolving threat intelligence and attack patterns. Threat hunting, facilitated by AI, involves proactively searching for signs of malicious activity within an organization's network. Machine learning algorithms can assist threat hunters in identifying subtle indicators of compromise and uncovering hidden threats that may elude automated detection mechanisms.

Quantum computing poses a potential threat to traditional cryptographic algorithms, prompting the development of quantum-safe cryptographic methods. AI and ML technologies are employed in the advancement of quantum-resistant cryptographic solutions, ensuring that cryptographic systems remain secure in the era of quantum computing. The integration of AI in quantum-safe cryptography involves the exploration of algorithms that can withstand the computational power of quantum computers, providing a foundation for securing sensitive data in the face of evolving technological landscapes.

In conclusion, the role of artificial intelligence and machine learning in threat detection represents a transformative leap in cybersecurity capabilities. From behavioral analytics and anomaly detection to network traffic analysis, endpoint security, and malware detection, AI and ML technologies empower organizations to proactively identify and respond to a diverse range of cyber threats. The integration of threat intelligence, the evolution of email security, the application of natural language processing, and the advancement of deception and threat hunting techniques further highlight the versatility and adaptability of AI-driven threat detection strategies. As the cybersecurity landscape continues to evolve, organizations must leverage the power of AI and ML to stay ahead of emerging threats and ensure the resilience of their defenses in the face of a dynamic and ever-changing threat landscape.

Discuss the importance of effective incident response plans.

The importance of effective incident response plans in cybersecurity cannot be overstated, as organizations navigate an increasingly complex and dynamic threat landscape. Incident response is a systematic and organized approach to managing and mitigating security incidents, ranging from data breaches and malware infections to denial-of-service attacks. These plans serve as a strategic framework, outlining the steps and procedures that an organization will follow when a security incident occurs. The proactive development and implementation of incident response plans are crucial for minimizing the impact of security breaches, reducing recovery time, and safeguarding the confidentiality, integrity, and availability of sensitive data and critical systems.

A fundamental aspect of effective incident response plans lies in their ability to provide a structured and well-defined process for handling security incidents. By establishing clear roles, responsibilities, and communication channels, these plans enable organizations to respond swiftly and decisively when faced with a security event. The lack of a structured incident response framework can lead to confusion, delays in decision-making, and a fragmented approach to incident handling. Effective incident response plans establish a cohesive structure that ensures a coordinated and efficient response to security incidents, ultimately mitigating the potential damage and reducing the overall impact on the organization.

The timely detection and containment of security incidents are critical elements addressed by incident response plans. Rapid response is essential to prevent the escalation of a security event and to limit the potential damage to systems and data. Incident response plans provide organizations with predefined procedures for identifying and verifying security incidents promptly. By having a well-defined incident detection and assessment process, organizations can minimize the dwell time of attackers within their networks, reducing the window of opportunity for malicious activities. This proactive approach is essential in preventing the lateral movement of adversaries and limiting the scope of potential damage.

Incident response plans play a pivotal role in ensuring effective communication during a security incident. Clear communication channels, both internal and external, are vital for disseminating information, coordinating response efforts, and keeping relevant stakeholders informed. Effective incident response plans outline communication protocols, including notification procedures, escalation paths, and updates to key stakeholders. By establishing communication strategies in advance, organizations can streamline their response efforts, maintain transparency, and manage the expectations of internal and external parties, including customers, partners, regulatory bodies, and law enforcement agencies.

The integration of legal and regulatory considerations within incident response plans is essential in today's regulatory landscape. Organizations must comply with various laws and regulations governing the protection of sensitive information, and a security incident can have legal implications. Effective incident response plans incorporate a legal framework that outlines the steps to take in compliance with relevant regulations. This includes considerations such as data breach notification requirements, preservation of evidence for legal investigations, and collaboration with law enforcement agencies. The ability to navigate legal complexities in the aftermath of a security incident is crucial for mitigating legal risks and ensuring compliance with applicable laws.

Incident response plans contribute significantly to the preservation of digital evidence, a critical aspect of post-incident analysis and forensic investigations. The forensic analysis of a security incident is vital for understanding the root cause, identifying the extent of the compromise, and attributing the attack to specific threat actors. Effective incident response plans incorporate guidelines for preserving and collecting digital evidence in a forensically sound manner. This ensures that investigators have the necessary data to conduct a thorough analysis, aiding in the identification of vulnerabilities, tactics, techniques, and procedures (TTPs) employed by attackers. The insights gained from forensic analysis inform organizations on how to enhance their security posture and resilience against future incidents.

The importance of continuous improvement and learning from incidents is emphasized by effective incident response plans. Post-incident reviews, also known as after-action reviews or lessons learned sessions, allow organizations to assess the effectiveness of their response efforts and identify areas for improvement. By systematically analyzing each security incident, organizations can refine their incident response plans, update procedures, and enhance the skills of their incident response teams. This continuous improvement cycle is critical for staying ahead of evolving threats, adapting to new attack vectors, and ensuring that the incident response capability remains robust and effective over time.

Incident response plans contribute to organizational resilience by fostering a proactive and adaptive cybersecurity posture. The ability to respond swiftly and effectively to security incidents enhances an organization's capacity to withstand and recover from cyber threats. This resilience is particularly important in the face of advanced and persistent adversaries who continually evolve their tactics. Effective incident response plans empower organizations to learn from each incident, adapt their defenses, and build a culture of security awareness and preparedness. In doing so, organizations can minimize the impact of incidents, protect their reputation, and demonstrate a commitment to safeguarding the interests of their stakeholders.

The role of incident response plans in mitigating financial and reputational damage cannot be overstated. Security incidents, if not handled effectively, can result in significant financial losses, legal liabilities, and damage to an organization's reputation. The costs associated with a data breach, including legal fees, regulatory fines, and expenses related to remediation and recovery, can be substantial. Moreover, the loss of customer trust and confidence can have long-term consequences for the organization's brand. Effective incident response plans are instrumental in containing the impact of incidents, reducing the associated costs, and demonstrating to customers and partners that the organization is capable of responding to and recovering from security challenges.

The regulatory landscape emphasizes the importance of incident response plans as a key component of a comprehensive cybersecurity program. Many industries and regions have implemented data protection regulations that mandate organizations to have robust incident response capabilities. Compliance with these regulations requires organizations to not only develop incident response plans but also regularly test and update them. Regulatory authorities often assess an organization's incident response preparedness in the event of a security incident, and non-compliance may result in severe penalties. As such, incident response plans are not just best practices; they are essential components of regulatory compliance and risk management.

The collaboration and coordination fostered by incident response plans extend beyond the organization itself. Effective incident response plans facilitate collaboration with external entities, including other organizations, industry groups, and law enforcement agencies. The sharing of threat intelligence, indicators of compromise, and insights gained from incident response efforts enhances the collective defense against cyber threats. Additionally, collaboration with law enforcement can aid in the investigation and attribution of cybercriminal activities, contributing to the broader effort to combat cybercrime. Incident response plans that include provisions for external collaboration strengthen the overall cybersecurity ecosystem and contribute to a more resilient and secure digital landscape.

In conclusion, the importance of effective incident response plans in cybersecurity is multifaceted, encompassing the need for structured processes, rapid detection and containment, clear communication, legal compliance, forensic analysis, continuous improvement, organizational resilience, financial protection, regulatory compliance, and external collaboration. These plans serve as a linchpin in an organization's ability to navigate the complexities of the modern threat landscape and respond effectively to security incidents. As cyber threats continue to evolve, incident response plans remain a foundational element of cybersecurity resilience, enabling organizations to safeguard their assets, maintain stakeholder trust, and demonstrate a commitment to proactive and effective cybersecurity practices.

Explore the concept of cyber hygiene and its role in preventing cyber attacks.

The concept of cyber hygiene is a fundamental and proactive approach to maintaining a secure and resilient digital environment. Rooted in the analogy of personal hygiene that emphasizes the routine practices individuals adopt to preserve their health, cyber hygiene entails a set of habitual behaviors and practices aimed at safeguarding digital systems and data from cyber threats. At its core, cyber hygiene is about instilling a culture of security consciousness, promoting awareness, and fostering responsible behaviors among individuals, organizations, and society at large. The significance of cyber hygiene lies in its role as a foundational element in the prevention of cyber attacks, mitigating vulnerabilities, and minimizing the risk of security incidents.

One of the central tenets of cyber hygiene involves the regular and meticulous updating of software and operating systems. Software vulnerabilities are a common entry point for cybercriminals, and maintaining up-to-date systems is an essential practice in mitigating these risks. Regular software updates, patches, and security fixes issued by software vendors address known vulnerabilities and bolster the overall resilience of digital systems. Neglecting these updates leaves systems exposed to exploitation by cyber attackers who often exploit unpatched software as a means of unauthorized access, data theft, or the deployment of malicious payloads. Thus, the routine application of updates is a fundamental cyber hygiene practice that serves as a first line of defense against a wide range of cyber threats.

Password management is another core aspect of cyber hygiene that plays a pivotal role in preventing unauthorized access and data breaches. The use of strong, unique passwords for each account, coupled with regular password changes, is essential in thwarting common cyber attack methods such as brute-force attacks and credential stuffing. Cyber hygiene practices related to password management also include the avoidance of easily guessable passwords, the use of multi-factor authentication (MFA), and refraining from the reuse of passwords across multiple accounts. By cultivating strong password habits, individuals and organizations can significantly reduce the risk of unauthorized access and protect sensitive information from compromise.

In the context of cyber hygiene, the awareness and education of users emerge as critical components in preventing cyber attacks. Training programs that focus on cybersecurity awareness equip individuals with the knowledge and skills to recognize phishing attempts, social engineering tactics, and other common cyber threats.

Users who are educated about the risks of clicking on suspicious links, sharing sensitive information, or falling victim to scams contribute to a more secure digital environment. Cyber hygiene practices extend to cultivating a skeptical mindset among users, promoting a healthy level of caution when interacting with emails, websites, and digital communications. Through ongoing education and awareness initiatives, organizations can empower users to be active participants in their own cyber defense.

The judicious use of antivirus and anti-malware solutions constitutes a fundamental aspect of cyber hygiene. These security tools serve as a protective barrier against a myriad of malicious software, including viruses, worms, Trojans, and ransomware. Regular scans, updates, and real-time monitoring provided by antivirus solutions contribute to the early detection and removal of malware, minimizing the potential damage it can inflict on systems and data. Cyber hygiene practices in this context involve not only the installation of reputable security software but also the regular updating of virus definitions and the performance of comprehensive system scans. Proactive defense against malware is a crucial element of cyber hygiene, preventing infections that could lead to data loss, system disruptions, or compromise of sensitive information.

The practice of secure web browsing is integral to cyber hygiene, considering the prevalence of web-based threats and malicious activities. Cyber hygiene in the context of web browsing includes exercising caution when visiting unfamiliar websites, avoiding clicking on suspicious links, and refraining from downloading files from untrusted sources. The use of secure and encrypted connections (HTTPS) is emphasized as part of web browsing hygiene to protect against man-in-the-middle attacks and eavesdropping. Additionally, the regular clearing of browser caches and cookies contributes to a more secure browsing experience by minimizing the exposure of sensitive information. By instilling secure browsing habits, individuals and organizations fortify their defenses against a range of web-based threats, including phishing, drive-by downloads, and other online attacks.

Data backup and recovery practices are integral components of cyber hygiene, providing a failsafe mechanism in the event of data loss or ransomware attacks. Regular and automated backups of critical data ensure that organizations can quickly restore their systems to a pre-incident state, reducing downtime and mitigating the impact of cyber attacks. Cyber hygiene practices related to data backup involve the implementation of robust backup policies, including the frequency of backups, the verification of backup integrity, and the secure storage of backup copies. The ability to recover from data loss or ransomware incidents is contingent on the effectiveness and regularity of backup practices, emphasizing the proactive nature of cyber hygiene in preserving the integrity and availability of data.

Endpoint security measures, such as firewalls and intrusion detection systems, are key components of cyber hygiene, acting as a protective barrier between internal systems and external threats. Cyber hygiene practices in this context include configuring firewalls to restrict unauthorized access, monitoring network traffic for suspicious activities, and promptly addressing any detected anomalies. Additionally, the use of virtual private networks (VPNs) and encryption technologies enhances the security of data transmitted over networks, safeguarding against eavesdropping and man-in-the-middle attacks. The integration of endpoint security measures within a broader cyber hygiene framework reinforces the defense-in-depth approach, fortifying the perimeter and minimizing the risk of unauthorized access and data exfiltration.

Mobile device security is an essential facet of cyber hygiene, given the ubiquity of smartphones and tablets in both personal and professional settings. Cyber hygiene practices for mobile devices encompass the use of strong passcodes or biometric authentication, regular software updates, and the installation of security applications. Individuals and organizations must exercise caution when downloading apps, ensuring they originate from reputable sources and have undergone security vetting. The implementation of mobile device management (MDM) solutions further enhances cyber hygiene, allowing organizations to enforce security policies, remotely wipe devices in case of loss or theft, and monitor for potential security threats. By extending cyber hygiene principles to mobile devices, users can mitigate the risks associated with mobile-specific threats and protect sensitive information stored on these devices.

The secure configuration of systems and networks is a foundational cyber hygiene practice that involves minimizing unnecessary services, closing unused ports, and implementing the principle of least privilege. Cyber hygiene practices in this domain include conducting regular security audits and vulnerability assessments to identify and remediate configuration weaknesses. Secure configuration practices also extend to the timely removal of unnecessary software or services, reducing the attack surface and potential points of exploitation. By adhering to secure configuration principles, organizations bolster their cyber hygiene posture, creating a more resilient infrastructure that is less susceptible to exploitation and unauthorized access.

Incident response planning is an integral component of cyber hygiene, addressing the need for a structured and well-coordinated approach to handling security incidents. Cyber hygiene practices related to incident response involve the development of incident response plans, the identification of key stakeholders, and the establishment of communication protocols. Regular testing and simulation exercises ensure the readiness of incident response teams, allowing organizations to refine their response strategies and identify areas for improvement. The integration of incident response practices within the broader cyber hygiene framework enables organizations to respond effectively to security incidents, minimizing the impact on systems, data, and overall business operations.

The adoption of a risk management mindset is inherent in the concept of cyber hygiene, emphasizing the ongoing assessment and mitigation of cybersecurity risks. Cyber hygiene practices involve conducting risk assessments to identify potential threats, vulnerabilities, and their associated impacts. Risk management extends to the prioritization of security controls and measures based on the level of risk they address. By aligning cyber hygiene practices with risk management principles, organizations can focus their efforts on addressing the most critical and impactful risks, ensuring a targeted and effective approach to cybersecurity. This risk-aware mindset is essential for adapting cyber hygiene practices to the evolving threat landscape and the dynamic nature of digital ecosystems.

The role of cyber hygiene in the prevention of cyber attacks extends beyond individual and organizational practices to broader societal considerations. Public awareness campaigns, educational initiatives, and collaborative efforts within the cybersecurity community contribute to a culture of cyber hygiene at the societal level. By fostering a collective commitment to responsible and secure digital practices, society can create a more resilient and secure digital environment. Governments, industry associations, and educational institutions play a crucial role in promoting cyber hygiene awareness, providing resources, and establishing frameworks that facilitate the adoption of secure practices across diverse sectors of society.

In conclusion, the concept of cyber hygiene embodies a comprehensive and proactive approach to preventing cyber attacks. From the routine application of software updates to secure web browsing habits, password management, data backup practices, and incident response planning, cyber hygiene encompasses a broad spectrum of habits and practices. Its role in preventing cyber attacks extends from individual users to organizations and society as a whole, emphasizing the collective responsibility to cultivate a secure digital environment. The dynamic and ever-evolving nature of the cyber threat landscape underscores the importance of cyber hygiene as a foundational element in the ongoing effort to safeguard systems, data, and critical infrastructure against a diverse range of cyber threats.

Discuss the importance of information sharing and collaboration among cybersecurity professionals.

The importance of information sharing and collaboration among cybersecurity professionals cannot be overstated in the dynamic and evolving landscape of cyber threats. Cybersecurity, as a field, faces an ever-expanding array of sophisticated adversaries and rapidly changing attack vectors. In this context, effective information sharing serves as a linchpin for enhancing collective defense, threat intelligence, incident response capabilities, and the overall resilience of organizations and the broader cybersecurity community. Collaboration fosters a proactive and adaptive ecosystem that empowers professionals to stay ahead of emerging threats, respond swiftly to incidents, and collectively strengthen the global cybersecurity posture.

One of the primary benefits of information sharing in the cybersecurity domain is the ability to pool collective knowledge and experiences to identify emerging threats and vulnerabilities. By sharing insights into the tactics, techniques, and procedures (TTPs) employed by cyber adversaries, professionals can build a more comprehensive understanding of the evolving threat landscape. This collaborative intelligence gathering allows organizations and cybersecurity practitioners to proactively adapt their defenses, prioritize mitigation strategies, and enhance their overall security posture. In essence, information sharing creates a force multiplier effect, leveraging the collective expertise of the cybersecurity community to stay ahead of the curve.

Threat intelligence sharing, a subset of information sharing, plays a pivotal role in bolstering the capabilities of cybersecurity professionals. Threat intelligence encompasses actionable information about potential and current cyber threats, including indicators of compromise (IoCs), malware signatures, and attack patterns. When shared collaboratively, threat intelligence provides early warnings and insights that enable organizations to fortify their defenses. This shared intelligence helps cybersecurity professionals to anticipate, detect, and respond to threats more effectively, reducing the dwell time of adversaries within networks and minimizing the potential impact of cyber attacks.

In the realm of incident response, collaboration and information sharing are indispensable components of an effective defense strategy. During a security incident, time is of the essence, and rapid response is critical. By sharing information about ongoing incidents, indicators of compromise, and forensic insights, cybersecurity professionals can collaborate to coordinate a swift and targeted response. This collaborative approach enables organizations to leverage the experiences and expertise of others who may have encountered similar incidents, accelerating the resolution process and minimizing the impact on affected systems and data.

Information sharing extends beyond specific incidents to include broader insights into threat actors, campaigns, and attack methodologies. By understanding the motivations, tactics, and infrastructure of threat actors, cybersecurity professionals can develop more robust defenses and strategies to counteract malicious activities. This collective knowledge helps to build a proactive defense posture that anticipates and mitigates potential threats before they materialize. In essence, information sharing transforms isolated incidents into valuable learning opportunities, contributing to the continuous improvement and evolution of cybersecurity practices.

The collaborative sharing of best practices and lessons learned is a cornerstone of professional development within the cybersecurity community. As professionals encounter and overcome various challenges, sharing their experiences contributes to a collective body of knowledge that benefits the entire community. This collaborative learning environment allows practitioners to stay abreast of emerging technologies, methodologies, and defensive strategies. It also fosters a culture of continuous improvement, where cybersecurity professionals are encouraged to adapt and refine their approaches based on the shared insights and experiences of their peers.

Cross-sector collaboration is particularly vital in the realm of cybersecurity, where interconnectedness is pervasive across industries. Threat actors often target vulnerabilities that transcend sector boundaries, and their tactics can be replicated across diverse environments. Collaborative efforts that span different industries enable the identification of sector-agnostic threats and the development of more comprehensive and effective defense strategies. Forums, working groups, and collaborative initiatives that bring together professionals from various sectors create a synergistic environment where shared insights contribute to a more resilient and interconnected cybersecurity ecosystem.

The sharing of threat intelligence and incident data becomes even more critical in the context of nation-state cyber threats and geopolitical cyber activities. Nation-state actors often operate with significant resources and employ advanced techniques that can have global implications. Collaborative efforts at the national and international levels allow cybersecurity professionals to pool their resources, share threat intelligence, and collectively respond to state-sponsored cyber threats. Such collaboration enhances the ability of the global cybersecurity community to attribute attacks, apply diplomatic pressure, and implement coordinated responses against malicious actors that operate across borders.

Public-private partnerships represent a crucial avenue for information sharing and collaboration in cybersecurity. Private sector organizations often possess valuable threat intelligence and incident data, while government agencies can provide broader contextual information and contribute to a more comprehensive understanding of the threat landscape. Collaborative initiatives that facilitate the sharing of information between the public and private sectors contribute to a more robust cybersecurity ecosystem. These partnerships enhance the ability to detect, respond to, and mitigate cyber threats, leveraging the strengths of both sectors for the greater good of national and global cybersecurity.

Information sharing also plays a pivotal role in addressing the cybersecurity skills gap. By sharing knowledge, resources, and best practices, experienced professionals can mentor and guide those newer to the field. This collaborative mentoring not only accelerates the learning curve for aspiring cybersecurity professionals but also fosters a culture of knowledge transfer and skill development within the community. Collaborative training programs, workshops, and educational initiatives contribute to the cultivation of a diverse and skilled cybersecurity workforce equipped to tackle the challenges of the digital age.

The importance of information sharing and collaboration is further underscored by the rise of threat-sharing platforms and Information Sharing and Analysis Centers (ISACs). These platforms provide dedicated spaces where organizations within specific industries or regions can share anonymized threat intelligence, incident reports, and defensive strategies. ISACs serve as trusted forums where participants can openly discuss and collaboratively address cybersecurity challenges specific to their sectors. The establishment of such collaborative platforms reflects a growing recognition of the value that collective insights and experiences bring to enhancing the cybersecurity resilience of participating organizations.

Legal and regulatory frameworks also play a role in shaping the landscape of information sharing and collaboration in cybersecurity. Legislation that encourages or mandates the sharing of cybersecurity information between organizations and with government agencies aims to create a more cooperative and transparent environment. By providing legal protections for organizations that share threat intelligence, these frameworks seek to overcome potential barriers to collaboration, such as concerns about liability or competitive disadvantage. The legal framework, when supportive, fosters a climate where organizations are more willing to actively engage in information sharing initiatives.

Challenges and barriers to effective information sharing and collaboration in cybersecurity still exist and need to be addressed. Concerns related to privacy, data protection, and competitive advantage can inhibit the free flow of information. Striking a balance between transparency and safeguarding sensitive information is crucial. Establishing trust among participants is equally important, as organizations need assurance that shared information will be handled responsibly and ethically. Additionally, technical challenges related to interoperability and standardization of data formats can impact the seamless exchange of threat intelligence. Overcoming these challenges requires ongoing dialogue, the development of best practices, and a commitment to a collaborative cybersecurity culture.

In conclusion, the importance of information sharing and collaboration among cybersecurity professionals is paramount for building a resilient and effective defense against the myriad of cyber threats. From threat intelligence sharing and incident response coordination to collaborative learning, cross-sector partnerships, and public-private initiatives, the impact of collaboration reverberates throughout the cybersecurity ecosystem. The collective knowledge and experiences shared within the cybersecurity community not only empower individual organizations but contribute to the overall strength and adaptability of the global cybersecurity posture. In an era where cyber threats transcend borders and industries, a collaborative approach becomes not just a best practice but an essential strategy for confronting the dynamic challenges of the digital age.

Explore initiatives that promote global cooperation against cyber threats.

Initiatives promoting global cooperation against cyber threats are critical in addressing the complex and interconnected challenges presented by the evolving cyber landscape. Recognizing the transnational nature of cyber threats, numerous international efforts have emerged to foster collaboration, information sharing, and coordinated responses among nations, private sector entities, and other stakeholders. One of the prominent initiatives is the Budapest Convention on Cybercrime, also known as the Council of Europe Convention on Cybercrime. This international treaty, adopted in 2001, aims to harmonize national laws, improve investigative techniques, and facilitate international cooperation in combating cybercrime. The Budapest Convention promotes a unified legal framework and encourages nations to work together to address cyber threats, enhance digital forensics capabilities, and facilitate the extradition of cybercriminals across borders.

The United Nations (UN) has played a significant role in promoting global cooperation against cyber threats through various initiatives. The UN Group of Governmental Experts (GGE) on Developments in the Field of Information and Telecommunications in the Context of International Security has been instrumental in providing a forum for member states to discuss and develop norms, rules, and principles for responsible state behavior in cyberspace. The GGE's work contributes to building consensus on issues such as the applicability of international law to cyberspace, confidence-building measures, and the prevention of conflicts stemming from cyber activities. The UN's efforts underscore the importance of diplomatic dialogue and the development of norms to prevent the escalation of cyber threats into larger geopolitical conflicts.

Another notable initiative is the Paris Call for Trust and Security in Cyberspace, launched in 2018 under the auspices of the French government. The Paris Call brings together governments, the private sector, and civil society to commit to principles aimed at securing cyberspace and preventing malicious cyber activities. Signatories pledge to work together to prevent and recover from cyber incidents, protect against intellectual property theft, and promote responsible behavior in cyberspace. The Paris Call reflects a multi-stakeholder approach, emphasizing the shared responsibility of governments, industry, and civil society in addressing cyber threats on a global scale.

The Global Forum on Cyber Expertise (GFCE) is another initiative fostering international collaboration in the field of cybersecurity. The GFCE, launched in 2015, provides a platform for countries, organizations, and experts to share knowledge, best practices, and capacity-building efforts. By facilitating cooperation on cyber capacity-building, the GFCE aims to enhance the capabilities of countries to prevent, respond to, and recover from cyber threats. The GFCE's inclusive approach recognizes the diverse challenges faced by nations and encourages the exchange of expertise to bridge gaps in cybersecurity capabilities around the world.

The Organization for Security and Co-operation in Europe (OSCE) has been active in promoting cybersecurity norms and confidence-building measures among its participating states. The OSCE recognizes the interconnectedness of security in the physical and cyber domains and emphasizes the importance of building trust among nations. The OSCE's efforts include promoting the implementation of voluntary norms of responsible state behavior in cyberspace, encouraging information exchange, and fostering dialogue on cybersecurity policies. Through its inclusive approach, the OSCE contributes to the development of a common understanding of norms that promote stability and security in cyberspace.

The Cybersecurity Tech Accord represents an industry-driven initiative aimed at promoting global cooperation among technology companies to protect users and customers from cyber threats. Launched in 2018, the accord encourages signatories to commit to key principles, including protecting users and customers from cyberattacks, avoiding the assistance of cyberattacks, and empowering users and developers to strengthen cybersecurity. The collaboration among major technology companies through the Cybersecurity Tech Accord demonstrates the industry's commitment to collective action in addressing common threats and challenges.

Interpol, the International Criminal Police Organization, plays a crucial role in facilitating international police cooperation against cybercrime. Interpol's Global Complex for Innovation (IGCI) serves as a hub for coordinating efforts to combat cyber threats and provides support to member countries in conducting cybercrime investigations. Interpol's initiatives include the establishment of a secure global police communications platform, the facilitation of joint operations, and the provision of capacity-building programs to enhance the skills of law enforcement agencies in tackling cybercrime. By leveraging its global network of member countries, Interpol contributes to strengthening international collaboration in the fight against cyber threats.

The Financial Action Task Force (FATF), an intergovernmental organization focused on combating money laundering and terrorist financing, recognizes the nexus between financial crimes and cyber threats. In response to the evolving landscape, FATF has expanded its focus to include the regulation and oversight of virtual assets and cryptocurrencies. The organization provides guidance to countries on addressing the risks associated with virtual assets, ensuring that the global financial system is equipped to handle the challenges posed by cyber-related financial crimes.

The United States has been active in fostering international collaboration against cyber threats through various initiatives. The U.S. Department of State's Bureau of International Security and Nonproliferation leads efforts to engage with international partners on cyber diplomacy. Through bilateral and multilateral engagements, the United States seeks to promote a secure and open cyberspace, advance responsible state behavior, and address shared challenges in cyberspace. The U.S. Cyber Command, as part of the Department of Defense, also plays a role in defending U.S. interests in cyberspace and collaborating with allies and partners to enhance collective cybersecurity.

The Global Commission on the Stability of Cyberspace (GCSC) is an independent initiative that brings together experts from various fields, including government, industry, and academia, to develop norms and policies aimed at enhancing the stability and security of cyberspace. The GCSC's work focuses on addressing the issue of state-sponsored and non-state actors engaging in cyber activities that may undermine the stability and integrity of the internet. By developing a framework of norms and policies, the GCSC contributes to global efforts to establish rules for responsible behavior in cyberspace.

The North Atlantic Treaty Organization (NATO) has recognized the significance of cyberspace as a domain of operations and has taken steps to strengthen its cyber defense capabilities. NATO's Cooperative Cyber Defence Centre of Excellence (CCDCOE) serves as a hub for research, training, and exercises in the field of cybersecurity. NATO's cyber defense policy emphasizes collective defense and the integration of cyber capabilities into the alliance's overall defense posture. By enhancing its cyber resilience, NATO contributes to deterring and responding to cyber threats that may impact the security of its member countries.

The Global Cybersecurity Alliance (GCA), a collaborative initiative between the World Economic Forum (WEF) and leading cybersecurity companies, aims to counter systemic cyber risks and improve the security and resilience of digital ecosystems. The GCA focuses on developing practical tools and initiatives that address key cybersecurity challenges, with an emphasis on scalability and global impact. Through public-private collaboration, the GCA seeks to drive collective action against cyber threats, recognizing the need for a coordinated and inclusive approach to address the challenges posed by malicious actors in cyberspace.

The ASEAN CERT Incident Drill (ACID) is an initiative within the Association of Southeast Asian Nations (ASEAN) that promotes regional cooperation in incident response and cybersecurity capacity-building. ACID brings together computer emergency response teams (CERTs) from ASEAN member states to participate in simulated cyber attack scenarios. The drill enhances the coordination and communication capabilities of participating countries, fostering a collaborative approach to addressing cyber threats in the Southeast Asian region.

The European Union Agency for Cybersecurity (ENISA) plays a key role in promoting collaboration and enhancing cybersecurity capabilities across the European Union (EU). ENISA supports member states in developing their national cybersecurity strategies, facilitates information sharing and cooperation, and provides expertise to strengthen the EU's overall cybersecurity posture. The agency's work encompasses a wide range of activities, including threat intelligence sharing, capacity-building, and the development of cybersecurity standards and best practices.

The World Economic Forum's Centre for Cybersecurity serves as a platform for public-private collaboration on global cybersecurity challenges. The Centre brings together leaders from government, business, academia, and civil society to develop and implement cybersecurity solutions. The Centre's initiatives include the Partnering for Cyber Resilience program, which encourages organizations to adopt cybersecurity principles and collaborate in addressing shared risks. By fostering cross-sector collaboration, the World Economic Forum contributes to building a more secure and resilient global digital ecosystem.

In conclusion, initiatives that promote global cooperation against cyber threats are essential in addressing the multifaceted challenges presented by the dynamic and interconnected nature of cyberspace. From international treaties and diplomatic engagements to industry-driven collaborations, the initiatives outlined above highlight the diverse and concerted efforts to enhance cybersecurity on a global scale. As cyber threats continue to evolve and transcend borders, the need for sustained and inclusive cooperation becomes increasingly critical to ensuring the security and stability of the digital world. The success of these initiatives lies in their ability to foster trust, build consensus, and facilitate meaningful collaboration among diverse stakeholders with a shared commitment to a secure and resilient cyberspace.

Chapter 8: Ethical Hacking and Cybersecurity Defense

Define ethical hacking and its role in cybersecurity defense.

Ethical hacking, often referred to as penetration testing or white-hat hacking, is a cybersecurity practice where skilled professionals, known as ethical hackers, simulate cyber attacks on computer systems, networks, applications, and other digital assets to identify vulnerabilities and weaknesses. The primary goal of ethical hacking is to proactively discover and address security flaws before malicious hackers can exploit them. Ethical hackers use the same tools, techniques, and methodologies employed by malicious hackers but with explicit authorization and adherence to a strict code of ethics. The role of ethical hacking in cybersecurity defense is multifaceted, encompassing proactive risk management, vulnerability assessment, incident prevention, and the continuous improvement of security postures.

Ethical hacking serves as a proactive and preventive measure to identify and remediate vulnerabilities before they can be exploited by malicious actors. By mimicking the tactics of potential adversaries, ethical hackers help organizations identify weaknesses in their defenses, ranging from software vulnerabilities and misconfigurations to inadequate access controls. The insights gained from ethical hacking engagements enable organizations to patch, mitigate, or otherwise address these vulnerabilities, reducing the attack surface and enhancing overall cybersecurity resilience. The proactive nature of ethical hacking aligns with the principle of "defense in depth," where multiple layers of security are implemented to thwart potential threats.

Vulnerability assessment is a key component of ethical hacking, involving the systematic identification, classification, and prioritization of potential weaknesses in a system or network. Ethical hackers employ a combination of automated tools and manual testing to simulate real-world attack scenarios, ensuring a comprehensive evaluation of an organization's security posture. Through vulnerability assessment, organizations gain a detailed understanding of their susceptibility to various cyber threats and can prioritize remediation efforts based on the severity and potential impact of identified vulnerabilities. This risk-based approach allows for the allocation of resources to address the most critical security issues first, optimizing the organization's overall cybersecurity strategy.

The role of ethical hacking extends to the identification and testing of specific security controls and mechanisms, such as firewalls, intrusion detection systems, and encryption protocols. By subjecting these controls to simulated attacks, ethical hackers evaluate their effectiveness in detecting and mitigating threats. This process helps organizations assess the robustness of their security infrastructure and fine-tune configurations to ensure optimal protection. Ethical hackers may also examine the resilience of incident response mechanisms, evaluating how well an organization can detect, contain, and respond to security incidents. This holistic evaluation contributes to the creation of a more robust and adaptive cybersecurity defense.

Ethical hacking plays a crucial role in securing web applications, which are frequent targets for cyber attacks. Web application vulnerabilities, such as SQL injection, cross-site scripting (XSS), and insecure authentication mechanisms, can expose sensitive data and compromise the integrity of online services. Ethical hackers assess the security of web applications by attempting to exploit these vulnerabilities in a controlled environment. This process helps organizations identify and rectify coding errors, configuration issues, and design flaws that could be leveraged by malicious hackers. As web applications continue to be integral to business operations, ethical hacking serves as a proactive measure to ensure their resilience against evolving cyber threats.

The continuous evolution of technology and the dynamic nature of cyber threats necessitate ongoing testing and assessment of an organization's cybersecurity defenses. Ethical hacking, as a recurring practice, provides organizations with the means to adapt to emerging threats and evolving attack vectors. Regularly scheduled ethical hacking engagements, often conducted as part of a broader cybersecurity strategy, help organizations stay ahead of potential adversaries by identifying and addressing vulnerabilities in a timely manner. This proactive approach aligns with the principle of continuous improvement, recognizing that cybersecurity is an ongoing process that requires vigilance and adaptability to effectively mitigate risks.

Ethical hacking also contributes to regulatory compliance by assisting organizations in meeting the security requirements outlined in various industry standards and data protection regulations. Many regulatory frameworks mandate regular security assessments, and ethical hacking serves as a valuable tool for demonstrating compliance. By identifying and addressing vulnerabilities, organizations can demonstrate their commitment to safeguarding sensitive information and maintaining the confidentiality, integrity, and availability of data. Ethical hacking engagements provide organizations with documented evidence of their cybersecurity efforts, aiding in regulatory audits and ensuring adherence to legal and industry-specific requirements.

The education and awareness aspects of ethical hacking are integral to its role in cybersecurity defense. Ethical hackers often collaborate with internal teams, including developers, system administrators, and security professionals, to share insights and knowledge gained during assessments. This collaborative approach fosters a culture of security awareness within organizations, empowering personnel to understand the implications of security decisions and adhere to best practices. Ethical hacking engagements also serve as valuable training opportunities, allowing organizations to enhance the skills of their cybersecurity teams and build internal expertise in identifying and addressing security vulnerabilities.

Ethical hacking goes beyond technical assessments and also encompasses social engineering testing. Social engineering involves manipulating individuals to divulge sensitive information, such as passwords or confidential data. Ethical hackers may conduct simulated phishing attacks, impersonate employees, or attempt to exploit human factors to assess an organization's susceptibility to social engineering tactics. By identifying weaknesses in employee awareness and training, organizations can implement measures to educate staff about the risks associated with social engineering and reinforce a security-conscious culture.

The role of ethical hacking extends to the assessment of emerging technologies, including the Internet of Things (IoT), cloud computing, and artificial intelligence. As these technologies become integral to modern business operations, they introduce new attack surfaces and potential vulnerabilities. Ethical hackers play a crucial role in assessing the security of IoT devices, cloud environments, and AI systems, ensuring that organizations can harness the benefits of these technologies without compromising security. The proactive evaluation of emerging technologies aligns with the principle of anticipating and mitigating risks associated with the adoption of innovative solutions.

Ethical hacking contributes to incident prevention by identifying vulnerabilities and weaknesses that could be exploited by malicious actors. The proactive nature of ethical hacking, combined with timely remediation efforts, helps organizations preemptively close security gaps, reducing the likelihood of successful cyber attacks. By addressing vulnerabilities before they can be exploited, ethical hacking serves as a strategic component in an organization's overall risk management strategy, minimizing the potential impact of security incidents and enhancing the organization's cybersecurity posture.

The transparency and accountability inherent in ethical hacking contribute to building trust with stakeholders, including customers, partners, and regulatory bodies. Organizations that engage in ethical hacking demonstrate a commitment to cybersecurity and a willingness to invest in proactive measures to protect sensitive information. Ethical hacking reports, detailing the findings and recommendations from assessments, provide stakeholders with transparency into the organization's security efforts and serve as a basis for ongoing dialogue about cybersecurity risk management.

Ethical hacking also plays a critical role in validating the effectiveness of security awareness training programs. By simulating real-world attack scenarios, ethical hackers assess how well employees recognize and respond to phishing attempts, social engineering tactics, and other security threats. This validation process enables organizations to tailor their training programs to address specific areas of weakness and enhance the overall security awareness of personnel. Ethical hacking, in this context, serves as a valuable tool for organizations seeking to strengthen the human element of their cybersecurity defenses.

In conclusion, ethical hacking occupies a central role in cybersecurity defense by serving as a proactive and preventive measure to identify and address vulnerabilities before they can be exploited by malicious actors. The multifaceted contributions of ethical hacking include vulnerability assessment, security control testing, web application security, continuous improvement, regulatory compliance, education and awareness, social engineering testing, and the evaluation of emerging technologies. The ethical hacking process aligns with the principles of defense in depth, continuous improvement, and risk management, contributing to the overall resilience of organizations in the face of evolving cyber threats. As a transparent and accountable practice, ethical hacking fosters a culture of security awareness and trust, positioning organizations to adapt and respond effectively to the dynamic challenges of the cybersecurity landscape.

Discuss the ethical hacker's mission to identify and patch vulnerabilities.

The ethical hacker's mission to identify and patch vulnerabilities is a critical and proactive endeavor within the realm of cybersecurity. Rooted in the fundamental principle of fortifying digital defenses, ethical hackers, also known as white-hat hackers, embark on a mission to systematically assess and shore up the security posture of computer systems, networks, applications, and other digital assets. This mission is underpinned by a commitment to safeguarding sensitive information, protecting against cyber threats, and ensuring the integrity, confidentiality, and availability of data. The ethical hacker's journey unfolds through a series of strategic steps, encompassing reconnaissance, vulnerability identification, exploitation simulation, and ultimately, the crucial task of patching or mitigating the identified weaknesses.

The mission begins with reconnaissance, a phase where ethical hackers gather information about the target system or network. This mimics the initial stages of a potential cyber attack, where adversaries seek to understand the target's infrastructure, technologies, and potential points of entry. Ethical hackers leverage both passive and active reconnaissance techniques, scanning for publicly available information, conducting network discovery, and probing for open ports. This information forms the foundation for subsequent phases of the mission, guiding the ethical hacker in identifying potential vulnerabilities specific to the target environment.

Vulnerability identification represents a pivotal aspect of the ethical hacker's mission. Through meticulous analysis and testing, ethical hackers aim to uncover weaknesses in the target's defenses. This involves employing a diverse array of tools and methodologies, ranging from automated scanning tools to manual testing procedures. Common vulnerabilities, such as software bugs, misconfigurations, weak access controls, and known security loopholes, become targets for ethical hackers to scrutinize. The mission involves a comprehensive examination of the target's attack surface, leaving no stone unturned in the quest to expose potential entry points for malicious actors.

Once vulnerabilities are identified, ethical hackers simulate the exploitation process to understand the extent of potential damage that could be inflicted by malicious actors. This simulation involves attempting to exploit the identified vulnerabilities in a controlled environment, mirroring the tactics that real-world attackers might employ. By doing so, ethical hackers gain insights into the severity of the vulnerabilities and their potential impact on the confidentiality, integrity, and availability of the target's data and systems. This phase not only validates the vulnerabilities discovered but also informs the ethical hacker's strategy for subsequent steps in the mission.

The ethical hacker's mission takes a crucial turn as they transition from exploration to action, moving beyond identification to the core task of patching or mitigating vulnerabilities. Patching involves the application of fixes, updates, or security measures designed to remediate the identified weaknesses. This step is not merely about pointing out flaws; it is about actively contributing to the enhancement of the target's cybersecurity defenses. Ethical hackers collaborate with the organization's IT and security teams to implement patches, configuration changes, and other measures aimed at closing the gaps that could be exploited by cyber adversaries. The ethical hacker's expertise becomes an integral part of the organization's proactive defense strategy, preventing potential security breaches.

The patching process is not a one-size-fits-all solution; instead, it requires a nuanced approach tailored to the specific vulnerabilities and the organization's operational context. Ethical hackers work closely with IT teams to prioritize vulnerabilities based on their severity and potential impact. This risk-based approach ensures that scarce resources are directed toward addressing the most critical security issues first. The mission involves not only technical acumen but also a keen understanding of the broader risk landscape, allowing ethical hackers to guide organizations in making informed decisions about where to allocate their efforts and resources for maximum impact.

Beyond the technical aspects, the ethical hacker's mission involves effective communication with stakeholders. Clear and concise reporting of findings, risks, and recommended remediation measures is a crucial part of the mission. Ethical hackers translate technical details into actionable insights for non-technical decision-makers, enabling organizations to make informed choices about risk tolerance and mitigation strategies. This communication aspect is essential for fostering a collaborative cybersecurity culture within the organization, where all stakeholders understand their role in maintaining a robust security posture.

The ethical hacker's mission is not confined to a one-time event but aligns with the principles of continuous improvement and ongoing vigilance. Cyber threats evolve, and new vulnerabilities may emerge over time. Ethical hackers advocate for a proactive and iterative approach to cybersecurity, encouraging organizations to engage in regular assessments and patching cycles. This iterative aspect of the mission acknowledges that cybersecurity is a dynamic and evolving discipline, requiring constant adaptation to stay ahead of emerging threats.

The ethical hacker's mission extends beyond individual systems and networks to include the security of web applications, a prominent target for cyber attacks. Web applications often handle sensitive data, making them attractive targets for malicious actors. Ethical hackers assess the security of web applications by scrutinizing code, testing for common vulnerabilities such as SQL injection and cross-site scripting (XSS), and evaluating the effectiveness of authentication mechanisms. The mission involves not only identifying vulnerabilities but actively contributing to the development of secure coding practices and robust application security measures.

In the mission to identify and patch vulnerabilities, ethical hackers also delve into the realm of social engineering testing. This aspect acknowledges the human factor as a potential vulnerability in the cybersecurity landscape. Ethical hackers simulate social engineering tactics, such as phishing attacks or impersonation, to assess how well employees recognize and resist manipulative techniques. By addressing vulnerabilities in human behavior and awareness, ethical hackers contribute to the creation of a holistic cybersecurity defense that encompasses both technical and human-centric elements.

The ethical hacker's mission recognizes the critical role of education and awareness in cybersecurity. Beyond identifying and patching vulnerabilities, ethical hackers collaborate with organizations to implement effective training programs. These programs aim to enhance the cybersecurity awareness of employees, empowering them to make informed decisions and recognize potential security threats. The mission involves not only strengthening technical defenses but also building a resilient human firewall that acts as an additional layer of protection against cyber threats.

Ethical hackers often find themselves at the forefront of assessing emerging technologies, including the Internet of Things (IoT), cloud computing, and artificial intelligence. As organizations adopt innovative technologies to streamline operations, new attack surfaces and potential vulnerabilities emerge. The ethical hacker's mission extends to evaluating the security implications of these technologies, providing insights into how organizations can harness their benefits without compromising security. The proactive assessment of emerging technologies aligns with the mission's overarching goal of anticipating and mitigating risks associated with the evolving digital landscape.

In conclusion, the ethical hacker's mission to identify and patch vulnerabilities is a multifaceted and dynamic endeavor within the broader landscape of cybersecurity. From reconnaissance to vulnerability identification, exploitation simulation, and the crucial task of patching or mitigating weaknesses, ethical hackers contribute significantly to enhancing the security posture of organizations. The mission goes beyond technical proficiency, encompassing effective communication, risk-based prioritization, continuous improvement, social engineering testing, education, and the evaluation of emerging technologies. Ethical hackers embody the proactive spirit of cybersecurity, embodying a mission that not only identifies weaknesses but actively contributes to fortifying digital defenses in the face of evolving cyber threats.

Explore the shift in perception from hacking as a criminal act to ethical hacking as a valuable profession.

The evolution of hacking from a perceived criminal act to the recognition of ethical hacking as a valuable and legitimate profession reflects a transformative journey shaped by changing perspectives, technological advancements, and the imperative for robust cybersecurity measures in the digital age. Historically, hacking was synonymous with unauthorized intrusion into computer systems, often associated with malicious intent and criminal activities. The early pioneers of hacking were often motivated by curiosity, a desire to explore the capabilities of computer systems, and, in some cases, a rebellious spirit challenging established norms. However, as the digital landscape expanded and cyber threats became more sophisticated, the negative connotations of hacking intensified, leading to a perception of hackers as cybercriminals posing a serious threat to individuals, organizations, and even national security.

The shift in perception began to take shape as the consequences of malicious hacking became increasingly apparent. High-profile cyberattacks, data breaches, and the exploitation of vulnerabilities for financial gain or political motives highlighted the urgent need for a more proactive and ethical approach to cybersecurity. Organizations, facing the escalating challenge of defending against cyber threats, started to recognize that understanding the mindset and techniques of hackers could be instrumental in fortifying their defenses. This realization marked the emergence of ethical hacking as a constructive and invaluable profession within the broader field of cybersecurity.

Ethical hacking, also known as penetration testing or white-hat hacking, involves authorized and controlled attempts to simulate cyber attacks on systems, networks, and applications. The goal is to identify vulnerabilities and weaknesses before malicious hackers can exploit them for nefarious purposes. The recognition of ethical hacking as a valuable profession stems from its capacity to provide a proactive and preventative approach to cybersecurity. Ethical hackers, armed with a deep understanding of hacking techniques, work collaboratively with organizations to assess their security posture, identify potential risks, and recommend measures to strengthen defenses.

One of the pivotal factors in reshaping the perception of hacking was the realization that not all individuals with hacking skills were malicious actors. Ethical hackers demonstrated that the same technical acumen used by cybercriminals could be repurposed for positive and constructive purposes. The narrative began to shift from viewing hackers solely as adversaries to acknowledging them as allies in the ongoing battle against cyber threats. Ethical hacking positioned itself as a solution to the growing challenges posed by the evolving tactics of cybercriminals, offering organizations a proactive means to stay one step ahead in the ever-changing landscape of digital security.

As the demand for skilled cybersecurity professionals grew, ethical hacking emerged as a specialized and sought-after profession. Certifications such as Certified Ethical Hacker (CEH) gained prominence, providing standardized recognition of individuals possessing the skills and knowledge required for ethical hacking roles. Educational institutions and training programs started offering courses specifically tailored to ethical hacking, reflecting the industry's acknowledgment of the profession's significance. Ethical hackers became integral members of cybersecurity teams, contributing their expertise to vulnerability assessments, penetration testing, and the development of robust security strategies.

The collaboration between ethical hackers and organizations marked a paradigm shift, transforming the perception of hacking from a clandestine and potentially criminal activity to a legitimate and necessary practice within the cybersecurity domain. Recognizing the ethical hacker's role as a proactive defender rather than an adversary aligned with the broader industry shift toward a more holistic and preemptive cybersecurity approach. This transformation also underscored the ethical hacker's commitment to operating within legal and ethical boundaries, obtaining explicit authorization before conducting assessments and adhering to a strict code of conduct.

Another crucial aspect of reshaping perceptions was the ethical hacker's focus on constructive engagement with the broader cybersecurity community. Ethical hackers actively participated in information sharing, knowledge dissemination, and collaborative initiatives aimed at enhancing the overall cybersecurity posture. By contributing to the collective understanding of emerging threats, vulnerabilities, and countermeasures, ethical hackers fostered a sense of community resilience. This collaborative ethos not only strengthened the profession's legitimacy but also facilitated a cultural shift in which ethical hacking became synonymous with responsible and cooperative cybersecurity practices.

The emergence of bug bounty programs further reinforced the positive perception of ethical hacking. Organizations, recognizing the limitations of traditional security measures, began incentivizing ethical hackers to identify and report vulnerabilities by offering financial rewards, recognition, or other incentives. Bug bounty programs provided a structured and mutually beneficial framework for collaboration, allowing ethical hackers to leverage their skills in a transparent and constructive manner. This approach not only helped organizations fortify their defenses but also showcased the value of ethical hacking as a proactive and cost-effective security strategy.

The regulatory landscape also played a role in legitimizing ethical hacking. Recognizing the importance of cybersecurity in safeguarding sensitive information, regulatory authorities started acknowledging the role of ethical hacking in compliance frameworks. Industry-specific regulations and standards began to include provisions for regular security assessments, penetration testing, and vulnerability management, implicitly endorsing the proactive measures employed by ethical hackers. This alignment with regulatory requirements further contributed to the profession's acceptance and integration into mainstream cybersecurity practices.

The media's portrayal of hacking also underwent a transformation, reflecting the changing narrative surrounding ethical hacking. Rather than exclusively highlighting cybercrime and unauthorized intrusions, media outlets began to cover stories of ethical hackers making positive contributions to cybersecurity. Profiles of ethical hackers who played pivotal roles in identifying and mitigating critical vulnerabilities became more common, helping to dispel the negative stereotypes associated with hacking. This shift in media representation contributed to a more nuanced and informed public perception of hacking as a diverse field with both malicious and ethical dimensions.

The growing recognition of ethical hacking was not limited to the private sector; governmental and law enforcement entities also began to appreciate the value of ethical hackers in the broader context of national cybersecurity. Some governments initiated programs to recruit and train ethical hackers to enhance their cyber defense capabilities. Collaborative efforts between ethical hackers and law enforcement, such as coordinated vulnerability disclosure programs, provided a legal framework for responsible vulnerability reporting and further legitimized the profession.

The perception of hacking as a criminal act transformed into an understanding of ethical hacking as a valuable profession due to a combination of factors: the industry's need for proactive cybersecurity measures, the ethical hacker's commitment to operating within legal and ethical boundaries, the collaborative ethos within the cybersecurity community, bug bounty programs, regulatory recognition, media representation, and governmental acknowledgment. Ethical hacking has evolved from being viewed with suspicion to being embraced as an essential and constructive component of the cybersecurity landscape. As organizations continue to face evolving cyber threats, ethical hacking remains a cornerstone of their defense strategy, contributing to a more resilient and secure digital environment.

Discuss the ethical considerations of hacking for defensive purposes.

The ethical considerations surrounding hacking for defensive purposes are complex and multifaceted, requiring a nuanced examination of the principles, practices, and implications associated with this approach to cybersecurity. Hacking, traditionally perceived as a malicious activity, takes on a different ethical dimension when employed for defensive purposes. Defensive hacking involves the authorized and controlled exploration of computer systems, networks, and applications to identify vulnerabilities, weaknesses, and potential exploits. The ethical considerations revolve around issues such as transparency, consent, proportionality, accountability, and the broader impact on privacy, individual rights, and the digital ecosystem as a whole.

Transparency is a foundational ethical principle when engaging in hacking for defensive purposes. Organizations and individuals conducting defensive hacking activities must operate transparently, providing clear communication about the nature, scope, and objectives of their efforts. This transparency extends to obtaining informed consent from relevant stakeholders, including system owners, users, and any parties potentially affected by the defensive hacking activities. Transparency helps build trust and ensures that defensive hacking is conducted with the knowledge and understanding of those impacted, mitigating concerns about unauthorized intrusion or potential privacy violations.

Informed consent is a crucial aspect of ethical defensive hacking. Obtaining explicit permission from system owners and relevant stakeholders is essential to ensure that defensive hacking activities remain within legal and ethical boundaries. Informed consent acknowledges the rights of individuals and organizations to control access to their systems and data. Without proper consent, defensive hacking can inadvertently infringe on privacy rights and legal boundaries, raising ethical concerns about unauthorized access and potential misuse of information. Therefore, ethical defensive hacking requires a robust framework for obtaining and documenting informed consent from all relevant parties.

Proportionality is an ethical principle that emphasizes the necessity of defensive hacking measures being proportionate to the identified risks and vulnerabilities. Defensive hacking activities should be aligned with the severity of potential threats, avoiding unnecessary intrusiveness or disruption. The ethical hacker must carefully balance the need to identify and address vulnerabilities with the potential impact on the targeted systems and the broader digital environment. Overly aggressive or disproportionate defensive hacking measures may cause unintended harm, disrupt legitimate activities, and compromise the overall integrity of the digital ecosystem.

Accountability is a cornerstone of ethical defensive hacking. Those engaging in defensive hacking activities must be accountable for their actions, adhering to legal frameworks, industry standards, and ethical guidelines. Accountability involves taking responsibility for the consequences of defensive hacking, including any inadvertent impact on systems, data, or users. Ethical hackers should be transparent about their methods, report findings responsibly, and collaborate with relevant stakeholders to address and remediate identified vulnerabilities. The lack of accountability in defensive hacking practices can erode trust, undermine the credibility of security professionals, and lead to unintended negative consequences.

Respect for individual privacy is a paramount ethical consideration in defensive hacking. While the primary goal is to enhance cybersecurity by identifying and mitigating vulnerabilities, defensive hacking activities may involve accessing and analyzing sensitive information. Ethical hackers must prioritize the protection of privacy rights, ensuring that their actions are focused solely on security objectives and do not involve unnecessary intrusion into personal or confidential data. Safeguarding privacy requires ethical hackers to implement measures such as anonymization, data minimization, and secure handling of any information accessed during defensive hacking assessments.

The ethical considerations of defensive hacking extend to the potential collateral impact on third parties and the broader digital ecosystem. Defensive hacking activities may inadvertently affect systems, networks, or individuals not directly involved in the assessment. Ethical hackers must take precautions to minimize collateral damage, avoid disruption to critical services, and ensure that their actions do not have unintended consequences for unrelated parties. This ethical responsibility requires careful planning, risk assessment, and collaboration with relevant stakeholders to mitigate any potential negative impacts on the broader digital landscape.

Collaboration and information sharing are integral ethical considerations in defensive hacking. Ethical hackers often work in collaboration with organizations, industry peers, and the cybersecurity community to share insights, best practices, and threat intelligence. This collaborative approach contributes to a collective defense strategy, enhancing the overall resilience of the digital ecosystem. Ethical hackers should prioritize responsible disclosure, sharing findings with relevant stakeholders in a timely and transparent manner. By fostering a culture of collaboration, ethical defensive hacking becomes a collaborative effort to address shared cybersecurity challenges and protect against evolving threats.

The ethical considerations of defensive hacking also encompass the responsible handling of discovered vulnerabilities. Ethical hackers must follow established disclosure processes, providing organizations with adequate time to address and remediate identified vulnerabilities before making findings public. Responsible disclosure balances the need for transparency with the potential risks associated with immediate public disclosure, allowing organizations to implement patches and protective measures before cybercriminals can exploit the vulnerabilities. This ethical approach ensures that defensive hacking contributes to improved cybersecurity without unduly exposing systems to potential harm.

Continual self-assessment and professional development are essential ethical considerations for those engaged in defensive hacking. The rapidly evolving nature of technology and cyber threats requires ethical hackers to stay current with industry trends, emerging vulnerabilities, and evolving best practices. Regular training, education, and adherence to professional codes of conduct contribute to the ethical foundation of defensive hacking. By maintaining a commitment to ongoing learning and ethical conduct, defensive hackers can navigate the complexities of the cybersecurity landscape responsibly and contribute positively to the field.

The ethical considerations of defensive hacking also extend to the geopolitical context. Defensive hacking activities may intersect with national security concerns, and ethical hackers must be mindful of the potential implications of their work within a broader geopolitical framework. Collaboration with law enforcement, adherence to relevant legal frameworks, and an awareness of the geopolitical context are crucial aspects of ethical defensive hacking. Ethical hackers must navigate these complexities with diligence, recognizing the potential impact of their actions on national and international cybersecurity.

In conclusion, the ethical considerations of hacking for defensive purposes involve a delicate balance of principles, practices, and accountability. Transparency, informed consent, proportionality, accountability, respect for privacy, consideration of collateral impact, collaboration, responsible disclosure, ongoing professional development, and awareness of the geopolitical context are integral components of ethical defensive hacking. Ethical hackers play a crucial role in enhancing cybersecurity, and their commitment to ethical conduct ensures that defensive hacking contributes positively to the protection of digital systems, networks, and data while respecting individual rights and the broader integrity of the digital ecosystem.

Explore prominent certifications for ethical hackers, such as Certified Ethical Hacker (CEH) and Offensive Security Certified Professional (OSCP).

Prominent certifications for ethical hackers play a pivotal role in validating the skills, knowledge, and expertise required to navigate the complex landscape of cybersecurity. Among these certifications, the Certified Ethical Hacker (CEH) and the Offensive Security Certified Professional (OSCP) stand out as widely recognized and respected credentials that contribute to the professional development of ethical hackers.

The Certified Ethical Hacker (CEH) certification, offered by the EC-Council, is a foundational credential that establishes a baseline of knowledge for ethical hackers. The CEH certification is designed to equip individuals with the skills needed to assess and fortify the security posture of computer systems and networks. The certification covers a comprehensive range of topics, including penetration testing methodologies, footprinting and reconnaissance, scanning networks, enumeration, system hacking, and web application penetration testing. The CEH certification also delves into areas such as social engineering, cryptography, and incident response, providing a well-rounded curriculum that reflects the diverse skill set required for ethical hacking.

The CEH certification process includes a rigorous exam that assesses the candidate's understanding of ethical hacking principles and techniques. Successful candidates demonstrate proficiency in identifying vulnerabilities, exploiting weaknesses, and recommending appropriate security measures. The CEH certification is widely recognized in the industry and serves as a valuable credential for individuals seeking roles such as ethical hacker, penetration tester, security analyst, or information security professional. The ongoing updates to the CEH curriculum reflect the dynamic nature of cybersecurity, ensuring that certified professionals remain current with emerging threats and best practices.

On the other hand, the Offensive Security Certified Professional (OSCP) certification, offered by Offensive Security, is renowned for its hands-on and practical approach to assessing and securing systems. The OSCP certification is often considered an advanced credential, attracting individuals seeking a more immersive and challenging experience in ethical hacking. The certification focuses on practical skills, emphasizing the ability to perform real-world penetration testing rather than merely memorizing theoretical concepts.

The OSCP certification process includes a grueling 24-hour practical exam where candidates must compromise a series of machines within a specified time frame. This exam, known as the OSCP exam, is a hallmark of the certification and tests candidates' skills in areas such as information gathering, vulnerability analysis, exploitation, post-exploitation, and reporting. The hands-on nature of the OSCP exam distinguishes it from other certifications, requiring candidates to apply their knowledge in a realistic and dynamic environment.

The OSCP certification aligns with Offensive Security's ethos of "Try Harder," encouraging candidates to persevere through challenges, think creatively, and develop problem-solving skills. The certification not only validates technical proficiency but also instills a mindset of persistence and resilience, qualities essential for effective ethical hackers. OSCP-certified professionals are often sought after for roles that involve conducting penetration tests, vulnerability assessments, and red teaming exercises.

While both the CEH and OSCP certifications contribute significantly to the field of ethical hacking, they cater to different preferences, skill levels, and career aspirations. The CEH certification is an excellent starting point for individuals entering the field, providing a solid foundation in ethical hacking principles and methodologies. It is recognized by employers globally and can open doors to entry-level and intermediate positions in cybersecurity.

On the other hand, the OSCP certification is ideal for individuals seeking a more challenging and practical experience. The emphasis on hands-on labs and the 24-hour exam sets the OSCP apart as a certification that goes beyond theoretical knowledge, focusing on the application of skills in real-world scenarios. OSCP-certified professionals are often viewed as having a deep understanding of penetration testing and are well-suited for roles that require advanced technical expertise.

In addition to the CEH and OSCP certifications, other notable certifications contribute to the diverse landscape of ethical hacking. The Certified Information Systems Security Professional (CISSP) certification, offered by (ISC)^2, is a widely recognized credential that covers various domains of information security, including ethical hacking. CISSP-certified professionals often hold managerial or leadership roles and possess a holistic understanding of cybersecurity principles.

The Offensive Security Certified Expert (OSCE) certification, also offered by Offensive Security, is an advanced credential that builds upon the OSCP. The OSCE certification focuses on advanced penetration testing techniques, exploit development, and understanding the intricacies of various operating systems. Professionals holding the OSCE certification are adept at conducting sophisticated penetration tests and are often sought after for roles that demand a high level of technical expertise.

The Certified Penetration Tester (CPT) certification, offered by the Information Assurance Certification Review Board (IACRB), is another certification that validates the skills of penetration testers. The CPT certification emphasizes practical skills, requiring candidates to demonstrate their ability to identify and exploit vulnerabilities in a controlled environment. It is recognized as a hands-on certification that reflects real-world penetration testing scenarios.

Certifications such as the EC-Council Certified Security Analyst (ECSA), CompTIA PenTest+, and GIAC Penetration Tester (GPEN) also contribute to the diverse ecosystem of ethical hacking certifications. Each of these certifications has its unique focus and objectives, catering to the varying needs of professionals in the field.

In conclusion, the landscape of ethical hacking certifications offers a variety of options for individuals seeking to validate their skills and advance their careers in cybersecurity. The CEH and OSCP certifications, in particular, stand out as prominent credentials that cater to different skill levels and preferences. While the CEH provides a solid foundation and is suitable for those entering the field, the OSCP offers a challenging and hands-on experience for individuals seeking a more advanced certification. As the field of ethical hacking continues to evolve, certifications play a crucial role in establishing professional standards, fostering ongoing learning, and validating the expertise of ethical hackers worldwide.

Discuss the importance of ongoing training in the rapidly evolving field.

In the rapidly evolving field of cybersecurity, the importance of ongoing training cannot be overstated. The dynamic nature of technology, coupled with the ever-expanding threat landscape, necessitates a continuous learning approach for professionals to stay ahead of emerging challenges, adapt to new technologies, and maintain the highest standards of expertise. Ongoing training serves as a cornerstone for cybersecurity professionals, fostering a culture of resilience, innovation, and preparedness in an environment where the only constant is change.

One of the primary reasons for the critical role of ongoing training in cybersecurity is the relentless pace of technological advancement. As new technologies emerge, they bring with them novel attack surfaces, vulnerabilities, and potential exploits. Cybersecurity professionals must continually update their skills and knowledge to effectively navigate and secure these evolving landscapes. Whether it be the adoption of cloud computing, the proliferation of Internet of Things (IoT) devices, or the integration of artificial intelligence into cybersecurity defenses, ongoing training ensures that professionals remain well-versed in the latest tools, techniques, and best practices.

The ever-expanding threat landscape further underscores the importance of ongoing training. Cyber threats continually evolve in sophistication, ranging from traditional malware and phishing attacks to more advanced tactics such as ransomware, zero-day exploits, and supply chain attacks. To effectively combat these threats, cybersecurity professionals must stay abreast of the latest attack vectors and tactics employed by malicious actors. Ongoing training provides the necessary insights into emerging threats, enabling professionals to proactively enhance security measures and develop effective counter-strategies.

Moreover, the regulatory landscape surrounding cybersecurity is subject to constant changes and updates. Various industries and regions establish new compliance requirements and standards to address emerging threats and safeguard sensitive information. Cybersecurity professionals must stay informed about these regulatory developments to ensure organizational compliance and mitigate legal risks. Ongoing training not only covers the intricacies of existing regulations but also prepares professionals for upcoming changes, helping them adapt policies, procedures, and security controls accordingly.

The importance of ongoing training is further emphasized by the need for professionals to specialize in specific areas within cybersecurity. The field encompasses diverse domains, including but not limited to penetration testing, incident response, threat intelligence, secure coding, and security architecture. Ongoing training allows professionals to deepen their expertise in chosen specialties, contributing to a more comprehensive and effective cybersecurity strategy. Specialized training programs, certifications, and workshops enable professionals to acquire in-depth knowledge and hands-on experience, enhancing their ability to address specific challenges within their chosen domains.

Continuous learning is integral to the development of a proactive cybersecurity mindset. As the saying goes, "The best defense is a good offense." Ongoing training empowers cybersecurity professionals to adopt a proactive approach, anticipating potential threats and vulnerabilities before they can be exploited. This proactive mindset is essential in an environment where cyber threats are not only persistent but also increasingly sophisticated. By staying ahead of the curve through ongoing training, professionals are better equipped to identify and mitigate risks, reducing the likelihood of successful cyber attacks.

The rapidly evolving field of cybersecurity demands not only technical proficiency but also a keen understanding of the human factors involved in cyber threats. Social engineering, phishing attacks, and insider threats are persistent challenges that require a nuanced understanding of human behavior and psychology. Ongoing training in areas such as cybersecurity awareness, secure behavior, and ethical decision-making is crucial for building a human firewall within organizations. Training programs that simulate real-world scenarios and educate employees about potential risks contribute to a cybersecurity culture that is resilient to social engineering tactics.

The interconnectedness of the global digital landscape introduces another layer of complexity to cybersecurity. Professionals must be well-versed in the intricacies of managing and securing interconnected systems, networks, and devices. Ongoing training in areas such as network security, secure communication protocols, and the Internet of Things (IoT) security is essential for professionals to navigate this complexity successfully. Additionally, the rise of remote work and the increased reliance on virtual collaboration tools underscore the need for ongoing training in securing distributed environments and mitigating the associated risks.

The field of cybersecurity is not only about preventing and responding to cyber threats but also about promoting a culture of ethical conduct and responsible hacking practices. Ongoing training in ethical hacking, penetration testing, and vulnerability assessment is essential for professionals to understand the methodologies employed by malicious actors and, in turn, develop effective defensive strategies. Ethical hacking certifications and training programs, such as the Certified Ethical Hacker (CEH) and Offensive Security Certified Professional (OSCP), empower professionals to test systems for vulnerabilities in a controlled and ethical manner, contributing to a more robust security posture.

Furthermore, ongoing training is essential for fostering innovation and adaptation within the cybersecurity field. As cyber threats evolve, so must the defensive strategies employed by organizations and professionals. Ongoing training cultivates a mindset of innovation, encouraging professionals to explore new technologies, methodologies, and tools that can enhance security measures. Training programs that encourage experimentation, hands-on learning, and collaboration contribute to a culture of innovation that is essential for staying ahead of the curve in the rapidly changing cybersecurity landscape.

The importance of ongoing training extends beyond technical skills to encompass soft skills and effective communication within the cybersecurity profession. Cybersecurity professionals often interact with stakeholders across various departments, from IT and legal to executive leadership and end-users. Effective communication, risk management, and the ability to translate technical jargon into understandable terms are crucial skills that ongoing training can enhance. Training programs that focus on communication, leadership, and collaboration contribute to the development of well-rounded cybersecurity professionals capable of addressing both technical and organizational challenges.

The cybersecurity profession is characterized by a global shortage of skilled professionals. Ongoing training plays a pivotal role in addressing this shortage by not only upskilling existing professionals but also attracting new talent to the field. Training initiatives that emphasize inclusivity, diversity, and accessibility contribute to a more vibrant and diverse cybersecurity community. By investing in ongoing training, organizations and educational institutions can create pathways for individuals from diverse backgrounds to enter and thrive in the cybersecurity field, thereby strengthening the overall resilience of the industry.

In conclusion, the importance of ongoing training in the rapidly evolving field of cybersecurity cannot be overstated. The dynamic nature of technology, the evolving threat landscape, regulatory changes, specialization within cybersecurity domains, the need for a proactive mindset, the human factors involved in cyber threats, the interconnectedness of digital environments, ethical hacking practices, fostering innovation, developing effective communication skills, and addressing the global skills shortage are all compelling reasons for professionals to engage in continuous learning. Ongoing training not only enhances technical proficiency but also cultivates a holistic and adaptable approach to cybersecurity, ensuring that professionals are well-equipped to navigate the complexities of the ever-changing cybersecurity landscape.

Define penetration testing and its role in identifying vulnerabilities.

Penetration testing, often referred to as ethical hacking or pen testing, is a proactive and controlled cybersecurity practice designed to assess the security of computer systems, networks, applications, and infrastructure by simulating real-world cyber attacks. The primary objective of penetration testing is to identify vulnerabilities and weaknesses within an organization's information technology (IT) environment before malicious actors can exploit them for nefarious purposes. This strategic and methodical approach helps organizations understand their risk posture, enhance their security measures, and fortify defenses against potential cyber threats.

At its core, penetration testing involves the authorized and systematic attempt to exploit vulnerabilities in a manner similar to how actual attackers would. It is crucial to emphasize the authorized nature of penetration testing—organizations engage certified and skilled ethical hackers to conduct these assessments within legal and ethical boundaries. The overarching goal is not to cause harm or disruption but to identify and prioritize vulnerabilities, ultimately leading to a more robust security posture.

Penetration testing encompasses a diverse set of methodologies and approaches, adapting to the specific characteristics of the target environment. One common distinction is between black-box, white-box, and grey-box testing. In black-box testing, the ethical hacker has little or no prior knowledge of the target system, simulating the perspective of an external attacker. White-box testing, on the other hand, involves full knowledge of the target system, allowing the ethical hacker to delve deep into its internal architecture. Grey-box testing strikes a balance, providing partial information about the target system, reflecting a scenario where some details are known, typically mimicking the perspective of an insider.

The penetration testing process typically follows a systematic and well-defined methodology. It begins with scoping, where the goals, rules of engagement, and target systems are clearly defined. This phase is crucial for aligning the assessment with the organization's objectives and ensuring that ethical hackers focus on the most critical assets. Following scoping, the ethical hackers proceed with information gathering, aiming to understand the target environment's architecture, systems, and potential points of weakness. This reconnaissance phase involves passive and active techniques, such as network scanning, enumeration, and open-source intelligence (OSINT) gathering.

Once armed with a comprehensive understanding of the target, ethical hackers move to the vulnerability analysis phase. Here, they systematically assess and analyze the identified information for potential vulnerabilities. This analysis spans the entire attack surface, including network infrastructure, operating systems, web applications, databases, and any other components that may be susceptible to exploitation. Common vulnerability assessment tools, manual testing, and expertise in various domains are employed to ensure a thorough examination of the target's security posture.

The next phase involves actual exploitation, where ethical hackers attempt to leverage identified vulnerabilities to gain unauthorized access or control over systems and data. This step often includes techniques such as privilege escalation, SQL injection, cross-site scripting (XSS), and other methods commonly employed by malicious actors. Importantly, this phase adheres to strict rules of engagement to prevent unintended disruptions and to maintain a controlled testing environment.

Post-exploitation activities follow the exploitation phase, allowing ethical hackers to assess the extent of the potential impact if an attacker were to successfully compromise a system or network. This involves examining the ability to move laterally within the environment, escalate privileges, and access sensitive information. Understanding the potential consequences of a successful attack is critical for organizations to prioritize remediation efforts effectively.

The final phase of penetration testing is reporting, where ethical hackers provide a detailed and comprehensive report to the organization. This report typically includes an executive summary for leadership, a technical breakdown of identified vulnerabilities, their potential impact, and recommended mitigation strategies. The report serves as a roadmap for organizations to prioritize and address vulnerabilities based on their severity and potential impact on business operations.

The role of penetration testing extends beyond merely identifying vulnerabilities—it contributes to a proactive and adaptive cybersecurity strategy. By simulating real-world attack scenarios, penetration testing goes beyond automated vulnerability scanning tools by leveraging the creativity and expertise of ethical hackers. This human-centric approach allows for the discovery of nuanced vulnerabilities that automated tools might overlook. Additionally, penetration testing provides insights into the effectiveness of existing security controls, helping organizations understand their strengths and weaknesses in defending against various attack vectors.

Furthermore, penetration testing serves as a critical component of a comprehensive risk management strategy. It enables organizations to make informed decisions about allocating resources to address the most pressing security concerns. Through a prioritized approach, organizations can focus on remediating vulnerabilities that pose the greatest risk to their business operations, sensitive data, and overall security posture. This risk-centric methodology aligns with industry best practices and regulatory requirements, facilitating compliance with standards such as the Payment Card Industry Data Security Standard (PCI DSS) and the Health Insurance Portability and Accountability Act (HIPAA).

The iterative nature of penetration testing is also essential for organizations to adapt to the evolving threat landscape. Cyber threats are dynamic, and new vulnerabilities are constantly discovered. Regular penetration testing allows organizations to stay ahead of emerging risks, ensuring that their security measures are continually refined to address the latest threats. This adaptability is crucial for organizations operating in industries where the confidentiality, integrity, and availability of information are paramount, such as finance, healthcare, and critical infrastructure.

The benefits of penetration testing extend beyond risk mitigation—they include building a resilient security culture within organizations. Engaging in penetration testing fosters a mindset of continuous improvement and vigilance against evolving cyber threats. It promotes a proactive approach to cybersecurity, where organizations actively seek to understand and address their vulnerabilities before adversaries can exploit them. Additionally, penetration testing provides an opportunity for collaboration between security teams and other stakeholders within an organization, reinforcing the importance of shared responsibility for cybersecurity.

In conclusion, penetration testing plays a pivotal role in identifying vulnerabilities within an organization's IT environment. Through its systematic and ethical approach, penetration testing enables organizations to understand their risk posture, prioritize remediation efforts, and build a resilient security culture. By simulating real-world attack scenarios, ethical hackers contribute valuable insights that go beyond automated vulnerability scanning tools. The iterative and proactive nature of penetration testing is essential for organizations to adapt to the evolving threat landscape and stay ahead of emerging risks. Ultimately, penetration testing is a cornerstone of effective cybersecurity, providing organizations with the knowledge and tools needed to fortify their defenses and protect against a diverse range of cyber threats.

Discuss real-world examples of successful penetration tests.

In the realm of cybersecurity, real-world examples of successful penetration tests showcase the importance of proactive testing, the identification of vulnerabilities, and the subsequent reinforcement of defenses. These examples highlight the diverse ways in which ethical hackers emulate malicious actors to uncover weaknesses in systems, networks, and applications, ultimately contributing to the enhancement of overall cybersecurity posture.

One notable real-world example involves the penetration testing of a large financial institution's network infrastructure. In this case, ethical hackers were engaged to assess the organization's security measures comprehensively. Through a combination of automated tools and manual testing, the ethical hackers discovered a critical vulnerability in the organization's web application, which handled sensitive financial transactions. This vulnerability, if exploited, could have allowed unauthorized access to user accounts and potentially resulted in financial losses. The penetration testing team promptly reported their findings to the organization's security team, who swiftly implemented a patch to address the vulnerability. This example illustrates how penetration testing can uncover critical issues that may have otherwise gone unnoticed, preventing potential financial harm and reinforcing the organization's commitment to safeguarding sensitive information.

Another compelling example involves a penetration test conducted on a healthcare provider's network. With the increasing prevalence of cyber threats targeting the healthcare sector, the organization sought to proactively identify and address vulnerabilities in its systems. Ethical hackers, simulating the tactics of malicious actors, discovered a series of weaknesses in the organization's network infrastructure and database systems. Notably, they identified an unpatched software vulnerability in the hospital's patient records system, potentially exposing sensitive patient information. The findings prompted the organization to promptly apply patches, update security protocols, and reinforce access controls. This real-world example underscores the crucial role of penetration testing in the healthcare sector, where the protection of patient data is paramount, and the consequences of security lapses can be severe.

In a corporate environment, a multinational technology company conducted a penetration test to assess the security of its internal systems and proprietary software. Ethical hackers were tasked with identifying potential vulnerabilities that could be exploited by both internal and external threat actors. The penetration testing team employed a combination of social engineering techniques, network scanning, and application testing to emulate real-world attack scenarios. During the assessment, they discovered a previously unknown vulnerability in the company's flagship software product that could have allowed unauthorized access to user data. The ethical hackers worked closely with the company's development team to address the issue promptly, ensuring that a patch was deployed before the vulnerability could be exploited maliciously. This example highlights the value of penetration testing not only for external threats but also for identifying internal vulnerabilities that may pose risks to proprietary software and sensitive corporate data.

A notable example in the realm of cloud security involves a global e-commerce platform that sought to evaluate the resilience of its cloud infrastructure to cyber threats. Ethical hackers were engaged to perform a penetration test with a focus on the organization's cloud-based services, including web applications, databases, and storage systems. Through a combination of reconnaissance, vulnerability analysis, and simulated attacks, the ethical hackers identified misconfigurations in the cloud environment that could have exposed sensitive customer data. The organization promptly rectified the misconfigurations, implemented additional security controls, and conducted a thorough review of its cloud security practices. This real-world scenario underscores the importance of including cloud environments in penetration testing initiatives, considering the increasing adoption of cloud services and the unique security challenges they present.

In the financial sector, a multinational bank conducted a penetration test to assess the security of its online banking platform. The ethical hacking team, emulating potential adversaries, identified a critical vulnerability in the authentication mechanism of the platform. This vulnerability could have allowed attackers to compromise user accounts and gain unauthorized access to sensitive financial information. The bank swiftly addressed the issue, enhancing its multifactor authentication system and implementing additional security measures to protect customer accounts. This example illustrates the targeted nature of penetration testing in the financial industry, where the stakes are high, and the protection of customer assets is a top priority.

In the energy sector, a utility company commissioned a penetration test to evaluate the security of its supervisory control and data acquisition (SCADA) systems, which are critical for the operation of power plants and distribution networks. Ethical hackers, simulating potential cyber threats, identified vulnerabilities in the SCADA systems that could have allowed unauthorized manipulation of power distribution. The findings prompted the utility company to implement enhanced security measures, segment its network infrastructure, and deploy intrusion detection systems to monitor for potential anomalies. This real-world example underscores the vital role of penetration testing in safeguarding critical infrastructure, where the consequences of cyber attacks can extend beyond data breaches to impact the reliability of essential services.

In the context of software development, a leading software company conducted a penetration test on its flagship application to ensure the security of customer data and intellectual property. Ethical hackers, adopting the perspective of external adversaries, identified a series of vulnerabilities in the software's codebase, including injection flaws and inadequate input validation. The software company collaborated with the ethical hacking team to remediate the vulnerabilities, conduct code reviews, and implement secure coding practices. This example highlights the significance of integrating penetration testing into the software development lifecycle to identify and address security issues before software is deployed to customers, preventing potential exploitation by malicious actors.

A particularly illustrative example involves the penetration testing of a government agency's network infrastructure. Ethical hackers, simulating sophisticated threat actors, identified vulnerabilities in the agency's systems that could have allowed unauthorized access to sensitive government data. The findings prompted the agency to reevaluate its security policies, conduct additional training for personnel, and implement advanced security measures to defend against targeted cyber threats. This example underscores the importance of penetration testing in the public sector, where the protection of sensitive government information is of paramount importance, and the consequences of security breaches can have far-reaching implications.

In the education sector, a university engaged ethical hackers to conduct a penetration test on its IT infrastructure, including student information systems and research databases. The penetration testing team, emulating various attack scenarios, discovered vulnerabilities that could have exposed sensitive student records and intellectual property. The university responded by enhancing access controls, implementing encryption measures, and conducting cybersecurity awareness training for faculty and students. This real-world example emphasizes the relevance of penetration testing in educational institutions, where the protection of student data and academic research is crucial.

These real-world examples collectively illustrate the diverse applications and impact of penetration testing across different industries and sectors. Whether assessing the security of financial institutions, healthcare providers, multinational corporations, e-commerce platforms, utility companies, software developers, government agencies, or educational institutions, penetration testing serves as a proactive and essential practice to identify vulnerabilities, strengthen defenses, and mitigate potential cyber threats. The lessons learned from these examples underscore the ongoing need for organizations to prioritize and invest in penetration testing as a fundamental component of their cybersecurity strategies.

Explore the concept of bug bounty programs and their role in crowdsourcing cybersecurity testing.

Bug bounty programs represent a dynamic and innovative approach to cybersecurity testing by leveraging the collective expertise of a global community to identify and address vulnerabilities in software, applications, and digital platforms. These programs, also known as vulnerability reward programs, invite ethical hackers, security researchers, and cybersecurity enthusiasts to actively search for and report security flaws in exchange for financial rewards or other incentives. The essence of bug bounty programs lies in the recognition that security testing is not solely the responsibility of an organization's internal security teams but can be enhanced through collaboration with external individuals who bring diverse perspectives and skill sets to the table.

One of the fundamental roles of bug bounty programs is to tap into the vast pool of cybersecurity talent that exists beyond the confines of a single organization. By crowdsourcing cybersecurity testing, organizations can harness the collective intelligence of a global community with diverse backgrounds, experiences, and expertise. This diversity is a strength, as it allows for a comprehensive examination of software and systems from various angles, often uncovering vulnerabilities that internal teams may overlook. The inclusivity of bug bounty programs democratizes the process of cybersecurity testing, welcoming contributions from individuals worldwide and fostering a collaborative environment where security is a shared responsibility.

Bug bounty programs operate on the principle of incentivizing ethical hackers to responsibly disclose vulnerabilities they discover during their testing activities. The concept of responsible disclosure is key to the success of these programs, as it encourages participants to report their findings to the organization in a transparent and timely manner, allowing the organization to remediate the issues before they can be exploited maliciously. In turn, ethical hackers receive recognition for their contributions, financial rewards, and the satisfaction of knowing they have played a crucial role in enhancing cybersecurity.

The financial rewards offered by bug bounty programs serve as a powerful motivator for ethical hackers to actively engage in security testing. Organizations typically structure their bug bounty programs with tiered reward systems, where the severity and impact of a reported vulnerability determine the payout. Critical vulnerabilities that could lead to severe consequences, such as data breaches or system compromises, command higher rewards. This tiered approach not only incentivizes ethical hackers to focus on high-impact issues but also aligns with the risk prioritization that organizations must undertake when addressing security vulnerabilities. The financial incentives act as a recognition of the value contributed by ethical hackers and help establish a mutually beneficial relationship between the security community and organizations.

Beyond financial rewards, bug bounty programs often offer additional incentives and recognition to participants. These can include public acknowledgment, certificates of achievement, invitations to exclusive events, and even opportunities for future collaboration or employment. The recognition component is essential in building a positive and engaging community of ethical hackers who feel valued for their contributions. Many ethical hackers participate in bug bounty programs not solely for financial gain but also for the opportunity to showcase their skills, build a professional reputation, and contribute to the broader goal of improving cybersecurity globally.

Bug bounty programs contribute significantly to the proactive identification and remediation of vulnerabilities, enabling organizations to stay ahead of potential cyber threats. Traditional security testing approaches, such as automated scanning tools and internal assessments, may not always replicate the diverse and creative tactics employed by malicious actors. Ethical hackers participating in bug bounty programs bring a human-centric approach to testing, using their ingenuity to explore potential attack vectors that automated tools might miss. This proactive stance aligns with the overarching philosophy of shifting from a reactive to a preventive cybersecurity posture, where vulnerabilities are discovered and addressed before they can be exploited.

The scope of bug bounty programs extends across a wide range of digital assets, including websites, mobile applications, APIs, network infrastructure, and even hardware devices. This broad scope reflects the evolving nature of cyber threats, which can target various facets of an organization's digital presence. By allowing ethical hackers to test diverse components, bug bounty programs provide organizations with a comprehensive evaluation of their security posture. Additionally, the flexibility of bug bounty programs allows organizations to adapt to emerging technologies, ensuring that even cutting-edge systems and applications undergo rigorous testing.

Bug bounty programs also offer an avenue for organizations to engage with the cybersecurity community and establish positive relationships with ethical hackers. This collaborative model contrasts with the traditional perception of hackers as adversaries and positions them as valuable allies in the collective effort to improve cybersecurity. Organizations that embrace bug bounty programs signal a commitment to transparency, accountability, and a willingness to learn from the wider community. This collaborative approach not only enhances the organization's security but also contributes to a culture of continuous improvement and shared responsibility within the cybersecurity ecosystem.

One of the key advantages of bug bounty programs is their scalability. Organizations of varying sizes and industries can leverage bug bounty platforms to tailor testing initiatives to their specific needs. Whether a startup or a multinational corporation, bug bounty programs provide a flexible and scalable solution for organizations to receive targeted and thorough security assessments. The scalability is particularly beneficial for organizations with complex and rapidly evolving digital landscapes, allowing them to maintain a proactive cybersecurity stance without the constraints associated with traditional testing methods.

The success of bug bounty programs is evident in the numerous impactful discoveries that have resulted from the collaboration between ethical hackers and organizations. High-profile vulnerabilities, such as those affecting widely used software, services, or platforms, have been responsibly disclosed through bug bounty programs. For example, critical security flaws in popular web browsers, content management systems, and communication platforms have been identified by ethical hackers participating in bug bounty programs. These discoveries showcase the real-world impact of bug bounty initiatives in mitigating potential risks for millions of users globally and highlight the crucial role of external contributors in securing digital ecosystems.

Bug bounty programs also play a vital role in the context of the Internet of Things (IoT), where the proliferation of connected devices introduces new challenges and security considerations. Ethical hackers engaged in bug bounty programs have uncovered vulnerabilities in smart home devices, industrial control systems, and wearable technologies. These discoveries underscore the importance of proactive security testing in an era where the interconnectivity of devices creates a complex attack surface. Bug bounty programs provide a valuable mechanism for organizations to fortify the security of IoT ecosystems and address vulnerabilities before they can be exploited to compromise user privacy or disrupt critical infrastructure.

In conclusion, bug bounty programs represent a paradigm shift in cybersecurity testing by embracing the power of crowdsourcing and collaboration. These programs leverage the collective intelligence of ethical hackers from around the world, providing organizations with a scalable, proactive, and diverse approach to identifying and addressing vulnerabilities. The financial incentives, recognition, and positive engagement offered by bug bounty programs create a mutually beneficial relationship between organizations and the global cybersecurity community. As cyber threats continue to evolve, bug bounty programs stand as a dynamic and effective strategy for organizations to fortify their security postures, build positive relationships with ethical hackers, and contribute to the broader goal of enhancing cybersecurity across digital ecosystems.

Discuss the benefits and challenges of bug bounty initiatives.

Bug bounty initiatives, while transformative in enhancing cybersecurity, present a nuanced landscape with both notable benefits and inherent challenges. These programs leverage the collective wisdom of a global community of ethical hackers to identify vulnerabilities, but their effectiveness is contingent on careful program design, ongoing communication, and adaptability. The benefits of bug bounty initiatives are substantial, encompassing increased security resilience, diverse skill sets, scalability, positive community engagement, and a proactive stance in cybersecurity. However, challenges such as program management, false positives, legal complexities, and the potential for unintended consequences necessitate thoughtful consideration to optimize the impact of bug bounty initiatives.

A primary benefit of bug bounty initiatives lies in their ability to significantly bolster an organization's security resilience. By harnessing the diverse expertise of ethical hackers worldwide, organizations can identify and rectify vulnerabilities that may have eluded traditional security testing methodologies. Ethical hackers bring a fresh perspective, creativity, and an array of skill sets to the table, probing systems and applications in ways that automated tools or in-house security teams might overlook. This proactive identification and remediation of vulnerabilities contribute to a robust security posture, reducing the likelihood of successful cyber attacks and minimizing potential damage to an organization's reputation and operations.

The inclusivity inherent in bug bounty initiatives offers a unique advantage by tapping into a broad spectrum of skills and backgrounds within the cybersecurity community. Ethical hackers participating in bug bounty programs come from diverse geographic locations, industries, and professional backgrounds, bringing varied experiences and insights to the testing process. This diversity is a strength, as it allows for a comprehensive examination of digital assets from multiple perspectives. It enhances the likelihood of discovering intricate vulnerabilities and reflects the real-world landscape where cyber threats manifest in multifaceted ways. The collaboration between organizations and a global community of ethical hackers fosters an environment where collective intelligence and shared responsibility become central tenets of cybersecurity.

Scalability is another key benefit of bug bounty initiatives, enabling organizations to adapt to the dynamic nature of their digital landscapes. As organizations evolve, introducing new technologies, applications, and services, bug bounty programs provide a flexible and scalable approach to security testing. Unlike traditional testing methodologies, bug bounty initiatives can easily accommodate changes in scope, allowing organizations to maintain a proactive stance in cybersecurity without being constrained by the limitations of internal resources. This scalability is particularly crucial in industries characterized by rapid technological advancements, where the attack surface is continually expanding, and traditional testing approaches may struggle to keep pace.

Positive community engagement is a hallmark of successful bug bounty initiatives. These programs foster collaboration, communication, and mutual respect between organizations and ethical hackers. By recognizing and rewarding ethical hackers for their contributions, organizations establish positive relationships within the cybersecurity community. This engagement extends beyond financial incentives to include public acknowledgment, certificates of achievement, invitations to exclusive events, and opportunities for future collaboration or employment. The recognition provided by bug bounty programs not only enhances an ethical hacker's professional reputation but also creates a sense of camaraderie and shared purpose in improving cybersecurity globally.

Furthermore, bug bounty initiatives represent a proactive stance in cybersecurity, allowing organizations to stay ahead of potential threats. Rather than waiting for malicious actors to exploit vulnerabilities, organizations engage ethical hackers to actively search for and report security flaws. This proactive approach aligns with the principles of risk management and prevention, minimizing the likelihood of security breaches and their associated consequences. Bug bounty programs encourage organizations to continuously evaluate and enhance their security postures, fostering a culture of vigilance and adaptability in the face of evolving cyber threats.

However, bug bounty initiatives come with their share of challenges that necessitate careful consideration and management. Program management is a critical aspect that requires dedicated resources to define clear guidelines, establish effective communication channels, and ensure the timely resolution of reported vulnerabilities. Inadequate program management can lead to misunderstandings, delays in addressing reported issues, and a diminished experience for ethical hackers. Organizations must invest in the infrastructure and processes necessary to manage bug bounty programs effectively, including a secure platform for reporting, a structured reward system, and a responsive communication framework.

The challenge of false positives poses another complexity in bug bounty initiatives. Ethical hackers may occasionally misinterpret normal behavior as a security vulnerability, leading to false reports. Discerning between genuine security risks and false positives requires expertise and thorough analysis. Organizations must establish robust mechanisms to triage reported vulnerabilities, separating credible findings from inaccuracies. A streamlined and transparent process for assessing and validating reported issues ensures that ethical hackers receive fair and accurate feedback, maintaining the credibility and effectiveness of bug bounty programs.

Legal complexities represent a persistent challenge in bug bounty initiatives, particularly concerning the disclosure of vulnerabilities and adherence to relevant laws and regulations. Organizations must navigate the delicate balance between encouraging ethical hackers to report vulnerabilities responsibly and mitigating potential legal risks. Legal considerations include compliance with data protection laws, intellectual property rights, and contractual obligations. Creating clear terms of engagement, defining responsible disclosure policies, and seeking legal counsel can help organizations navigate these complexities and establish a framework that encourages collaboration while safeguarding legal interests.

The potential for unintended consequences is an additional challenge that organizations must address in bug bounty initiatives. While ethical hackers participate with good intentions, the discovery of vulnerabilities may lead to unforeseen consequences, such as service disruptions, data exposure, or unintentional disclosure of sensitive information. Organizations need robust contingency plans to manage and mitigate any unintended impacts that may arise during the course of bug bounty testing. Communication channels between ethical hackers and the organization must remain open and responsive to ensure a coordinated and responsible approach to addressing discovered vulnerabilities.

A key consideration in bug bounty initiatives is the dynamic nature of cybersecurity and the evolving sophistication of malicious actors. Organizations must continually adapt their bug bounty programs to align with emerging technologies, attack vectors, and industry-specific challenges. Stagnation in program design or a failure to incorporate lessons learned from previous engagements may diminish the effectiveness of bug bounty initiatives over time. Regular assessments, updates to program guidelines, and ongoing communication with ethical hackers are essential components of a successful bug bounty program that remains relevant and responsive to the evolving threat landscape.

In conclusion, bug bounty initiatives offer a transformative approach to cybersecurity testing, leveraging the collective intelligence of ethical hackers to enhance security resilience, tap into diverse skill sets, achieve scalability, foster positive community engagement, and maintain a proactive stance in cybersecurity. However, the challenges associated with program management, false positives, legal complexities, and the potential for unintended consequences require careful consideration and strategic mitigation. By addressing these challenges thoughtfully, organizations can optimize the benefits of bug bounty initiatives, establishing a collaborative and effective model that contributes to the continuous improvement of cybersecurity across digital ecosystems.

****